DRAMATIC

MISCELLANIES.

VOL. I.

AMS PRESS
NEW YORK

Engraved by J Wooding

THOMAS BETTERTON.

From an Origional Picture by Sr. Godfory Kneller, in the possession of Saml. Ireland. Esql

DRAMATIC MICELLANIES:

CONSISTING OF

CRITICAL OBSERVATIONS

ON SEVERAL

PLAYS OF SHAKSPEARE:

WITH

A REVIEW OF HIS PRINCIPAL CHARACTERS, AND
THOSE OF VARIOUS EMINENT WRITERS,

AS REPRESENTED

BY MR. GARRICK, AND
OTHER CELEBRATED COMEDIANS.

WITH ANECDOTES OF DRAMATIC POETS, ACTORS, &c.

By THOMAS DAVIES,

AUTHOR of MEMOIRS of the LIFE of
DAVID GARRICK, Esq.

IN THREE VOLUMES.

VOL. I.

Μισω πλυτον ανυν, κολακων τροφον, υδε παρ' οφρυν
Στησομαι· οιδ' ολιγης δαιτος ελευθεριην. Epig. Græc.

LONDON:
Printed for the AUTHOR, and fold at his Shop, in
GREAT RUSSELL-STREET, COVENT-GARDEN.

M.DCC.LXXXIV.

Library of Congress Cataloging in Publication Data

Davies, Thomas, 1712?-1785.
 Dramatic micellanies [sic] consisting of critical
observations on several plays of Shakespeare.

 1. Shakespeare, William, 1564-1616--Stage history.
2. Shakespeare, William, 1564-1616--Criticism and
interpretation. 3. Theater--England--History.
I. Title.
PR3095.D3 1973   822.3'3   75-163675
ISBN 0-404-01991-9 (v. 1)

Reprinted from an original in the collections
of The Newark Public Library

From the edition of 1784, London
First AMS edition published in 1973
Manufactured in the United States of America

International Standard Book Number:
Complete Set: 0-404-01990-0
Volume One: 0-404-01991-9

AMS PRESS INC.
NEW YORK, N. Y. 10003

T O

HIS ROYAL HIGHNESS,

GEORGE,

PRINCE OF WALES,

SIR,

PERMIT me to intreat your patronage for the Dramatic Miscellanies; in which the characters of Shakspeare, and other celebrated authors, are confidered and reviewed.

The portraits of our old monarchs, drawn by the great father of the Englifh ftage, merit the attention of the heir apparent to the crown of Great-Britain; the pencil of the divine poet has thrown a light on their characters, far fuperior to the compofition of the moft elaborate narratives. What the hiftorian coldly relates, Shakfpeare, by the glow of genius, animates and realizes.

The calamities, which befel certain princes of the Plantagenet line, as reprefented in the fcenes of this admired writer, were principally owing to their contempt of thofe laws, which they had folemnly engaged to maintain. The oppreffion of the people created rebellion to the prince, and brought ruin to the kingdom. Thefe, fir, are hiftorical facts, painted in the moft lively colours by the fkill of the great dramatift, which will ever claim the ferious regard of monarch and fubject in this free country.

The

The illuftrious houfe of Hanover was called to the throne of thefe realms, by the voice of the people, to fupport that fabric of government, by which the limits of the crown and the claims of the fubject were unalterably fixed and eftablifhed at the Revolution.

From that happy period, the fovereign of England acquired the moft glorious of all titles, A KING OF FREEMEN!

The many amiable qualities of your Royal Highnefs, which endear you to a great and generous nation, will invariably ftimulate you to emulate the virtues of your anceftors, to ftand forth the friend of liberty, and the advocate of thofe rights, the enjoyment of which can alone bring fecurity to the prince and happinefs to the people!

When it fhall pleafe Divine Providence, at a diftant period, to call your Royal Highnefs to the throne of thefe kingdoms, that you may reign in the hearts of a free and united people, is the earneft prayer of,

SIR,

Your ROYAL HIGHNESS's

Moft obedient

And

Moft humble fervant,

THOMAS DAVIES.

ADVERTISEMENT.

T O publifh my remarks on Shakfpeare, after the approved labours of fo many eminent critics, will, 1 fear, be termed prefumption. The laft edition of the great dramatift, by Dr. Johnfon and Mr. Steevens, which includes, befides their own notes, the obfervations of their friends, men of name in the learned world, ought to have deterred me, it will be faid, from trying my ftrength upon a fubjèct fo beaten, and fo well underftood and explained.

In the interpretation of Shakfpeare's phrafeology, fo many commentators have differed widely from each other, fo many plaufible reafons have been fuggefted to fupport their feveral opinions, that no apology feems needful for one who fubmits his fentiments to the general cenfure ; and who, in prefuming to think for himfelf, is fo far from treating thofe who have gone before him with arrogance, that he is ever ready to own their pre-eminence, and to acknowledge his obligations to their uncommon induftry, learning, and fagacity.

In

In carefully examining my folutions of fome difficult texts, a few of them, I am obliged to own, are of little import; others are fcarcely more than tranfcripts from former commentators, which had efcaped my obfervation or memory. In both thefe particulars, I have not, I believe, often offended.

But the explaining Shakfpeare's text was but the fmalleft part of my defign.

The plays of Shakfpeare, which are founded on Englifh hiftory, and which exhibit the actions and characters of our monarchs, I have always confidered as a valuable treafure to Englifhmen, and of great importance to king and fubject. In them, as in a mirror, future events, incidental to a mixed government, may be forefeen, or, at leaft, with probability conjectured.

In a free ftate, like our's, encroachments of prerogative on privilege, and, vice verfa, of privilege on prerogative, muft occafionally happen. The confequences, arifing from both, no hiftorian or political writer has painted in more lively colours than our great poet. He lived at a time, it is true, when the limits of the crown and the liberties of the fubject had not been duly fixed, and before the principles of the conftitution had gained a firm eftablifhment by a legal fettlement.

But the paffions of men will be the fame at all times, and no laws can be made fo obligatory as to prevent the confequence of their exceffes on certain occafions. The unhappy fate of mifguided arbitrary princes, and the mifchiefs which attend fedition and rebellion in the people, will be fubjects to intereft this nation for ever.

The

The characters of Shakfpeare are the boaft and honour of the Englifh ftage. Of the heroes and demi-gods, of the Greek and Roman drama, we have no refemblances in our own minds to compare them with. The French theatre, which approaches neareft to our own, delineates the perfons of their heroes in conformity to the manners of France. Let them be Greeks, Romans, or Turks, they have always fomething in them of the Frenchman.

Shakfpeare prefents men to us as they really exifted, and fuch as are congenial to our common nature.

When I undertook to write remarks on the principal characters of Shakfpeare, I found my plan too large for my canvas ; for I could not, confiftently with my promife of giving obfervations on other dramatic poets, comprehend half the principal portraits of the great father of the Englifh ftage ; nor can I, at the very advanced age of feventy, I fear, make any fupplement to the Dramatic Mifcellanies, if they fhould happen to pleafe.

The comparing the merits of our principal comedians coft me no fmall attention to their difcriminative faculties. I wifh this part of my book may prove as enter-taining to the public, and as profitable to the gentlemen and ladies of the theatre, as it was laborious to me.

Such books and pamphlets, as have furnifhed me with facts and anecdotes relating to authors and actors, I have generally referred to in the margin ; fome I have given from my own knowledge and obfervation ; many of them I gleaned from old actors, long fince deceafed. The principal of thefe, as well as my memory can recollect, were Mr. John Roberts, a man of confiderable reading and obfervation, who wrote an anfwer to that part of

A 4 Pope's

Pope's preface to Shakſpeare which related to Burbage
and other players of his time; Mr. Morgan, commonly
called Drib Morgan; Mr. Aſton, ſon of the famous itinerant actor, Tony Aſton; and Mr. Nathaniel Clarke.
My acquaintance with Mr. Crofs, late prompter of
Drury-lane theatre, has been of ſervice to me: he had
known the ſtage long; and had recorded many facts of the
actors in his days, which he occaſionally acquainted me
with. Some obligations of this kind I owe Mr. Macklin,
and more to Mr. Victor. Mr. Ebenezer Forreſt, the attorney, who had been long converſant with Covent-
garden theatre, very kindly ſupplied me with ſome intereſting anecdotes.

The unexpected encouragement, given to the Memoirs
of the Life of Mr. Garrick, by a generous public, demands my ſincere and grateful acknowledgement.

That the Memoirs were not agreeable to Mrs. Garrick
gives me little uneaſineſs. Her diſlike of them may be
accounted for, much to her honour, without reflecting
any diſgrace on me.

In writing the life of a great and good man, (and
ſuch, I preſume, with ſome allowance of human infirmi-
ty, I have deſcribed Mr. Garrick,) the honeſt biographer
muſt relate ſome circumſtances of conduct which a tender
and affectionate wife cannot peruſe with complacency.

I was not inattentive to the feelings of Mrs. Garrick. — When I was preparing a ſecond edition of my
book, I wrote a letter to the gentleman who is the acting
executor of Mr. Garrick's will; in which I deſired
him to communicate any miſtakes or overſights I might
have incurred in the Memoirs, and to point out any

paſſage

paffage in it that might have given juft offence to Mrs. Garrick or any of Mr. Garrick's family; promifing, at the fame time, to rectify any thing amifs, in the new edition. To this letter I received no anfwer.

It is with pleafure I can farther eftablifh a moft valuable part of Mr. Garrick's character; I mean his charity and generofity.

Dr. Ramfden, the worthy mafter of the Charterhoufe, very lately informed me, that a defcendant of Grotius, who, by the intereft of Dr. Johnfon, (a man who is never fo well pleafed as in relieving the diftreffes of the indigent and promoting the happinefs of mankind,) was enabled to partake the excellent charity of that houfe, told him, that, by the death of Mr. Garrick, he had loft a very great friend; and, being defired to explain himfelf, he affured the mafter, that Mr. Garrick had fettled a penfion on him of 10l. per annum during his own life.

I could mention a noble act of generofity of this truly benevolent man; but refpect to the living reftrains me.

I might, indeed, juftly fay, that the charities of David Garrick were not only very extenfive, but many of them concealed from the world.

By the kind partiality of the public, I fhall be enabled, very foon, to publifh a fourth edition of the Memoirs of the Life of David Garrick.

S U R.

SUBSCRIBERS.

A.

ARchard, Reverend Mr.
Allen, Mr. Edmund.
Aldridge, Dr.
Abington, Mrs.
Adamfon, Mr.
Ayleward, Mr,
Almon, Mr.   2 fets.
Adolphins, Mr.
Anderfon, Mr.
Andrews, Mr. Jofeph.
Ackworth, Mr.
Ayton, Mr.
Aickin, Mr. James.

B.

Briftol, Right honourable Earl of,
Beauchamp, Right Honourable Lord,
Beauchamp, Lady.
Beauchamp-Proctor, Lady, of Bruton-ftreet.
Beaumont, Sir George.
Beaumont, Percival, Efq.

Barnard,

Barnard, John, Efq.

Blake, Mr. Henry,

Barnard, William, Efq.

Bofwell, James, Efq.

Booth, Benjamin, Efq.

Bowles, Oldfield, Efq.

Beard, John, Efq.

Byng, J. Efq.

Bathoe, J. Efq.

Bate, Mr.

Burney, Dr.

Brodie, Dr.

Brocklefby, Dr.

Beaver, Dr.

Beattie, Dr.

Blair, Dr. Hugh.

Bowle, Reverend Mr.   3 fets.

Bowles, Mr.   4 ditto.

Barnard, Rev. Mr. Benjamin.

Brereton, Mr.

Berry, Mr.

Baynes, Mr.

Berry, Mr.   10 fets.

Bennett, Mrs.

Beattie, Mr. James Hay.

Barwell, Mr. Nathaniel.

Baldwin, Mr. Henry.

Brook, Mr. Edward.

Benfley, Mr.

Bennett, Mr.

Blythe, Mr.

                               Bannifter,

Bannifter, Mr. John.
Baker, Mr.
Baddeley, Mr.
Baden, Mr.
Brereton, Owen Salifbury, Efq.
Barbut, Mr. Stephen.
Booth and Son, Meffrs.
Barker, Mr. William.
Beardmore, Thomas, Efq.
Bourdillon, Mr. Thomas.
Baldwin, Mr. Robert.
Bate Dudley, Reverend Mr.
C.
Carmarthen, Marquis of, 2 fets.
Chedworth, Lord.
Cholmondeley, Honourable Mrs.
Cradock, Jofeph, Efq.
Caldwin, ———, Efq.
Currer, John, Efq.
Crofbie, Andrew, Efq.
Corett, Thomas, Efq.
Colman, George, Efq.
Cooper, Dr.
Cornthwaite, Reverend Mr.
Clerke, Reverend Mr.
Crompton, Captain.
Clerk, Lieutenant.
Crompton, Mr.
Campbell, Mr.
Chapman, Mr. William.
Cradock, Mrs.
Catton, Mr.
Campbell, Mr. Walter.
Cadell, Mr. Thomas.

Clayton,

Clayton, Mr. Henry.
Conant, Mr.
Campbell, Mr.   2 fets.
Cook, Mr. William.
Crookſhanks, Mr. J.
Corſbie, Mr.
Clarke, Mr.
Chapman, Mr. William Francis.
Cummins, Mr. Th. R. York.
Calverly, Mr. John, jun.
Cattley, Mr. John.
Cadell, Mrs.
Conſt, Mr. Francis.
Copley, Mr.
Cadby, ———, Efq.
Caldwell, Andrew, Efq.

D.

Douglas, Dr.
Dunbar, Dr.
De Salis, Dr.
Du Val, Dr.
Dulany, Captain.
Dodſley, Mr. James.
Davis, Mr. Lockyer.
Dilly, Mr. Charles.
Dempſter, George, Efq.
Dent, Mr.   2 fets.
Dance, Mr.
Dick, Mr.
Dodd, Mr.
Dinwoody, Mr.
Debrett, Mr.

E.

E.

Eccles, Ifaac Ambrofe, Efq.　6 fets.
Evanfon, Mr.
Evans, Mr. Thomas.
Egerton, Mr. John.
Efte, Mr.　　　　　　　　2 fets.
Ewfden, Mr.
Elliot, Mr.
Edwin, Mr.
Elmfly, Mr.

F.

Fitzwilliams, Honourable William.
Franklin, Dr.
Forbes, Sir William.
Farmer, Rev. Dr. Mafter of Emanuel-college, Cambridge.
Frafer, Honourable Archibald.
Fountain, Mr.
Felton, Mr.
Farren, Mifs.
Foy, Mifs.
Forfbrook, Mr. Leonard.
Forfbrook, Mr.
Fector, William, Efq.
Farren, Mr.
Fletcher, Mr. George, jun.

G.

Graham, Marquis of.
Gordon, Honourable Mr. Baron.
Giffard, William, Efq.

Glasford,

Glasford, William, Efq.
Glover, Dr.
Glynne, Dr.
Garrick, Reverend Mr.
Goate, Colonel.
Gibfon, Mr.
Green, Mr. Henry.
Griffith, Mr. Arthur.
Galabin, Mr.
Gwatkin, Mrs.
Gilbert, Mr. William.
Glasford, Mr. James.
Garton, Jonathan, Efq.
Griffiths, Mr. R.
Glover, Mifs.   2 fets.

H.

Holden, ———, Efq.
Harris, ———, Efq.
Hopkins, Thomas, Efq.
Holden, Robert, Efq.
Horn, Dr.
Hamilton, Mr.   16 fets.
Hull, Mr. Thomas.
Henderfon, Mr.
Hoole, Mr.
Hird, Mr. Thomas.
Howard, Samuel, Efq.
Hervey, Colonel.
Hammond, Peter, Efq.
Haffel, Mr.

                                        Henry,

Henry, Mr. J.
Hawkins, Mr. Abraham.
Hotchkin, Mr.
Heavifide, Mr. J.
Hodges, Mr. Chriftopher.
Harrifon, Mr.
Hill, Mr. Edward.
Hingifton, Mr. John.
Hilderfley, Mrs.
Hughes, Mr.

J.

Johnfon, Dr.   2 fets.
Jervis, Reverend Mr.
Jeffreafon, Reverend Mr.
Ives, Reverend Mr.
Ireland, Samuel, Efq.
Ireland, Mr. J.
Jones, Mr.
Jorden, Mr. John.
Jorden, Mr. George.
Jackfon, George, Efq.

K.

King, John, Efq.
King, Thomas, Efq.   6 fets.
King, Mr. William,   2 fets.
Kemble, Mr.
Kelly, Mr.
Kettle, Captain,   2 fets.

L.

Lawſon, Sir William.
Langton, Bennett, Eſq.
Lawſon, Welfrid, Eſq.
Locker, William, Eſq.
Lort, Reverend Dr.
Lewis, Mr.
Lawrence, Mr. William, jun.
Lawrence, Mr.
Leigh, Mr.
Lobb, Mr. Richard.
Ledger, Mr.
Lindſey, Mr.
Lennard, Mr. Peregrine.
Longman, Mr.
Law, Mr.
Lee Lewes, Mr.

M.

Mountſtuart, Lord.
Maclaurin, John, Eſq.
Muſgrove, Richard, Eſq.
Merrick, James, Eſq.
Merier, Captain James.
Moore, Miſs Hannah.
Morley, Mrs.
Murray, Mrs.
Morriſſon, Mr.
Meredith, jun. Mr.
Maſcall, Mr.

Moody,

Moody, Mr.
Macklin, Mr.
Malone, Mr.
Murphy, Mr. Arthur,   4 fets.
Meyer, Mr.
Mainfton, Mr.
Mathias, Mr. Gabriel.
Merrill, Mr.
Murray, Mr.
Marfhall, Mr. Thomas.
Marfhall, Mrs.
Mattocks, Mr.
Manager of the theatre, Norwich.

N.

Norfolk, his Grace the Duke of.
Newling, John, Efq.
Nicoll, Mr.
Nichols, Mr. John.
Nicol, Mr. George.
Noble, Mr.
Naylor, Mr.
Naffau, Mr.
New Society of Nottingham.

P.

Payne, Sir Ralph.
Pique, Edward, Efq.
Percy, (Dr.) Lord Bifhop of Dunmore.
Pennick, Reverend Dr.
Pegge, Reverend Mr.
Peach, Reverend Mr.

Payne, Mr.
————, Mr. Thomas, jun.
————, Mr. James.
————, Mifs.
————, Mifs Sally.
Palmer, Mr.
————, Robert, Efq.
Parnell, Hugh, Efq.
Powell, Mr.
Paradife, Mr.
Peterfon, Mr.
Perkin, Mr.
Povoleri, Mr.
Parfons, Mr.
Pearce, William, Efq.
Pytts, Jonathan, Efq.
Parker, Mr.
Perry, Mrs.
Popham, Mr. Biggs.
Priaulx, Mrs.
Phillips, Mr. Peregrine.
Payne, John, Efq.

Q.

Quick, Mr.

R.

Reynolds, Sir Jofhua.
Rufh, ————, Efq.
Rolfie, ————, Efq.
Roberts, William, Efq.
Row, Nathaniel, Efq.
Richardfon, William, Efq.
Rofe, Dr.   4 fets.

Robertfon,

Robertſon, Dr. Regius Profeſſor.

Richardſon, Reverend Mr.

Rouſe, Reverend Mr.

Reave, Reverend Mr.

Robertſon, Mr. James.

Ritſon, Mr.

Rockcliff, Reverend Mr.

Richardſon, Mr.

Robſon, Mr.

Robinſon, Mr. G.

Royer, Mr. Edward.

Raim, Mr. J.

Rivington, John, Eſq.

S.

Smith, Sir John.

Strahan, William, Eſq.

Stuart, James, Eſq.

Sheldon, Richard, Eſq.

Sheridan, Thomas, Eſq.

Stephens, Francis, Eſq.

Shepherd, Reverend Dr.

Smallbrook, Dr.

Steward, Mr.

Steward, Mr. John.

Seward, Mr.

Stuart, Colonel James.

Swan, Mr. John.

Stacie, Mr.

Spreckley, Mr. George.

Siddons, Mrs.

Story, Mr. George William.

Spilſbury,

Spilfbury, Mr.

Smart, Mr.

Sewell, Mr. Thomas.

Sole, Mr. C.

Spicdell, Mr.

Skirret, Mr. Thomas.

Saftree, Mr.

Suttell, Mr. George.

Sheldon, Mr.

Swan, Mr. John.

Sevans, Mr.

Scott, Mr. Samuel.

Strahan, Reverend Mr.

Scourfield, Reverend Mr.

Smith, William, Efq.

T.

Tyers, J. Efq.

Tighe, Edward, Efq.

Tooke, Reverend Mr.

Twift, Mr.

Thompfon, Mr. Edward.

Truflove, Thomas, Efq.

Tickell, Richard, Efq.

Tinckler, Mr. John.

Thomkinfon, Mr.

Turner, Mr. Richard.

Twygge, Mr. T. F.

Taylor, Mifs Frances.

Thrale, Mrs.

U.

V.

Vincent, Sir Francis.
Vanbrugh, Edward, Efq.

W.

Weddal, Thomas, Efq.
Winter, Ralph, Efq.
Wilkinfon, Tate, Efq.
Wright, Dr.
Warner, Reverend Mr.
White, Major,
Waring, Captain.
Winder, Captain.
Walter, Mr.
Wray, Mr.
Walcot, Mr.
Woodfall, Mr. H. S.
Wright, Mr.
Winder, Mr.
Wefton, Mr. Ambrofe.
Winter, Mr. William.
Whitmore, Mr.
Wyndham, Mr. Thomas.
Walker, Mr. J.
Wingrave, Mr.
Wife, Mr. J.
Wilfon, Mr.
Way, Benjamin, Efq.
Weller, Mr. John.

Wallis,

Wallis, Mr.
Whitmore, Mr.
Wilkie, fen. Mr.
Wrighten, Mrs.
Woodminſton, Mr.
Woodfall, Mr. William.
Walter, Mr.
White, Mr. Benjamin.
White, Mr. Benjamin, jun.

Y.

York, John, Eſq.
Yates, Mrs.
Young, Miſs.
Younger, Mr.

DRAMATIC

DRAMATIC

MISCELLANIES.

King John.

CHAPTER I.

Three plays written on the subject of K. John. — When Shakspeare's K. John was first published. — Shakspeare indebted to the Troublesome Reign of K. John. — Colley Cibber's Fatal Tyranny. — Cibber's arrogance. — Theatrical progress of the Fatal Tyranny. — Line in Pope's Dunciad upon it. — Revival of Shakspeare's K. John by Rich. — Its success, and an account of the actors, particularly Walker, Hale, and Mrs. Hallam. — Sarcasm of Quin. — Mistake of Mr. Steevens and Mr. Theobald. — Scene of Bastardy. — Queen Eleanor's logic in favour

VOL. I.					B					*of*

*of the Baſtard Falconbridge.—Explanation
of the word* trick.*—Mr. Garrick puzzled to
procure a contraſt.—Barry's perplexity.*

ON the ſubject of King John three plays have been written. That, which is called the Troubleſome Reign of King John, was attributed to Shakſpeare and Rowley by Mr. Pope, and by Mr. Steevens to Shakſpeare alone; but, on mature conſideration, this gentleman has retracted his opinion; Mr. Malone has, with great appearance of probability, aſcribed it to Marlow. Our author's K. John was firſt publiſhed, with the reſt of his works, in 1623. The late commentators have juſtly obſerved, that many of Shakſpeare's beſt pieces are formed on the ground-work of others. He ſeems more indebted to the author of the Troubleſome Reign of K. John, for his plot and characters, and even his ſentiments, than to any other writer. Colley Cibber's Papal Tyranny was taken from Shakſpeare's K.

John

John, but he was not so happy in his alterations of this tragedy as in his King
Richard the Third. In this last play, Colley very dextrously made up a very pleasing
pasticcio from a diligent perusal of all
Shakspeare's historical plays, scarcely making use of a line or thought which was his
own. His Papal Tyranny he pretends was
written to supply Shakspeare's deficiencies,
but more especially the want of warm resentment in a king of England when insul-
ted by a pope's nuncio; and, his play being acted in 1744, when the nation was a-
larmed with the threats of an invasion by a
popish pretender, the popular sentiments,
against the encroachments of papal influence, met with applause. Colley's
vanity so far transported him, that, in his
Dedication, he told Lord Chesterfield, he
had endeavoured to make his play more
like one ' than what he found it in Shakspeare.' But Cibber lived long enough to
see his Papal Tyranny entirely neglected,
and, what must have been more mortifying to

B 2   a

a man of his extreme vanity, the original
play revived with great fuccefs. His boun-
cing, though well-meant, declamation a-
gainft the infolent pretenfions of papal
power, could not make amends for his
mutilations of Shakfpeare: and efpecially for
his murdering two characters of our inimitable poet, not inferior perhaps to any
which fell from his pen ; Lady Conftance
and the Baftard Falconbridge. However,
it is to Cibber, I believe, we owe the revival of this tragedy, which had lain dormant
from the days of Shakfpeare till 1736.

The Fatal Tyranny had been offered to
Mr. Fleetwood, the manager of Drury-
lane theatre, about nine or ten years before
it was acted. This was no fooner known
to the public than Cibber was moft feverely
attacked by the critics in the newfpapers ;
Fielding wrote a farce upon the fubject,
which was played at the little theatre in
the Haymarket, though I do not believe it
is printed amongft his works. However,
the parts in the Fatal Tyranny were diftri-
buted,

buted, and a time fixed for its performance : but the clamour againſt the author,
whoſe preſumption was highly cenſured
for daring to meddle with Shakſpeare, in-
creaſed to ſuch a height, that Colley, who
had ſmarted more than once for dabbling
in tragedy, went to the playhouſe, and,
without ſaying a word to any body, took
the play from the prompter's deſk, and
marched off with it in his pocket. Pope,
in his new edition of the Dunciad, which
he had taken the pains to alter, in order to
dethrone Theobald and place Cibber in his
room, in the following line hints at the
cautious conduct of the poet-laureat :

King John in ſilence modeſtly expires.

Dunc. Book I.

So much was ſaid, and with propriety,
by the critics who wrote againſt Cibber in
the public prints, in commendation of
Shakſpeare's K John, that Mr. Rich very
wiſely determined to take the hint, and
reſolved to revive that long-forgotten tragedy. The principal parts, if I can truſt

my memory, were thus divided: King
John, Mr. Delane; the Baſtard, Tom
Walker, (the original Macheath;) Hale
acted the King of France, and Ryan Cardinal Pandulph; Lady Conſtance by Mrs.
Hallam. Of Delane, Walker, and Ryan, I have ſpoken at large in the Life of
Garrick; and in the courſe of this work
ſhall have frequent occaſion to mention
them. Hale was in perſon tall and well-
proportioned, his voice ſtrong and harmonious, his deportment manly, and his action not diſpleaſing; his ear was ſo un-
faithful, that he was generally monoto-
nous; he wanted that judgement which
alone knows how to give dignity to ſentiment or warmth and variety to paſſion.
His beſt performance was Hotſpur; he
was always to be endured when he re-
ſtrained himſelf from doing too much.
He was a favourite actor in Briſtol, where
I think he died in 1746. He was ſo fond of
wearing large full-bottomed wigs, that,
to the aſtoniſhment of the audience, he
                                    acted

acted the part of Charles the Firſt in one which was remarkably long and fair. *

Mrs. Hallam was an actreſs of ſuch uncommon merit, that ſhe deſerves to be particularly remembered. She had ſignalized herſelf ſo greatly as a member of the company acting at Norwich, when her name was Parker, that ſhe received an invitation from Mr. Rich to join his company at Lincoln's-inn Fields. There ſhe long ſtruggled with difficulties ; for I have

---

* It has been ſaid, that this actor was much hurt by Mr. Garrick's mimickry of him in the part of Bayes in the Rehearſal. Hale was preſent at the play, and laughing very heartily at the mimical exhibitions of Delane, Ryan, Bridgwater, and Giffard : when, on a ſudden, Garrick ſpoke three or four lines of Prince Prettyman, beginning with

" Oh ! what a ſtranger am I grown of late!"

in a ſtyle which conveyed ſuch an exact reſemblance of Hale's voice and manner, that the theatre echoed with loud laughter and thundering applauſe. Hale was ſhocked at the mortifying ſcene, and felt the folly and injuſtice of approving that ridicule of others which he could not bear himſelf.

B 4 been

been told fhe was by no means a favourite
of the manager: but, on the death of Mrs.
Boheme, many of her principal parts fell
to the lot of Mrs. Hallam.   The great encouragement, fhe conftantly met with from
the audience, at once raifed her reputation
and increafed her income.   Her merit, indeed, was indifputable ; for fhe fucceeded
a performer as remarkable for beauty as
fkill in her profeffion.   Mrs. Hallam was
unhappy in a large unweildy perfon : notwithftanding this unfavourable circumftance, the public always wifhed to fee her
in charaḑters which received no advantage
from her figure.   Monimia was a part
which her good underftanding would have
taught her to refign ; but neither the public nor the manager would permit it.   You
may guefs at the unfitnefs of her figure for
young and delicate ladies by Quin's farcafm.   He obferved one morning, at rehearfal, a large tub, or barrel, in which
the mad Englifhman in the Pilgrim rolls
about the ftage ; he afked the prompter
                                         what

what it was; but, before he could receive an anfwer, he cried out, *I fee what it is: Mrs. Hallam's ftays, in which fhe played Monimia laft night.* Her performance of Lady Conftance was natural and impaffioned; though fhe was not fo pathetic in utterance, fpirited in action, or dignified in deportment, as Mrs. Cibber in the fame part. Her principal characters in tragedy were Lady Macbeth, Belvidera, Roxana, Queen Elizabeth in the Earl of Effex, Zara in the Mourning Bride, Evadne in the Maid's Tragedy, the Queen in Hamlet; in comedy fhe excelled in Congreve's Lady Touchwood in the Double Dealer, his Marwood in the Way of the World, Amanda in Cibber's Love's laft Shift, Steele's Lady Brumpton in the Funeral, &c. Mrs. Hallam died about the year 1738.

King John was acted feveral nights with great applaufe; but the king was not remarkably well reprefented by Delane; he could not eafily affume the turbulent and gloomy paffions of the character.

Mr.

Mr. Steevens has fallen into a flight miftake, if that note be his, in which it is
faid, that Hall, Hollingfhead, and Stowe,
are clofely followed in the expreffions
throughout this, as well as feveral other
hiftorical plays of Shakfpeare : Hall begins his Chronicle about two hundred
years after the æra in which John began to
reign.   Mr. Theobald has likewife committed an error: he afferts, that, although
the play begins in the 34th year of K.
John's life, which was the firft of his
reign, yet that it takes in only fome tranfactions at the time of his death; whereas
the tragedy very properly begins with the
claim of John's nephew, Prince Arthur,
to the crown : this was one of the moft
material events in the king's life; and his
conduct, to Arthur, Shakfpeare very judicioufly makes the foundation of all his
misfortunes.

If I do not miftake, Mr. Steevens has
mifunderftood a paffage in a fpeech of Q.
Eleanor in the firft fcene of this play :

This

This might have been prevented, and made whole
With very eafy argument of love ;
Which now the *manage* of two kingdoms muft
With fearful bloody iffue arbitrate.

By the word *manage* I underftand the ftrength and power of France and England, rather than, according to Mr. Steevens, the conduct and adminiftration of them, which feems more remote from the author's meaning ; though perhaps the word may comprehend both.

The fcene between the two brothers, Robert and Philip Falconbridge, is a very extraordinary one, and hardly to be matched in dramatic poetry. One brother calls the other baftard, and accufes his mother of adultery ; which charge the other does not flatly deny, but is unwilling to part with his claim to the eftate. The original of this quarrel is to be found, I believe, in an old book, quoted by Mr. Steevens, called The Hiftory of Lord Falconbridge, Baftard-Son to Richard Cœur de Lion. Our author has followed the old play, with fuch alterations and ad-
ditions,

ditions as his genius fuggefted to him, which I think never fhone brighter than in his management of Falconbridge's character.

Shakfpeare has avoided a very grofs impropriety by not permitting the mother of Falconbridge to be prefent when her chaftity is called in queftion by her fon; an error which the author of the old play has fallen into. In that, too, Queen Eleanor exerts all her power in favour of the lady, and plays the cafuift fo acutely, that fhe merits the reputation of learning which hiftorians afcribe to her. The king obferves, in confirmation of what Robert Falconbridge had affirmed, that Philip the Baftard refembled King Richard, whom Robert afferts to have been his father; the queen's reply is, I think, curious, and worth preferving.

E L E A N O R.

Nay, hear you, fir: you run away too faft.
Know you not, *omne fimile non eft idem ?*

———— Hark you, good fir; 'twas thus, and no otherwife: fhe lay with Sir Robert, your father, and
thought

thought upon King Richard, my fon ; and fo your brother was formed in this fafhion.

In the old play, the Baftard draws his
fword upon his mother, and threatens to
kill her if fhe conceals the truth. In
Shakfpeare, the lady's confeffion is extorted by mirth and pleafantry. In Shakfpeare's King John, Queen Eleanor takes
notice that the Baftard

> Hath a *trick* of Coeur-de-Lion's face.

I am not fure that Mr. Steevens hath hit
the full meaning of the word *trick*, though
he has brought feveral authorities to fupport his interpretation of it.

In this and other places, by the word
trick Shakfpeare means fome diftinguifh-
ing air or feature of the face, in which
a ftrong refemblance of the parent may be
difcovered.

In the Winter's Tale, Paulina proves
the legitimacy of Queen Hermione's
daughter by *a trick of face* which fhe has in
common with her father :

Behold,

——————Behold, my lords,
The trick of's frown!————

WINTER'S TALE, Act. II.

So Falstaff, when reprefenting Henry the
Fourth, in a mock-fcene between the
Prince of Wales and himfelf, tells the
Prince,

Thou art my fon : I have partly thy mother's word,
partly my own opinion ; but chiefly *a villainous trick of
thine eye, and a foolish hanging of thy nether lip.*

In the fame fcene the Baftard exclaims,

With that half-face !

That this expreffion was taken from coins,
on which the profile only of our princes
was exhibited, Theobald has well enough
proved. An author, I think, is always
beft illuftrated by himfelf: Hotfpur, in
Henry the Fourth, Act I. in the midft of
his extravagant and wild flights, exclaims,

But out upon this half-fac'd fellowfhip!

Various

Various have been the actors of this brave, generous, romantic, and humourous, character, Falconbridge : but, though Garrick, Sheridan, Delane, and Barry, have attempted it, they all fell short of the merits of Tom Walker. In him alone were found the several requisites for the character : a strong and muscular person, a bold and intrepid look; manly deportment, vigorous action, and a humour which descended to an easy familiarity in conveying a jest or sarcasm with uncommon poignancy. Garrick had certainly much merit in the Bastard, but the want of the mechanical part was a deficiency not to be remedied by art.

He was at a loss, for some time, to fix upon a Robert Falconbridge, to set off his own figure ; at last he picked out poor Simson, a Scotchman, a modest and honest man, but as feeble in person as he was in acting. Frier John, the contrast to Frier Paul, in the Duenna, was scarce a greater skeleton than Simson. It was a matter of astonishment to every fpectator, that Barry, with the fuperior advantage of a fine perfon, could make fo little of the Baftard. He feemed, in that part, to be quite out of his road: all the humour, gaiety, eafe, and gallantry, of Falconbridge, were loft in Barry.

An odd circumftance happened on his endeavouring to repeat the following words in the firft act of the play :

Well now I can make any Joan a lady.

He was fo embarraffed in the delivery of this fingle line, that, not being able to repeat the words, he was forced to quit the ftage, amidft the general applaufes of the audience, who faw and felt his uneafinefs. But, what is ftill more furprifing, after going off and returning three feveral times, with the fame kind encouragement of the fpectators, he was forced to give it up ; and I believe he did not recover himfelf till he was relieved by the entrance of Lady Falconbridge.

CHAPTER

CHAPTER II.

The character of Philip Augustus. — Princes, of the present age, Trajans when compared to those in the reign of John.—Lymoges, duke of Austria.—Shakspeare oftener adheres to old ballads and romances than chronicle or history. —A vile groupe of sovereign princes.—Henry VI. emperor of Germany.—Popes in the eleventh and twelfth centuries.—The old man of the mountains.--Prince Arthur's right of primogeniture.—Character of Queen Eleanor, at large, from the French historians and Brantome.—An ass wearing shoes.—Reason why Eleanor prefers King John to Arthur. — Explanation of a term in hunting, from Turberville.—The word stay *explained.—Observation on Falconbridge's speech at the end of the third act.*

Act II. Scene I.

IN the second act of King John, the poet introduces, amongst other characters, Philip Augustus of France ; and, if ex-

C   treme

treme cunning, unbounded ambition, fraud, perfidy, perjury, rapine, and injuftice, could render a monarch a politician, he was certainly the greateft of his time. Shakfpeare was not obliged to fhew the whole of his character, and, indeed, it is fo comprehenfively odious, that no audience would have fuffered it. The princes, who now rule over the greateft part of Europe, though many of them are little attentive to the real interefts of their people, and more fond of power than willing to make a right ufe of it, may be termed by the honourable title of Trajans, if compared with the royal monfters of this period. Lymoges, archduke of Auftria, is, in this fcene, raifed from the dead to be punifhed for his bafe ufage of Richard I. whom he arrefted in his paffage through his dominions, and afterwards, for a ftipulated fum, delivered to the emperor of Germany. The offence, given by Richard, was fome fharp or proud expreffion he let fall againft the duke, when both were engaged in the

holy

holy wars. The old play could not lead Shakſpeare into the error of aſcribing the death of Richard to the duke of Auſtria, as Mr. Steevens has aſſerted; he was too well acquainted with our chronicles, and eſpecially Hollingſhead, to miſtake that event. But Shakſpeare oftener ſtudies ſtage effect than he adheres to the truth of hiſtory; and, in treating of remote ſtory, he is certainly juſtifiable for this deviation. But Shakeſpeare choſe too, in this play, and in moſt others, to follow old romance and ballad rather than chronicle or authenticated ſtory. Perhaps no æra ſince the creation produced ſuch a groupe of pernicious chief rulers as the time of which I am ſpeaking: beſides our own John, Philip, and the duke of Auſtria, we can reckon, amongſt them, Henry VI. emperor of Germany, ſeveral popes ſucceſſively in order, and a very remarkable potentate, called the Old Man of the Mountains. As for Henry, he, of all princes, was the leaſt ſcrupulous; perfidy, cru-

elty,

elty, oppreffion, and avarice, were his dar-
ling paffions; as foon as he got the poffeffion of Richard's perfon, he threw him into a dungeon; nay, to infult him more
confpicuoufly, he produced him before the
princes of Germany in a diet of the em-
pire: but Richard's undaunted fpirit and
convincing eloquence produced an effect
contrary to the emperor's intention; they
all interceded in his favour, and infifted he
fhould be delivered from confinement; but,
before he would grant him his liberty, he
exacted the immenfe fum of three hundred
thoufand pounds, equal to a million and a
half of our money. The meaneft dabbler
in hiftory will readily agree, that by far the
greateft part of the popes, who lived in the
eleventh and twelfth centuries, were inferior to no kings, that ever lived, in pride,
infolence, avarice, injuftice, and rapine.
If we fhould grant that in knowledge and
learning they were fuperior to the reft of
mankind, it muft likewife be owned, that
they perverted thefe acquirements to the
worft

worſt of purpoſes ; to the deceiving and robbing thoſe who put an implicit confidence in them.

The Old man of the mountains was called Chik Elchaffiffin, from which word Voltaire derives the word affaffin. This hoary ruffian had acquired ſuch an aſcendant over his fanatical ſubjects, that they paid an implicit obedience to his commands ; aſſaffination was meritorious with them, when under the ſanction of his royal mandate ; they carried their enthuſiaſtic zeal for his ſervice ſo far as to court all hazards, and even to ruſh wildly on to certain death in the execution of his orders*. Theſe miſerable wretches fancied that, when they ſacrificed their lives for his ſake, the gates of paradiſe would be open to them.

Every part of this digreffion will, I hope, be amuſing at leaſt, and ſome of it not uſeleſs, to the common reader of Shakſpeare's John.

C 3 Act

---

* Hume's Hift. of England, vol. II. p. 18.

Act II. Scene II.

CHATILLON.

With him along is come the mother queen,
An Até ftirring him to blood and ftrife.

The term, Até, is very properly beftowed upon this lady ; in her hufband
king Henry's life-time fhe was the trum-
pet of rebellion and treafon, and was
continually urging her fons to take up arms
againft their father.

PHILIP.

For thou haft underwrought its lawful king.

Thou haft prevented the lawful fucceffor from enjoying what belongs to
him, by cutting off the right of pofterity.
The feudal law, which was then in full
force over all Europe, had eftablifhed the
right of primogeniture. In England, as
well as elfewhere, the fon of the elder brother was entitled to fucceed to his grandfather, preferably to his uncles, though
they were nearer allied to the deceafed monarch. But the right line of fucceffion
had in no country, except Scotland, been

fo

fo often broken through, perhaps, as in ours, antecedent to this period. That order, or right, had been violated no lefs than three times in the fpace of about fourfcore years. Richard, when he fet out upon the holy war, declared his nephew Arthur, of Brittany, his fucceffor; but, notwithftanding John's ingratitude and rebellion, he, at the inftigation of his mother, by his laft will declared him heir to all his dominions: and this will the queen refers to, when, in anfwer to fome outrageous accufations of Lady Conftance, fhe replies,

> Thou unadvifed fcold, I can produce
> A will, that bars the title of thy fon.

LADY CONSTANCE.

> My boy a baftard! By my foul, I think
> His father never was fo true begot:
> It cannot be, and if thou wert his mother.

To underftand the propriety of Lady Conftance's fpeech, which contains fo heavy a charge, it is neceffary that the reader of this tragedy fhould be previoufly acquainted with Queen Eleanor's character.

This

This lady was daughter of the duke of Guienne, and wife to Louis VII. of France, to whom fhe brought in dowry fome of the richeft provinces of that kingdom. Her reputation for chaftity was far from being clear, when Louis took her with him on a crufade into the holy land. The French hiftorians, and, amongft the reft, Mezeray, an author whofe name I am furprifed not to find amongft the moft eminent French hiftorians, in one of the fineft poems which this age has produced*, tells us ftrange ftories of her inordinate and unfatisfied luft. It is faid fhe was particularly fond of Saladin, the emperor; others tell us, that it was Saladin, a private foldier, and a very handfome Saracen, of whom fhe was deeply enamoured. Let us hear what honeft Brantome fays, in his blunt, but expreffive, language.

" Our Queen Eleanor, duchefs of Guienne, who attended the king, her hufband, beyond fea, and who, by frequently converfing

---

* Hayley on Hiftory.

verfing amongft arms and the foldiery, gave
herfelf fuch a loofe at laft as to have to do
with the Saracens, for which the king divorced her, and which coft us dear. She
had a mind to try whether thefe warlike men
were as brave champions in a bed-cham-
ber as in the field of battle. Poffibly it
was her humour to love valiant men."

This plain-fpoken writer, in another
place, fays, that Queen Eleanor was not the
only one who went to the holy war in company with Louis ; ' *Plufieurs grandes dames
avec leur marys fe croisèrent, mais non leur
jambes, qu'elles ouvrirent, et les largirent à bon
efcient ; fi qu'aucunes y demeurerènt, et les au-
tres retournèrent, de très bonnes veffes.*'

Notwithftanding Eleanor's ill fame, and
her being divorced from her hufband for
lewdnefs, in reality, though pretendedly,
on account of too near confanguinity, our
King Henry II. was not fo fqueamifh as
to neglect the opportunity of adding
feveral noble and rich provinces to his
dominions by accepting her hand. They
were

were both in the prime and vigour of life, and their eagernefs to come together was evident by the quick journeys they took to meet each other. No couple of ardent lovers feemed more willing to be united in the nuptial bond than Henry and Eleanor. Their happinefs did not laft long; fhe was as jealous of Henry as her firft hufband had been of her, and with reafon: but Henry was not fo mild as Louis; he confined her in prifon during the greateft part of his reign. I fhall conclude this note with the remarkable words of Mezeray: " This woman, confummate in all forts of wickednefs, lived eighty years, kept up a war for above fixty years, and fettled a hatred between France and England, that has continued above three ages; fo that with reafon we may fay of her, what the Greek poet faid of Menelaus's wife, that we have fuffered not a ten, but a *four hundred, years war, with fire and fword, by means of this woman.*"

FALCONBRIDGE.
It lies as lightly on the back of him
As great Alcides' *shoes* upon an afs.

A more whimfical and ludicrous image cannot be prefented to the mind, than an afs trotting up and down, his hoofs covered over with fair large bufkins, fit for the foot of Hercules. The fenfe is very clear, but Theobald, fuppofing that the afs could carry fhoes no where but on his back, altered *fhoes* to *fhews*. Mr. Steevens has, from feveral parallel paffages of old authors, proved the frequent ufe of the term *Hercules' fhoes*, apparently from the old proverb, *ex pede Herculem*.

LADY CONSTANT.
Give grandam kingdom, and it grandam will
Give it a plum, a cherry, and a fig.

The inveterate hatred of thefe two ladies, the Queen and the Duchefs of Brittany, was founded on fomething more fubftantial than mere perfonal pique. Eleanor, it is faid by hiftorians, had a ftronger affection towards her nephew Arthur than her fon John; but fhe juftly apprehended,

if

if Arthur had fucceeded to the crown, his mother, who was a woman of an excellent underftanding and of an undaunted mind, would have had the direction of his affairs; this prompted the dowager to efpoufe the caufe of John, who paid great deference to her counfels.

ENGLISH HERALD.

And, like a jolly troop of huntfmen, come
Our lufty Englifh, all with purple hands,
Dy'd in the dying flaughter of their foes.

There is in Julius Cæfar, Act III. a paffage quite fimilar to this; Mark Antony, in an apoftrophe to the dead body of Cæfar, compares his murderers to hunters ftained with the blood of the flain deer.

Pardon me, Julius, here waft thou bay'd, brave hart!
Here didft thou fall, and here thy hunters ftand,
Sign'd in thy fpoil, and crimfon'd in thy lethe.

Dr. Johnfon, in a note upon the firft cited paffage, thinks it was one of the favage practices of the chace, for all the hunters to ftain their hands in the blood of the deer as a trophy.

Upon

Upon looking into Turberville's book of Hunting, I can fee no trace of that prac-tice; but there are two different accounts of the French and Englifh manner of dif-fecting or breaking up the deer. In divi-ding the feveral parts of the deer, the French employed the hand of the huntf-man alone; but our Englifh kings, ba-rons, and other great men, took part of that office upon themfelves. *Our order is,* fays Turberville, *that the prince or chiefe (if so pleafe them) do alight, and take affaye of the deere, with a fharpe knife, the which is done in this maner; the deere being layde upon his backe, the prince, chiefe, or fuch as they do appoint, comes to it, and the chiefe huntf-man, kneeling, if it be to a prince, doth hold the deere by the fore foot, while the prince or chiefe do cut a flit, drawn alongft the bryfket of the deere.*

The deer's head is alfo cut off by the prince or chief; in thefe operations, the diffecters muft neceffarily be fprinkled or befmeared with the blood of the animal, and

to

to this our author, in both paſſages, ſeems plainly to allude.

FALCONBRIDGE.

————————Here's a ſtay ;
That ſhakes the rotten carcaſs of old death
Out of his rags.

I muſt own, I ſee no great difficulty in the word *ſtay*; which means no more, notwithſtanding all the attributes given to it by the ſpeaker, than a very great and almoſt inſurmountable obſtacle. Perhaps the power of the word *ſtay* may be beſt known from a very old author ; from Gawin Dowglas's Tranſlation of Virgil take the four following lines :

Ane port there is whom the eſt fludis has
In manere of ane boule or bay,
With rochis ſet forgane the ſtreme *full ſtay*,
To brek the ſalt fame of the ſeyis ſtoure.

The very learned and modeſt author of the Gloſſary to this book, for no man knows to whom he is obliged for that excellent and learned commentary of old and difficult words, Scottiſh and Saxon, explains

ſtay

ſtay by *ſleep*, "as we ſay in Scotland, a *ſtay brae*, a high bank of difficult aſcent, from the verb *ſtay*, to ſtop or hinder, becauſe the ſteepneſs retards thoſe who climb it, as the Latins ſay, *iter impeditum, loca impedita*; or, from the Belgic, *ſtegigh, præruptus*."

Mr. Steevens and Mr. Malone have brought many paſſages from old writers to prove the uſe of the word *ſtay* in the ſenſe wherein it is applied by Shakſpeare.

BASTARD.

Mad world ! Mad kings ! Mad compoſition !

Theobald, with great propriety, finiſhes the ſecond act with this ſoliloquy of Falconbridge, which is a very humourous and ſatirical application to the ſelfiſh feelings of the far greateſt part of mankind. But why *mad* world ! *mad* kings ! and *mad* compoſition ? The treaty was a counterpart to almoſt all the treaties which have been made between princes for many ages paſt. Honour, faith, juſtice, and common honeſty, on theſe occaſions, are little regarded ; and intereſt, or commodity, as Shakſpeare

fpeare terms it, folely kept in view by the contractors. It is true, that treaties are entered into in the moft folemn manner, and in the name of the holy and undivided Trinity ; but this is matter of mere form, and, by many princes, as little remembered as a coronation-oath, which is always taken with great folemnity, and but feldom called to mind, except with a view to make free with it.

Had Shakfpeare faid *bad* world, &c. it would have been nearer the mark. But, in our author's language, which is equally copious and licentious, the word *mad* fome- times fignifies, as it does here, *ftrange ! odd! prepofterous ! abfurd !*

CHAP-

CHAPTER III.

Character of Lady Conflance. — Admirably acted by Mrs. Cibber. — Mrs. Butler set up as her rival. Quin's opinion of Mrs. Cibber.—High tides in the calendar.—Mrs. Cibber and Winstone.—Reasons why Mr. Macklin should not have acted Pandulph.— Quin's farcasm. — Cibber inferior, in the Pope's Legate, to Macklin, and why. — Mrs. Pritchard refuses Colley Cibber's advice. — Stephen Langton's character. — Shakspeare not a Roman Catholic.—Anecdote of Walker and Boman.

HITHERTO the character of Conflance has been seen to little advantage. Her speeches were rather more conformable to the scold or virago than the injured princess and afflicted mother. In the first scene of the third act she appears with the dignity of just refentment and majesty of maternal grief. To suppose that the art of acting was not amply, if

D   not

not perfectly, underftood and practifed, in the days of our author, would be an injury to the feelings of every intelligent reader. How many variations of action and paffion are in the firft fpeech of this fcene, confifting only of twenty fix lines, all naturally refulting from the agitations of a mind anxioufly inquiring into the truth of that which it dreads to know! Even the under character, Salifbury, is called upon, by the words of Conftance, to exprefs the different paffions of his mind by variety as well as juftnefs of action; as in the following lines:

> What doft thou mean by fhaking of thy head?
> Why doft thou look fo fadly on my fon?
> What means that hand upon that breaft of thine?
> Why holds thine eye that lamentable rheum?
> Be thefe fad fighs confirmers of thy words?

Lady Conftance's paffionate effufion of rage, grief, and indignation, from which fcarce a line or thought can be expunged, to his eternal difgrace, Cibber has either entirely fuppreffed, or wretchedly fpoiled, by vile

and

and degrading interpolations: nay, the whole scene is so deformed and mutilated, that little of the creative power of Shakspeare is to be seen in it.

To utter, with the utmost harmony and propriety, all the succeeding changes of grief, anger, resentment, rage, despondency, reviving courage, and animated defiance, incidental to Lady Constance, and to accompany them with correspondent propriety and vehemence of action, was a happiness only known to Mrs. Cibber. Mrs. Hallam wanted not spirit nor pathos in this part; nor would Mrs. Pritchard have fallen so below herself, if Cibber had not misled her. To speak the truth, Mrs. Cibber has had no successor in this part but Mrs. Yates, who yet, it must be confessed, notwithstanding her great and justly-applauded skill, is inferior.

When Mrs. Cibber threw herself on the ground in pronouncing

———Here I and sorrow sit:
Here is my throne, let kings come bow to it.

D 2 Her

Her voice, look, and perfon, in every limb, feemed to be animated with the true fpirit which the author had infufed into her character.

And yet I remember, when Cibber's King John was in rehearfal at Drury-Lane theatre, fo little was the merit of Mrs. Cibber known to the world, that, in oppofition to her, a party was formed in favour of Mrs. Butler, the original actrefs of Millwood, in Barnwell, who was faid to be an illegitimate daughter of a noble duke whofe monument is erected in Weftminfter-abbey. Nay, when the original play was afterwards revived in 1744, at the fame theatre, in oppofition to Cibber's Papal Tyranny, Mr. Garrick was fo little acquainted with the genuine powers of this charming Melpomene, that, accidentally meeting Mr. Quin at the Bedford Coffeehoufe, he told him he doubted of Mrs. Cibber's being able to do juftice to fo vigorous and trying a part as Lady Conftance: Quin thought otherwife; and faid to him, with

with fome warmth, ' Don't tell me, Mr. Garrick, *that woman has a heart, and can do any thing where paffion is required.*'

LADY CONSTANCE.

What hath this day deferv'd? What hath it done?
That it in golden letters fhould be fet
Among the high tides in the calendar?

High tides Mr. Malone cannot fuppofe is ufed by the poet as fynonimous to what Mr. Steevens very properly alledges they are, folemn feafons: Mr. Malone did not reflect that high tides bear a very different meaning from his intention. They are marks of ruin and defolation, not of profperity and feftivity; and, I believe, are oftener found in chronological tables than in the rubric of a calendar.

LADY CONSTANCE.

O Lymoges, O Auftria, thou doft fhame
That bloody fpoil: thou flave, thou wretch, thou
coward! &c.

This vehement charge of perfidy, cowardice, perjury, and every fpecies of villany, which is concluded with the moft ftinging reproach and contemptuous raillery, re-

D 3   quires

quires the utmoſt ſkill of the ſpeaker.
Mrs. Cibber's voice was ſo happily modu-
lated by a moſt accurate ear, that every
material word in this uncommon burſt of
indignation, was impreſſed ſo judiciouſly
and harmoniouſly upon the audience, that
they could not refrain a loud and repeated
teſtimony of their approbation. But part
of the pleaſure to be obtained from this
ſcene muſt be owing to the correſpon-
ding behaviour of Auſtria ; if he does not
contribute to the general deception by feeling the reproaches of Conſtance, the vigour of the ſentiments will be weakened,
and the intention of the anthor diſappoin-
ted. The character of Auſtria is very un-
amiable ; and Mrs. Cibber, when the play
was firſt in rehearſal, could not eaſily prevail on Winſtone to make Auſtria appear
as odious to an audience as he ought.
Winſtone was an actor of ſingular ſkill in
two or three parts : he was as honeſt and
aukward a country booby in John Moody,
in the Provoked Huſband, as the author
deſigned

defigned him ; and, in Ben Johnfon's Downright, he made an excellent grotefque picture of abrupt plain-dealing and unfafhionable fimplicity. He had the good fortune to gain a confiderable fum of money in a lottery about thirty years fince, and retired to live on an eftate which he purchafed in Monmouthfhire. But it was impoffible for any man long to refift the perfuafive manner of Mrs. Cibber. Winftone fully anfwered her idea of Auftria's character.

KING PHILIP.
Here comes the holy legate of the pope.

The character of Pandulph has not, as yet, been reprefented with that dignity and importance which it demands.

Macklin, whofe fkill in acting is acknowledged to be fuperior to that of any man, who is the beft teacher of the art, and is ftill, at a very advanced age, a powerful comedian, as well as a good comic writer, fhould have refufed this part; neither his perfon, voice, action, or deportment, conveyed any idea of a great

D 4   delegate

delegate from the head of the church, or the fpiritual monarch of Chriftendom. Quin, who was prefent at the revival of King John at Drury-lane, faid Macklin was like a cardinal who had been formerly a parifh-clerk. And yet, it muft be owned, Macklin underftood the logic of the part, if I may be allowed the expreffion, better than any body. But the man, who prefumes to controul the will of mighty mo-narchs, fhould have a perfon which be-fpeaks authority, a look commanding re-fpect, graceful action, and majeftic deport-ment. But Colley Cibber's Pandulph was lefs agreeable to an audience than Mack-lin's; the voice of the latter, though rough, was audible. The former's pipe was ever powerlefs, and now, through old age, fo weak, that his words were rendered inar-ticulate. His manner of fpeaking was much applauded by fome, and by others as greatly difliked, in the Pope's Legate, as in moft of his tragic characters. The unna-tural fwelling of his words difpleafed all

who

who preferred natural elocution to artificial cadence. The old man was continually advifing Mrs. Pritchard, who acted Lady Conftance, to *tone* her words; but fhe, by obeying her own feelings and liftening to her own judgement, gained approbation and applaufe; which was not the cafe with his fon Theophilus, who acted the Dauphin, and Mrs. Bellamy, who played Lady Blanch. They, by obeying their director's precepts, were moft feverely exploded. But Colley's deportment was, I think, as difgufting as his utterance. He affected a ftately magnificent tread, a fupercilious afpect, with lofty and extravagant action, which he difplayed by waving up and down a roll of parchment in his right hand; in fhort, his whole behaviour was fo ftarchly ftudied, that it appeared eminently infignificant, and more refembling his own Lord Foppington than a great and dignified churchman.

P A N-

P A N D U L P H.

—— —— And force per force
Keep Stephen Langton, chofen archbifhop
Of Canterbury, from that holy fee.

Stephen Langton, archbifhop of Canterbury, deferves to be held in everlafting remembrance by all Englifhmen ; to this generous and wife prelate we are more indebted than, perhaps, to any of the affo-
ciated barons, who obliged King John to
fign the great charter of our liberties.
Langton is a proof that every man of fenfe
will be independent if he can ; for, notwithftanding he owed his advancement to the fee
of Canterbury to the pope, as foon as
ever it was in his power, he became a ftre-
nuous oppofer of all meafures which tended to fubject the crown of England to a
foreign potentate. All the copies of Henry
the Firft's great charter, which had been
lodged in the capitularies of religious houfes, were loft, and it is fuppofed that
King John had made away with them.
Langton, by diligence or accident, found
one ;

one; and this was made the ground-work
of the new charter: but Langton had pa-
ved the way for this noble eftablifhment of
rights, by inferting, in the oath taken by
the king, when he abfolved him, the following article, " That he would re-efta-
blifh the good laws of King Edward the
Confeffor;" laws, which Hume, in the
earlier part of his hiftory, feems to over-
look or undervalue, though, in his reign
of John, he acknowledges their excellence.

KING JOHN.

Though you and all the kings of Chriftendom
Are led fo groflly by this meddling prieft,
Dreading the curfe that money may buy out,
And, by the merit of vile gold, drofs, duft,
Purchafe corrupted pardon of a man,
Who in that fale fells pardon from himfelf, &c.

From this and the former fpeech of
King John to the legate, many good Proteftants, and, amongft the reft, Colley Cibber, have brought ample proofs to difcre-
dit the belief of Shakfpeare's being a Roman Catholic, which feems to have taken
its rife from the defcription of purgatory by
the

the ghoft in Hamlet. Shakfpeare's contempt
of the fopperies and corruptions of Rome,
may be found in more places of his works
than this, and particularly in his Henry
VIII.

In uttering the refolute anfwer of John
to the legate, Garrick's fire and fpirit were
confpicuous; but, I think, from his deficiency of perfon, that it did not produce
fo ftrong an effect as the dignified figure
and weighty eloquence of Quin, or the e-
nergetic utterance of Moffop.

AUSTRIA.

Well, ruffian, I muft pocket up thefe wrongs,
Becaufe——

The perfon who acted Auftria, on the revival of King John at Covent-Garden, in
1736, was one Boman, a dyer. This actor, in anfwering Falconbridge's repeated
infult of

Hang a calf-fkin on thofe recreant limbs,

whether through ignorance, hafte, or
chance, inftead of uttering the reply to
Falconbridge

Falconbridge as he ought,—with a loud vulgar tone, pronounced it thus:

> Well, *ruffian,* I muſt *pockut* up theſe wrongs,
> Becauſe———

The audience did not obſerve the impropriety; but Walker, in the Baſtard, by changing the word *breeches* to *pockut,* imitated Boman's manner, look, action, and tone of voice, ſo archly and humourouſly, that he threw the audience into as merry a fit as ever Quick, or Parſons, or any actor, ever did, in the moſt comic ſituation: they were abſolutely convulſed with laughter for a minute or two, and gave ſuch loud applauſe to Walker, that poor Boman was thunderſtruck. In plain truth, Boman, though a jolly companion, a writer of Bacchanalian ſongs, the author of a play never acted, and a very honeſt man, was very deficient in the profeſſion of acting. He retired from the ſtage ſoon after, and filled the place of ſuperintendant to a brewhouſe with becoming dignity.

CHAPTER

CHAPTER IV.

Prince Arthur's age ascertained.—The Roman youth did not become warriors so early as the knights in the days of chivalry.—Arthur besieges Queen Eleanor.—Battle of Mirabel. — John endeavours to win his nephew to his interest.—Scene between Hubert and the king, who tempts him to murder Arthur, compared to one in Massinger's Duke of Milan.—Colley Cibber's presumption.— Astonishing power of sound, from Dante's Inferno.—Mrs. Cibber's great excellence in Lady Constance.—The merits of Quin, Garrick, Mossop, and Sheridan, in the celebrated scene between Hubert and John.— Garrick extolled.—Rumney's opinion of Æschylus.— Shakspeare the poet of painters.—Sir Joshua Reynolds, Mr. West, and Mr. Penny.—Anecdote of Quin and Bridgwater.—A discussion of John's guilt in the murder of Arthur. — Strange inattention of an audience to a beautiful actress.

THOUGH

THOUGH it cannot be doubted that Shakſpeare had peruſed the chronicles of King John's reign, at leaſt thoſe of Hollingſhead, yet, in drawing his portrait of Arthur, he has cloſely followed the old play; in which, he is repreſented to be a child of about ten or eleven years old; this circumſtance, he knew, would make thoſe ſcenes, in which Arthur and Lady Conſtance are introduced, more pathetic and diſtreſsful. But the prince was, at this time, in the ſixteenth or ſeventeenth year of his age, and had given, before his captivity, many ſignal proofs of valour. Though the Roman youth did not aſſume the manly habit till the ſeventeenth year of their age, the noble ſpirit of chivalry inſpired her ſons with an earlier ardour for the field. It was not an uncommon ſight to behold a young knight at the age of fourteen, clad in complete armour, mounting his ſteed, and ruſhing to the battle. Prince Henry, ſon of Henry IV. fought bravely at the battle of Shrewſbury, when

in

in the fifteenth year of his age; and, though wounded, refufed to retire from the field. The fame prince Henry had been knighted by King Richard II. three years before, for the proofs he gave of his prowefs in Ireland.

Arthur had been knighted by Philip, and prefented by him with certain territories in the Poictevin, with the view of detaching him for ever from the intereft of his uncle King John.

One of the young prince's firft enterprifes, after receiving this honour, was befieging his grandmother Queen Eleanor in the town of Mirabel; the fiege was fo clofely prefled, that the Queen was obliged to retire into the caftle; John, hearing of his mother's danger, haftened with an army to her relief. An obftinate battle was fought between the royalifts and the befiegers, in which the king was victorious: Arthur and a great number of his followers were taken prifon-ners. John was fo elated at this unexpect-ed good fortune, that he wrote to his ba-rons a particular and very exulting account

of

of his fuccefs, in terms not unlike thofe we
read of in a letter from a modern victorious
monarch to his minifters of ftate, commanding them to give God thanks and rejoice at
his fuccefs. The king endeavoured, by all
manner of foothing arts, to win over his
nephew to his party, by fetting forth to
him the mighty advantages of his compliance; but the young inexperienced prince
not only treated his uncle's offers of friendfhip with difdain, but imprudently infifted
upon his reftoring to him the crown of England, which he had ufurped. And the
writer of the old play puts into the mouth
of Arthur, when he is requefted by his
uncle to depend upon him,

ARTHUR.

Might hath prevailed, not right; for I
Am king of England, though you wear the diadem.

Upon this behaviour of Arthur, John confined him in the caftle of Falaife.

KING.

See thou fhake the bags of hoarding abbots.

E   In

In that play there is a ridiculous scene, where Falconbridge, in the rifling of a convent, calls upon a frier to open his chests and produce his treasure: he obeys, and, in the unlocking of one of them, a most beautiful nun unexpectedly jumps out: she promises to open another chest, where abundance of real treasure was to be found; but, upon the unlocking of one, a lusty frier proves to be the promised gold. This farcical scene, which Shakspeare has judiciously avoided, must have entertained the audience at a time when the Reformation was newly established on the ruins of Popery.

I do not recollect a third act, in any tragedy of Shakspeare, so rich in scenes, where pity and terror distress the soul of man, and govern it by turns with equal influence, as this of King John. The interview between John and Hubert, where the king solicits Hubert, more by looks and action than by words, to murder his nephew Arthur, is, in the opinion of every

very

very man of taſte, ſuperior to all praiſe.
A late editor of Maſſinger has indeed called upon the reader of a ſcene between
Sforza and Franciſco, in the Duke of Milan, to compare it with this between John
and Hubert, and boldly appeals to his
judgement for the deciſion.

The ſcene in Maſſinger is well conceived and highly finiſhed ; but the lightning
itſelf is not brighter or quicker in its flaſh,
nor more aſtoniſhing in its effects, than
the ſublime and penetrating ſtrokes of
Shakſpeare. In Maſſinger, eloquent language and unbroken periods give eaſy aſſiſtance to the ſpeaker, and calm and un-
diſturbed pleaſure to the hearer : In Shakſpeare, the abrupt hints, half-ſpoken
meanings, heſitating pauſes, paſſionate in-
terruptions, and guilty looks, require the
utmoſt ſkill of the actors while they a-
larm and terrify the ſpectator.

From Colley Cibber's long experience,
and perfect knowledge of the ſtage, we
might have expected that he would have

conſidered

confidered this fcene as a facred thing, and
have given confequence to his Papal Tyranny by tranfcribing it whole and un-
touched. But Colley's confidence in his
abilities was extreme; and he has not
only mixed his cold crudities and profaic
offals with the rich food of Shakfpeare,
but has prefumed to alter the œconomy
of the fcene by fuperfluous incident: for
John defires Hubert to draw the curtain,
that he may unfold his meaning to him in
the dark; and Hubert exacts an exculpa-
tory warrant from him to put Arthur to
death. In this latter management he has
borrowed from Maflinger. Francifco demands from Sforza a writing, figned by
him, to warrant the putting Marcelia to
death.

KING JOHN.

———If the midnight-bell
Did, with his iron tongue and brazen mouth,
Sound *one* unto the drowfy race of night.

Mr. Steevens, after having formerly ef-
poufed the old reading of "Sound *on* unto,"
&c. very candidly doubts the ftrength of
his

his argument, and with greater probability fuppofes that *one* fingle notice of a bell is more appofite to the purpofe of the king.

There is not, in all poetry, perhaps, a greater inftance of the aftonifhing and fublime effect of found, produced by a fingle word, than in Dante's Inferno. *The awful fentence of the Judge, in the laft great day*, fays that author, *will found for ever in the ears of the damned**. This he expreffes by RIMBOMBA *in Æternum*.

The feveral actors of John, in this fcene, had their different and appropriated fhares of merit. Quin's voice and manner of acting were well adapted to the fituation and bufinefs of it. His folemn and articulate whifperings were like foft notes in mufic, which fummon our deepeft attention; but, whether the action did not correfpond with the words, or the look did not affift the fpeech and action, the effect was not perfectly produced. If ever Garrick's quick intelligence of eye and varied

E 3   action

* Depart from me, ye curfed, into everlafting fire, prepared for the Devil and his angels. Matthew xxv. 41.

action failed him, it was here. Through the whole scene, his art was too visible and glaring ; his inclination and fear were not equally suspended ; the hesitations of a man big with murder and death were not happily and sublimely expressed.

Of Mossop, justice requires me to say, that he was nearer in feeling the throes of a guilty mind, and in conveying them to his auditors, than either Quin or Garrick. In my memoirs of Mr. Garrick, I have endeavoured, though faintly, to do justice to the skill of Mr. Sheridan, who, in this scene, bore away the palm from all competitors.

LADY CONSTANCE.
No! I defie all comfort! all redress!

The grief, anguish, and despair, of a mother, are no where so naturally conceived and so pathetically expressed, as in the Constance of Shakspeare. The Clytemnestra, Hecuba, and Andromache, of Euripides, though justly admired characters, have not those affecting touches, those heart-rending

rending exclamations of maternal diftrefs, with which Conftance melts the audience into tears. The modern imitations of the ancients are ftill more feeble. Nor can Crëufa or Merope approach the fublime pathos of our inimitable poet.

LADY CONSTANCE.

Oh amiable lovely death!——

This noble apoftrophe to death is fuperior to that fine invocation of the chorus in the Supplicants of Æfchylus to the fame power.

O thou, affigned the wretch's friend,
To bid his miferies end,
And in oblivion's balm to fleep his woe,
Come, gentle death, ere that fad hour
Which drags me to the nuptial bed,
And let me find, in thy foft power,
A refuge from the force I dread.

POTTER'S ÆSCHYLUS.

I have already taken notice of Mrs. Cibber's uncommon excellence in Conftance. It was indeed her moft perfect character. When going off the ftage, in this fcene, fhe uttered the words,

O Lord! my boy!

E 4 with

with fuch an emphatical fcream of **agony,** as will never be forgotten by thofe who heard her.

This admirable actrefs, during the re-prefentation of this tragedy at Covent-Garden Theatre, about the year 1750, was fuddenly taken ill. The play was, however, announced in the bills. Mrs. Woffington, who was ever ready to fhew her refpect to the public and her willingnefs to promote the intereft of her employer, came forward to the front of the pit, ready dreffed for the character of Conftance, and offered, with the permiffion of the audience, to fupply Mrs. Cibber's place for that night. The fpectators, inftead of meeting her addrefs with approbation, feemed to be entirely loft in furprize. This unexpected reception fo embarraffed her, that fhe was preparing to retire; when Ryan, who thought they only wanted a hint to roufe them from their infenfibility, afked them bluntly if they
would

would give Mrs. Woffington leave to act
Lady Conftance ? The audience, as if at
once awakened from a fit of lethargy, by
repeated plaudits ftrove to make amends
for their inattention to the moft beautiful
woman that ever adorned a theatre.

CHAPTER

CHAPTER V.

*Affecting interview of Hubert and Arthur.—
Who first introduced the practice of burning
out eyes in England. — Good effects of the
Great Charter. — Humanity of an executioner.—Marlow, in the story of John, nearer to history than Shakspeare.—Hubert o-
vercome by Arthur.—Marlow a competitor
with Shakspeare.—Passage from Marlow.—
Passions of the audience during the scene between Arthur and Hubert.—King John
crowned four times.—Method of doing homage.—The king's apprehensions.—Scene of
recrimination.—The several actors of John
compared.—Shakspeare the poet of painters.
—Actors of Hubert's character described.—
Anecdote of Quin and Bridgwater.—Difcuffion of John's guilt respecting the death
of Arthur.*

THE interview between Arthur and
Hubert, in the fourth act, involves
a subject so terrible to the imagination,
that

that it requires more than common fkill
and delicacy, in the writer, to treat it in
fuch a manner as neither to fhock the
reader, nor fill the fpectator with horror.
The cuftom of putting out a perfon's eyes
was unknown to our Britifh, Saxon,
and, I believe, our Danifh, anceftors.
The cruel practice of burning out the eye
was introduced by William the Conqueror.
That royal ruffian, (I cannot afford him a
fofter name,) we are affured by hiftorians,
punifhed the killing of a boar, a deer, or
even a hare, in his own forefts, (which
were fo widely extended that they contained almoft a twelfth part of the kingdom,) with the lofs of the offender's eyes.
The immediate fucceffors of this tyrant
did not abolifh this inhuman practice.
The great charter, extorted from John by
his barons, contributed to make man more
placid and humane, as well as generous
and free.

Shakfpeare has generally not only adhered to the plot of the old play, but has
borrowed

borrowed feveral fentiments from it. We
may fafely truft to the opinion of the accurate and induftrious Mr. Malone, who
fuppofes Marlow to have been the author;
for the verfification of the old play refem-
bles his more than that of any other writer. He has certainly more clofely followed hiftory than Shakfpeare; but I am
convinced that he alfo had read the fame
hiftorian; for the fpeech of the executioner, who declares himfelf well pleafed
to be abfent from the murder of Prince
Arthur, is judicioufly borrowed from a
paffage in Hollingfhead. John, having determined, for obvious reafons, to put his
nephew to death, tampered with certain
perfons, whom he tempted by the hopes
of reward, to execute his purpofe. Some
treated his propofals with difdain and horror: others endeavoured to accomplifh
the deed. The cries and ftruggles of the
young prince brought Hubert to them;
who, having difmiffed the ruffians, was
prevailed upon, by the tears of the unhappy

happy Arthur, to promife that he would fave and protect him. In order to effect this, he gave out that he was dead; and, ftill better to carry on the deceit, the burial fervice was performed for him. Thus far the hiftorian.

Notwithftanding that our author, in this fcene, unluckily falls into his old fond habit of quibbling and playing upon words, yet the ftrong pleadings of Arthur, in the natural language of youthful innocence in diftrefs, will touch the heart of every reader. To place Marlow as a competitor to Shakfpeare would revolt the mind of any reader; yet, in this fcene, he is no contemptible antagonift: the former is more affecting: the latter more eloquent. Some lines in Arthur's fpeech to Hubert, after reading the warrant for his death, ought not to be loft.

ARTHUR.

Heaven weeps, the faints do fhed celeftial tears;
They fear thy fall, and cite thee with remorfe:
They knock thy confcience, moving pity there,

Willing

Willing to fence thee from the rage of hell :
Hell ! Hubert ! Truſt me, all the plagues of hell
Hang on the performance of this damned deed !
This ſeal, the warrant of the body's bliſs,
Inſureth Satan chieftain of thy ſoul.
Subſcribe not, Hubert ! Give not God's part away !
I ſpeak not only for my eyes privilege,
The chief exterior that I would enjoy ;
But for thy peril, far beyond my pain,
Thy ſweet ſoul's loſs, more than my eyes lack,
A cauſe internal and eternal too :
Adviſe thee, Hubert, for the caſe is hard
To loſe ſalvation for a king's reward.

Hubert not ſeeming to be moved, Arthur ſubmits, and bids him obey his orders ; but ſtill endeavours to affect him with an imprecation.

Ye rolling eyes,* whoſe ſuperficies yet
I do behold with eyes that nature lent,
Send forth the terror of your mover's frown
To wreak my wrongs upon my murderers,
That rob me of your fair reflecting view.
Let hell to them, as earth they wiſh to me,
Be dark and direful guerdon of their guilt !
Delay not, Hubert, my oriſons are ended;

Begin,

---

* Orbs.

Begin, I pray thee, reave me of my fight :
But to perform a tragedie indeed,
Conclude the period with a mortal ftab!

Colley Cibber has done lefs injury to
Shakfpeare, in this fcene, than in any o-
ther of the play. Nay, it muft be confeffed, he has heightened the anguifh of
Hubert by a very fine and affecting incident. This man, after giving a folemn promife to his royal mafter that he would put
his nephew to death, inftantly prepares
to accomplifh the deed; but, as he is going about it, he overhears the prince putting up his prayers to heaven for him.
To hear the innocent victim praying for
his flaughterer ftaggers his refolution,
and throws him into an agony.

——— ———Ha! what is it that I hear!
Deftruction to my fenfe! He prays for me!
For Hubert! who has made his chains fit eafy!
And thanks high heaven he has fo kind a keeper!
What means this damp reluctance on my brows?
Thefe trembling nerves? This ague in my blood?

It

It had been well if Cibber had ftopt here:
but he goes on to compare that which will
bear no comparifon, the ftab of the affaffin with the wound which the brave man
gives and receives in the field of battle.
But let me not rob him of any juft claim
to merit. He puts a thought into the
mouth of Arthur, which, though not
unobvious, is exceedingly touching, from
the fituation of the character. Hubert enjoins Arthur to give, under his
hand, a formal acknowledgement that his
death was voluntary and inflicted by his
own hand.

ARTHUR.

Muft I do more than die! O mercy! mercy!

HUBERT.

Supprefs thy voice, or thou art days in dying.

ARTHUR.

I will, O fpare me, Hubert, but a moment!
But while I call once more on heaven. Indeed
I'll not be loud, *alas! I need not there*;
The fofteft fupplicating figh is heard in heaven.

The

The paffions of the audience, during this terrible fcene, are fufpended between hope and fear, between apprehenfion of the prince's death and expectation of Hubert's remorfe. It is with pleafure I have obferved a thoufand melting eyes refume their luftre, when Hubert quits the bloody purpofe and embraces the child.

The coronation of John follows.

Weak princes are ever fufpicious of the loyalty of their fubjects; John, who was confcious of his demerit, refolved to fence himfelf with the vows and promifes of his fubjects, by their repeated oaths and acts of allegiance. In this, he manifefted more confidence in the integrity of his peo‧ple than he ought. For he who flagrantly violates his own moft folemn adjuration when he is crowned, by which he binds himfelf to uphold the laws in their full force, and to maintain the rights of his people, emancipates them from their obligations. John was crowned no lefs than four times; once from the paltry fpirit of

F revenge,

revenge againft Hubert, archbifhop of
Canterbury, whom he hoped to involve in
confiderable expence, by the archbifhop's
incurring the neceffary charges attending
the ceremony. But the great motive for
thefe frequent coronations and other folemn affemblies was his receiving homage
from his vaffals, his barons, ecclefiaftical
and civil ; which was performed in the following manner : feated upon his throne,
in his royal robes, with his crown on his
head, and furrounded by his fpiritual and
temporal nobles, the king beheld his greateft
prelates and moft powerful barons, uncovered and unarmed, upon their knees. In
that humble pofture, they put both their
hands between his, and folemnly promifed
" To be his liegemen of life and limb, and
worldly worfhip ; to bear faith and truth
to him, to live and die with him, againft all
manner of men."

By this facred promife, given before all
the world, our monarchs imagined they
could fecure the fidelity and allegiance of
thofe

thofe whom they determined to injure, perfecute, and opprefs.

The conduct of the plot, in the fourth act, and efpecially that part of it which follows the difcourfe upon the new coronation, is very judicious. The king's fuppofed fecurity, arifing from this oftentatious piece of pageantry, is fuddenly fhaken to the foundation by the news of Arthur's death, and the ftrong reproaches and confequent defertion of the barons thereupon. The landing of the French adds to the king's perplexity, which is not diminifhed by the hermit's prophecy, ' That ere Afcenfion-day he would give up his crown.' In all the diftracted hurry of a man alarmed and terrified, John difpatches Falconbridge after the lords to foothe them, if poffible, and bring them to his prefence. Hubert, now left alone with the king, endeavours to magnify his apprehenfions by prodigies in the heavens, by prophecies, and by urging the univerfal difcontent of

the

the people, all owing to Arthur's death.
This is artfully contrived to reconcile the
king to Hubert's breaking his promise in
saving the life of the young prince. The
upbraidings of John,—who endeavours to
apply balm to his own wounded con-
science by recrimination on the enormous
guilt of his instrument, whom he describes
as an ugly monster, formed by nature for
acts of villany—Hubert's seizing the proper moment when the king's passion is at
an ebb, and restoring his peace by a single
word, with an artful, though false, vindi-
cation of his own innocence—These are
such paintings of the passions, and their
operations, on the human mind, as no o-
ther writer, ancient or modern, I suppose,
was acquainted with.

To enter into a long criticism upon the
several merits of the actors who have represented the last masterly scene between the
king and Hubert would be tedious and
unprofitable. It is not indeed loaded with
difficulty, like the former, between the
same

fame perfons in the third act. There the
paffions were over-awed, and durft not
fhew themfelves in full day, but fought
for a cover in nods and fhrugs, fearful
looks, disjointed phrafes, and broken fen-
tences : here they burft out with the vehemence of a torrent, and Nature is permitted to fpeak her own language with aftonifhing rapidity. Thofe actors who were
happy in the beft-toned voices, if they had
any fkill, were fure to excel. Delane and
Moffop wanted neither fire nor force to
exprefs anger, rage, and refentment, with
truth and vigour. Sheridan and Quin,
endowed with lefs power, were obliged to
fupply that requifite by art. Here Garrick reigned triumphant : he was greatly
fuperior to them all. His action was
more animated ; and his quick tranfitions
from one paffion to another gave an excellent portrait of the turbulent and diftracted mind of John. When Hubert
fhewed him his warrant for the death of
Arthur, faying to him, at the fame time,

F 3   Here

Here is your hand and feal for what I did,

Garrick fnatched the warrant from his hand; and, grafping it hard, in an agony of defpair and horror, he threw his eyes to heaven, as if felf-convicted of murder, and ftanding before the great Judge of the quick and dead to anfwer for the in-fringement of the divine command! Mr. Rumney, we are told by Dr. Potter, calls Æfchylus the poet of the painters: Shak-fpeare has furely as juft a title to that ap-pellation as any poet, ancient or modern. The tragedy of King John would fupply the fineft materials for difplaying the fkill of our moft eminent painters. The two fcenes in the third and fourth act, between John and Hubert, merit the noble pencil of a Sir Jofhua Reynolds or a Weft. My friend, Mr. Penny, has given the public fome valuable paintings from Shakfpeare, and particularly an exact picture of the fmith and the tailor, as defcribed by Hu-bert.

I faw

I faw a fmith ftand with his hammer thus,
With eager hafte fwallowing a tailor's news, &c.

Hubert is, by the poet, made a principal
agent in the play, and requires no fmall
art in the acting. The feveral players
whom I have feen in Hubert, Bridgwater,
Berry, and Benfley, very fkilfully difplayed the various paffions incidental to
the part. Quin was fo pleafed with Bridgwater, (who followed at the fame time the
different trades of coal-feller and player,)
that, upon going into the Green-room,
after the fcene in the fourth act, he
took him by the hand and thanked him,
telling him he was glad that he had drawn
his attention from his coal-wharf to the
ftage; " for fometimes, you know, Bridge,
that, in the midft of a fcene, you are thinking of meafuring out a bufhel of coals to
fome old crone, who you are fearful will
never pay you for them."

Arthur's death, by a fall from the walls
of Northampton-caftle, follows the important fcene of Hubert and Arthur. As

F 4 the

the death of this young prince is made of
great confequence in the tragedy, it will
not be an idle bufinefs to enter into a
fhort and impartial difcuffion of that fhare
of guilt which may be juftly imputed to
King John, for fo atrocious an action as
the murder of his nephew.

From the concurring teftimony of hiftorians who had the beft opportunity to
know the truth, it is paft doubt that Arthur was either killed by an exprefs order
of his uncle, or flain by the king's own
hand. Hume, an hiftorian not likely to
take things upon truft, and always a ready
vindicator of royalty, charges the king
himfelf with the perpetration of the bloody
deed; with ftabbing him, and then faften-
ing a ftone to his body, and throwing it
into the river Seine. The report of his
dying by a fall from the walls of his prifon was, in all probability, fpread by John
and his agents; and Shakfpeare has laid
hold of it as an hiftorical incident beft fuited to his purpofe.

All

All writers on this period report, that every body was ftruck with horror at the inhuman deed; and that, from that moment, the king was detefted, and his authority over his people and barons rendered very precarious. The world has ever loudly exclaimed againft the wretched John, as the moft execrable of men, for this murder. To be well affured that he merited the odium which fell upon him in confequence of the action, we ought to inquire into that predicament in which the king and his nephew ftood in relation to each other.

Although the feudal fyftem had admitted the right of inheritance by lineal defcent in the greateft part of Europe, it was not fo eftablifhed in England. From the conqueft to John, a period of one hundred and forty years, there had been no lefs than three fucceffions to the crown, without any regard to the right of reprefentation. John's title, as there was no law againft him, was as good as Arthur's, and the will

of

of King Richard in his favour rendered it
ftronger. Befides, the people of England,
having acknowledged John for their fovereign, put an end to all farther doubts with
refpect to his validity of claim. Lady Conftance and her fon were fo well fatisfied
with John's right to the throne of England, that they both refided for fome time
in his court. The policy of Philip, king
of France, who contrived to alarm the
prince and his mother for their fafety,
caufed them to leave England with terror,
and to throw themfelves under his protection; and this, I believe, was the ruin of
Arthur; for Philip had no other intention
then to ufe him as an inftrument in his
hands to difturb John. The young prince
was now become the profeffed rival of his
uncle, a competitor for the crown of England, as well as a claimant of all the dominions which our kings at that time enjoyed in France.

Arthur, when taken prifoner at the battle of Mirabel, was fo far from liftening to
the

the reafonable advice of his uncle, who intreated him to forfake the king of France,
and depend upon him, promifing, at the
fame time, to protect him in his due rights
to the utmoft of his power, that he very
imprudently and haughtily put the king
to defiance; nay, it is recorded that
he was fo far tranfported by paffion as to
tell his uncle, " That, to the laft moment
of his life, he would never ceafe feeking occafion to be revenged of him*." Notwithftanding all this provocation of Arthur, no
man will be fo daring or wicked as to juftify his murder; but fure the cafe will admit of confiderable mitigation.

Queen Ifabel, who caufed her hufband,
Edward II. to endure a moft painful and
fhocking death, may be juftly charged with
much greater aggravation of guilt. So
may Henry IV. who depofed, and ftarved
to death, his lawful fovereign, Richard II.
So may Richard III. who made away with
his

---

* Rapin, Life of John.

his nephews, King Edward V. and Richard, duke of York, his brother: yet the clamour against these delinquents has not been so outrageous as that against King John. After all, we may with great probability, in this case, make the same observation as Livy did upon the murder of Cicero by Mark Antony: " That Cicero met with the same fate from Antony, which he would have inflicted upon him if he had fallen into his power* Arthur's vehement expression of anger and resentment, when a prisoner to John, leaves no room to doubt that he would have gratified his revenge to the height, if his uncle had fallen into his hands.

A Dramatic Miscellany will, I hope, permit such an investigation of fact as relates to a principal character. This, indeed, is one main point I have in view; and it seemed to me more necessary, as I believe John's infamous conduct through

his

---

* Fragmentum Livii, tom. ult. ad fin.

his whole reign has hitherto been the caufe why the queſtion of Arthur's death has not been more nearly and impartially ſcrutinized.

CHAPTER

CHAPTER VI.

*The nobles revolt to Louis, Dauphin of France.
—Falconbridge viewing the dead body of
Arthur. — Variety of action exacted by
Shakſpeare.—Beautiful image in a ſpeech
of Falconbridge. — Remorſe explained.—
Meaning of* true defence, *and* Do not prove
me ſo.*—Garrick, in look and action, inferior to Tom Walker. Different deſcriptions
of the Devil. Hubert's character not ſo o-
dious as repreſented in the play. — Noble
imagery in a ſpeech of Falconbridge.—Meaning of* unowed intereſt.—*The raven's bone.
—Meaning of the word* England.

THE remainder of the fourth act is
employed by the poet to quicken
the revolt of the peers and their junction
with Louis the dauphin, who claims the
kingdom in right of his wife on the failure
of Arthur. The ſight of Arthur's dead
body confirms the barons in their reſolution of joining their forces to the dauphin.

phin. Falconbridge, with his ufual intrepidity, pleads the caufe of the king; but is ftruck with aftonifhment when the dead body is expofed to his view. His attitude of filent grief and furprife is well implied by Salifbury's queftions.

SALISBURY.

Sir Richard, what think you ? Have you beheld,
Or have you read or heard ? Or could you think ?
Or do you almoft think, although you fee,
That you do fee ? Could thought without this object
Form fuch another ?

By thefe feveral interrogatories, which Falconbridge is in no hafte to anfwer, the reader will fee what variety of action Shakfpeare exacts from the actors of his principal characters, and what opportunities he gives to the mafters of their profeffion to difplay their abilities. After a long paufe, the noble paffion of Falconbridge breaks forth, and he calls the deed by its proper name.

FALCONBRIDGE.

It is a damned and a bloody work.

SALISBURY.

SALISBURY.

This is the bloodieſt ſhame,
The wildeſt ſavagery, the vileſt ſtroke,
That ever wall-eye'd wrath or ſtaring rage
Preſented to the tears of ſoft remorſe.

This image is exceedingly beautiful :
but the word *remorſe* does not, in this
place, mean ſincere penitence for paſt
crimes or raſh actions, but is a term, not
unuſual with our author, to ſignify deep
ſorrow or violent affliction, independently
of remorſe ariſing from guilt. Hubert is
charged with the murder of the prince ;
Saliſbury draws his ſword upon him ; and
Hubert, ſtanding upon the defenſive, makes
uſe of an expreſſion, the meaning of which
I underſtand differently from Shakſpeare's
beſt commentator, Dr. Johnſon.

HUBERT.

I would not have you, lord, forget yourſelf,
Nor tempt the danger of my true defence.

Dr. Johnſon interprets *true defence* honeſt defence, or defence in a good cauſe ;
and certainly the words will well admit of
that

that fenfe : but I am of opinion that, in guarding himfelf againft this attempt upon his life, Hubert rather intended to bring the earl to a fenfe of his danger, in attacking one who was well fkilled in fighting, a brave man and a foldier, able to defend himfelf by art and ftrength as well as courage. However, I am not wedded to my opinion.

SALISBURY.

Thou art a murderer.

HUBERT.

Do not prove me fo.

" Do not make me a murderer, fays Dr. Johnfon, by compelling me to kill you." I rather believe, " Do not prove me fo," is as much as to fay, Do not bring me to a trial, or to the proof of it ; for the confequence will be, that yourfelf will be found a flanderer and a liar. I believe the phrafe or expreffion of " Do not prove me fo" is to be found, in this fenfe, in authors of Shakfpeare's age.

G   To

To prevent a farther fray, Falconbridge
interpofes between Salifbury and Hubert;
and, in this fcene, Mr. Garrick, notwithftanding his great power of action, (from
the deficiency of perfon, amongft men who
were of a larger fize than himfelf,) rendered the following animated fpeech of
Falconbridge unimportant and inefficient.

SALISBURY.

Stand by, or I fhall gall you, Falconbridge.

FALCONBRIDGE.

You had better gall the Devil, Salifbury.
If thou but frown on me, or ftir thy foot,
Or teach thy hafty fpleen to do me fhame,
I'll ftrike thee dead. ———

When Walker uttered thefe words, he
drew his fword, threw himfelf into a
noble attitude, fternly knit his black
brows, and gave a loud ftamp with his
foot; infomuch that, pleafed with the
player's commanding look and vehement
action, the audience confirmed the energy
of his conceptions by their approbation of
applaufe.

applaufe. Falconbridge, notwithftanding his defence of Hubert, tells him, as foon as the lords are departed, that he fufpects him very grievoufly ; and farther :

FALCONBRIDGE.
There is not fo ugly a fiend of hell,
As thou fhalt be, if thou didft kill this child.

Mr. Steevens has a curious note on this paffage, from a book printed in the reign of Henry VIII. where we are told that the deformity of the condemned, in the other world, is proportioned to the degrees of guilt in this. But it is from the conception of the fpeaker that the character of a Devil's uglinefs is formed here. With fome, one of the largeft fize, with branching horns, big faucer eyes, and a length of tail is the moft deformed and odious. But the brave man defines his Devil by giving him a quantity of fpite and malice, of which he fuppofes him to have a larger fhare than his brother fiends. So one of Shakfpeare's characters, fpeaking of his hatred to his enemy, fays,

I'll

> I'll fight with him with all the malice
> Of an under-fiend.

Hubert's exculpation of himfelf renders his character odious.   Not content with denying the commiffion of the murder, which he might have honeftly done, he fays, in exprefs terms,

> If I, in act, confent, or fin of thought,
> Be guilty of the ftealing that fweet breath,
> Let hell want pains enough to torture me.

This is a repetition of his impudent affirmation to the king :

> Within this bofom never enter'd yet
> The dreadful motion of a murderous thought.

Shakfpeare has drawn this man, in oppofition to all record, in a worfe light than he needed to have done.   Colley Cibber, on the other hand, caufes Falconbridge to ftab Hubert, on the accufation of the peers and the fight of the dead body of Arthur, without farther inquiry into his guilt ; and Hubert, dying, owns the juftice of his punifhment :

nifhment : for, though he did not commit the murder, he declares that he once intended it.

The fpeech of the Baftard, which concludes the act, is full of that noble imagery peculiar to Shakfpeare, and was uttered by Garrick with great force.

I cannot think that Mr. Steevens has hit the fenfe of *unowed* intereft, in the lines that follow :

> —————And England now is left
> To tug and fcramble, and to part by the teeth
> The *unow'd* intereft of proud fwelling ftate.

Unowed intereft, fays this commentator, is that which has no claimer to own it. But claimers there were, and enough.

By *England* I underftand John, who is often fo termed by himfelf, and the king of France, in the fecond act. In this very fpeech, Arthur, as rightful heir to the crown, is likewife called *England*.

> How eafy doft thou take all *England* up !

The king is now forced to fight and ftruggle for that dominion which he for-

merly

merly enjoyed, but which he does not now, in Shakſpeare's phraſe, *owe* or poſſeſs.

In the ſame ſenſe the word is uſed by Iago in Othello.

⸻⸻ Not poppy nor mandragora,
Nor all the drowſy ſyrups of the Eaſt,
Shall med'cine thee to that ſweet ſleep
Which thou ow'dſt yeſterday.

OTHELLO, Act III.

⸻⸻ Vaſt confuſion waits,
As doth a raven on a ſick-fallen beaſt,
The imminent decay of wreſted pomp.

Ravens and other birds of prey are not only ſaid to hover about the carcaſes of dying animals, in order to feaſt upon them, but to attend the diſſection of deer for a certain morſel, which hunters uſed formerly to call *the raven's bone.*

The following paſſage is tranſcribed from Turberville's Book of Hunting, page 135.

There is a little griſtle which is upon the ſpoon of the briſket, which we call the raven's bone, becauſe it is caſt up to the crows and ravens which attend hunters; and I have ſeen, in ſome places, a raven ſo accuſtomed to it, that

ſhe

ſhe would never fail to croak and cry for it all the while you were breaking up the deer, and would not depart till ſhe had it.

The imminent decay of wreſted pomp.

Wreſted pomp Dr. Johnſon explains by greatneſs obtained by violence. In a more correct writer, it would be ſo underſtood, but in Skakſpeare's broad and unconfined language, I believe, it is different. The imminent decay of wreſted royalty, is the ſpeedy deſtruction of a king whoſe power is wreſted from him by violence.

G 4   C H A P-

CHAPTER VI.

*John's refignation of his crown to the pope.—
The confequences of an interdict.—Interdict
defcribed.—The diftrefs of King John.—He
is obliged to refign his crown a fecond time.
—His infenfibility of difgrace.—He refufes
to grant a charter of liberty. — The pope
efpoufes John's caufe againft Louis of
France, who calls the refignation of his
crown voluntary.—Peter of Pomfret's prophecy accomplifhed.—He and his fon executed.—The humour of Falconbridge expires
with the difgrace of John.—Salifbury's noble
reluctance.—King Philip and his fon Louis
obliged to undergo penance. — Reafon why
Shakfpeare avoided the fubject of the Great
Charter.—Garrick's dying fcene of John.—
Shakfpeare, and Beaumont and Fletcher,
compared. — Remarkable quotation from The
Troublefome Reign of King John.—His character compared.—Why more odious than
any other Englifh monarch.—Conjecture concerning*

*cerning the original actors of King John,
—particularly Hubert.—Mr. Smith's Falconbridge.*

THE fifth act of this play opens with
the moſt diſgraceful event which could
poſſibly befall a crowned head and a great
kingdom. A powerful monarch reſigning
his crown and kingdom into the hands of
an imperious prieſt, and becoming his vaſ-
ſal by holding his dominions from him
and paying him an annual tax, was a new
and aſtoniſhing fight to John's own ſubjects, and to all the world. Shakſpeare
has connected this part of John's hiſtory
with the death of Arthur, concerning
whom the king interrogates Falconbridge
after the reſignation; but, in fact, ten
years had elapſed ſince the murder of Arthur. A ſeries of wicked and tyrannical
actions had alienated the barons of the
realm and the bulk of the people from
John: his quarrel with the pope had involved his ſubjects in all the miſeries of an
interdict,

interdict, a papal ordinance which deprived
the prieſt of his functions, and the community of religious worſhip: the churches
were ſhut up: neither baptiſm, marriage,
nor burial, permitted, except in particular
caſes and under certain reſtrictions. I give
the reader the deſcription of it in the lines
of Cibber, in his Papal Tyranny, which a-
grees pretty exactly with Hume's tranſcript
of that anathema, and, to the eternal
ſhame of the man, called by himſelf the
Servant of the Servants of God, who, in a
mean ſtruggle with the king for the nomination to a biſhopric, deprived a whole
kingdom of temporal and eternal happineſs, as far as it was in his power. Cibber's lines are not dignified with poetic
numbers, but they ſufficiently expreſs the
pope's malediction.

> O never was a ſtate ſo terrible!
> Now all the rights of holy function ceaſe!
> Infants unſprinkled want their chriſtian names!
> Lovers, in vain betrothed, reſume deſpair,
> Nor find a prieſt to ſanctify their vows!

In

In vain the dying finner groans for pardon !
Even penitence, depriv'd of abfolution,
In all the agonies of fear, expires !
Nor after death has at his grave a prayer,
Or for his parted foul a requiem fung.

John was now reduced to the laft extremity, hated and deferted by his fubjects, threatened with an invafion from
France, his kingdom groaning under an
interdict, himfelf excommunicated, and
his fubjects forbidden, under a curfe, to
pay him obedience. In this miferable ftate
his only refuge was fubmiffion to the pope's
mercy; and this could only be obtained
by giving up to him his crown and dignity. Shakfpeare feems to have fhrunk
from the detefted fubject : he knew the
juft reprefentation of fuch an event would
be fhocking to an Englifh audience, and
therefore paffes it over with as much ce-
lerity as poffible.

John fays, after delivering his crown
into the legate's hands,

Thus have I yielded up into your hand
The circle of my glory.

P A N D U L P H.

————————— Take again,
From this my hand, as holding of the pope,
Your fovereign greatnefs and authority.

This fhameful act, which rendered the king as contemptible in the eyes of the people as he had before made himfelf hateful to them, was performed with great ceremony, firft at Dover, before an innumerable multitude of nobles, bifhops, officers of ftate, and all forts of people. The contemptuous behaviour of the legate fhocked all who were prefent, though no man had the boldnefs to refent his infolence, or check his pride, except the archbifhop of Dublin, who alone ventured to incur the difpleafure of the Holy See, by giving vent to his honeft indignation. But, as if the king and kingdom had not been fufficiently humbled by this moft abject act of John, fome time after he was conftrained to make another refignation of

his

his crown and kingdom to the pope, at
Weſtminſter, before all the peers of the
kingdom, ecclefiaſtical and civil. Here
he figned another charter; which, to render it more authentic, was fealed with
gold, the firſt having been fealed with
wax only. This the king delivered into
the hands of the legate, for the uſe of his
maſter the pope.

KING JOHN.

Our people quarrel with obedience.

King John, like all other arbitrary princes, calls the people's ſeeking redreſs, from
oppreſſion and injuſtice, treaſon. Had he
condeſcended to liſten to the voice of e-
quity and reaſon, he need not have been
reduced to the neceſſity of yielding his
crown to the pope. But this prince, who
never knew the art of gaining the affections of his ſubjects, when defired by the
barons to grant them a charter of equal
laws, (ſuch as the people might juſtly
claim, and he beſtow without diminiſhing
his prerogative,) with a ſcornful ſmile,
demanded

demanded why the barons did not alfo afk for his dominions? what they defired, he faid, is foolifh and idle. Then, with an oath, he declared he would never grant them fuch privileges as would make him a flave. The meaning of which was, that he infifted upon their being bound to obey him in e-very thing, and himfelf to be free from all manner of reftraint. This conduct of John reduced the barons to the neceffity of calling in Louis the dauphin to their af-fiftance ; as, in later times, the principal men of the kingdom invited the Prince of Orange to redrefs the errors of King James's government, and to eftablifh their liberties on a fure foundation.

PANDULPH.

But, fince you are a gentle convertite —

It is obfervable that, from the time of John's fubmiffion to Rome, the language of that court, refpecting him, was greatly altered. He who had been painted, by the pope and his adherents, as an impious monfter, ftained with the worft of all vices, and

and more efpecially with herefy and difobedience to the holy fee, was now extolled
to the fkies as the beft of men, and the moft
religious and pious of all princes.

The word *convertite* is fo eafily derived
from *convert*, that Mr. Steevens needed not
to have authenticated it from Marlow. It
is no uncommon word with Shakfpeare
himfelf: he puts it into the mouth of
Jaques in As you like it, who wifhes to
converfe with a tyrant turned a penitent
and a hermit; for, fays he,

————— Out of thefe *convertites*
There is much matter to be heard and learn'd.

KING JOHN.

Is this Afcenfion-day? Did not the prophet
Say, that, before Afcenfion-day at noon,
My crown I fhould give off? Even fo I have.
I did fuppofe it fhould be on conftraint:
But, Heaven be thank'd! it was but voluntary.

How not by conftraint? Did he not
reduce himfelf to the abfolute neceffity of
yielding up his crown? Was there any
action lefs voluntary than this? But Shakfpeare,

fpeare, in drawing the picture of this prince, could not make him more brutal and abfurd than he really was. It appears from hiftory, that, though all Englifh-men long felt the fhame and difgrace of their king's meannefs of foul, he himfelf was the firft to forget it ; and, though treated by the pope's legate like a beaten flave, he feemed to triumph, becaufe his crown was reftored to him on any terms. But the tyrant's ridiculous joy was blended with an act of extreme cruelty : for, though Peter of Pomfret's prophecy was literally fulfilled in John's own opinion, yet this man of blood commanded that he, and his fon, who was no-ways concerned in the promulgation of his father's pre-diction, fhould both be taken out of pri-fon, where they had been long confined, and hanged, without any trial or farther proof; which unmerciful fentence was im-mediately executed.

Such heavy difgrace and dark melan-choly hang over the gloomy tranfactions

of

of John, that Shakſpeare cannot, even with
the unremitting ſpirit of a Falconbridge,
enliven the diſmal ſcene.

His ſpeech to John, beginning with

———Wherefore do you droop? Why look you ſad?
Be great in act as you have been in thought, &c.

is full of that noble ardor with which
the genius of Shakſpeare inſpires this
favourite character. But it is obſervable,
although Falconbridge retains his gallantry
to the laſt, that, after the murder of Arthur
and the reſignation of John, he drops his
vein of humour: John himſelf, after his abject ſubmiſſion to the pope, becomes lifeleſs
and deſponding.

In ſome of Shakſpeare's hiſtorical plays,
the laſt act is not ſupported with the ſame
vigour as thoſe which precede. King John
is conſtantly ſupplied with dramatic fuel,
which blazes brightly to the end. The
ſcenes between Louis and Saliſbury, and
Pandulph and Louis, are made important
by intereſting buſineſs. The character of

H   an

an Englifh nobleman, reduced by the out-
rage of tyranny to draw his fword againft
his fovereign, difplays a warm picture of
patriotifm, of gallantry, and tendernefs.
Louis, in contemning the threats of the
cardinal, appears a man of courage and a
politician.

DAUPHIN.

And come you now to tell me John hath made
His peace with Rome? What is that peace to me?

After John's fubmiffion to the
pope, hiftorians tell us that the legate
threatened King Philip and his fon Louis
with excommunication if they did not
refign their pretenfions to, and immediately
withdraw their forces from, England; for
that kingdom, he faid, was now become a
fief of the holy fee. Notwithftanding the
fpirited oppofition of Louis and his father
King Philip, they were obliged to fubmit
to the pope; who, not fatisfied with this
compliance, exacted a difgraceful penance
from them; and even with this laft mortifying injunction of papal authority they were
obliged

obliged to comply. Superftition had, in
thofe days, a ftrong hold on the minds of
the people. Great was the awe of the
priefthood. Altars, relics, and miracles,
fuppofed to be wrought at the fhrine of St.
Thomas-a-Becket, and other fuch faints,
were held in the greateft veneration. They
made an equal impreffion on all ranks of
people, and had more effect on their paffions than law, reafon, and humanity. It
was, perhaps, well for mankind that fuch
was the power of bigotry and fuperftition.
Let us fuppofe, for the fake of argument,
that our hard-hearted kings and their favage
barons had been *efprits forts*, or modern free-
thinkers! what would have been the lot of
the common people, who at that time, in all
parts of Europe, were little better than
flaves?

The fudden entrance of Falconbridge is
abrupt, and, with two or three lively ftric-
tures upon French courage, has rather too
much noife and parade; but his reproach to

the

the Englifh revolters is keen and farcafti-
cal.

BASTARD.

Their thimbles into armed gauntlets change ;
Their neelds to lances————

The word *neeld* is ftill ufed by the common people in Shropfhire.

In the fpeech of Salifbury, in this act,
and I think no where elfe through the
play, does the author hint at the true caufe
of the great quarrel between John and his
barons

———— Such is the infection of the time,
That, for the health and phyfic of our right,
We cannot deal but with the very hand
Of ftern injuftice and confufed wrong.

The murder of Arthur was not the caufe
of this conteft; for the death of that
young prince could not be a reafonable
pretence to diffolve the bonds of allegiance
between king and fubject. The fcene I
am fpeaking of, in order of time, was after
the king had figned the Great Charter
with his barons, and fworn to maintain all
its articles and covenants : his refolution

to

to break through his moſt ſolemn engagements, manifeſted by his invading the e-
ſtates of his nobles, drove them into the
arms of France.

Mr. Pennant, in his tour through Scotland, records an anecdote which will give
my readers a juſt idea of the eſtimation in
which John was held by his ſubjects.
" When the king was in his progreſs
northwards, to lay waſte the lands of the
nobility who had been the moſt active to
compel him to ſign the Great Charter of
Liberty, the inhabitants of Morpeth, as
ſoon as he approached the place, (ſo odious
had he rendered himſelf,) rather than
give entertainment to him and his forces,
ſet fire to their houſes, and conſumed
the town to aſhes." Pennant's Tour to
Scotland.

It may be aſked, perhaps, for what reaſon Shakſpeare did not embrace an occaſion ſo fairly given in the choice of the ſubject, to bring the great queſtion of liberty
upon the ſtage, by introducing the grand

H 3   diſpute

difpute between the king and kingdom.
The fubject is glorious, and the pen of
Shakfpeare would have adorned it. But
the poet produced his King John in
the days of prerogative, in an æra too,
when prerogative was popular. It was at
that remarkable period when the power of
the crown was at its height, and at the
fame time the prince was beloved, nay a-
dored, by the people: a people made happy by a wife and fteady adminiftration of
government, under a renowned and uni-
verfally-admired queen.

In a battle excurfion, John and Hubert
prepare the reader, by the ficknefs of the
king, for the clofe of the tragedy. Thefe
fhort fcenes are of real importance, though
often neglected by actors of fome merit, becaufe not attended with expected applaufe. It
was the great excellence of Garrick to hold
in remembrance the character he played,
through all its various ftages. No fituation of it whatever was neglected by him.
By his extreme earneftnefs to appear always
what

what he ought to be, he roufed the audience to a correfpondent approbation of his action. In this dialogue with Hubert, Garrick's look, walk, and fpeech, confeffed the man broken with inceffant anxiety, and difeafed both in body and mind. Defpair and death feemed to hover round him.

The difcovery of Louis's treachery, by Melun, to Salifbury and others, puts an end to the revolt of the Englifh peers, who return to the king.

An emendation of Theobald, in a line fpoken by Melun, deferves notice. Inftead of,

> Unthread the rude eye of rebellion,

he propofes to read,

> Untread the rude way of rebellion.

Mr. Steevens juftifies the old reading by a parallel paffage in Lear, fpoken by Regan to Glofter.

> Threading dark-ey'd night.

And yet it muft be confeffed that Theobald's conjecture feems to be fupported by

a line

a line of Salifbury in this very fcene :

We will *untread* the *fteps* of damned flight.

After all, Shakfpeare feems fond of introducing the word *eye* on many occafions ; as *the eye of death, he turned an* eye *of death upon me, my mind's* eye, &c. Unthread the rude eye of rebellion, may probably mean clearing the eye-fight of rebellion from all film or extraneous matter, fo that it may fee the path to duty with perfpicuity.

The laft Scene.

Shakfpeare has, in relating the death of the king, followed Caxton's Chronicle and the old play, though feveral hiftorians attribute his demife to a violent fever, occafioned by the lofs of all his baggage in the Lincoln marfhes, and his indifcreet and greedy eating of peaches to quench his thirft.* The poifoning of John at Swinfted-

---

* Speed, from various authors, charges the monks with poifoning John ; and quotes, in proof of it, a faying of Henry III. his fon and fucceffor, to the abbot of Clerkenwell — " Mean you to turn me out of the kingdom, and afterward to murder me, as my father was dealt with ?"

fted-abbey prefented to the poet's mind an interefting fcene of pity and terror. In this he has copied an idea of Marlow, if we fuppofe him to be the author of the old play.

KING JOHN.

Philip, fome drink. Oh! for the frozen Alps,
To tumble on and cool this inward heat
That rageth as a furnace feven-fold hot.

Mr. Seward, in the preface to his edition of Beaumont and Fletcher, prefers the poifoning of Alphonfo, in their play of A wife for a month, to Shakfpeare's fcene of King John.

The merit of that fcene is great; but the authors have furely faid more than was neceffary. It is true, their images correfpond with the fubject, and their lines in general are worked up to great perfection: but the fituation would not admit of fuch prolixity, or fuch nice defcriptions of heat and cold, with their feveral attributes. Shakfpeare knew human nature better than thefe his imitators and envious rivals. He

knew

knew where to ſtop. Their heads were at work, while his heart was buſy in its feelings.

One ſpeech of Alphonſo, in The Maid for a Month, and another from Shakſpeare's John, will perhaps convince the reader that I do not wrong the celebrated dramatic twins.

Wife for a Month.

ALPHONSO.

Give me more air, air, more air ; blow, blow !
Open, thou eaſtern gate, and blow upon me !
Diſtil thy cold dews, O thou icy moon,
And, rivers, run through my afflicted ſpirit !
I am all fire, fire, fire ! The raging dog-ſtar
Reigns in my blood ! Oh ! which way ſhall I turn me ?
Ætna and all his flames burn in my head.
Fling me into the ocean, or I periſh.
Dig, dig, dig, till the ſprings fly up ;
The cold, cold, ſprings, that I may leap into 'em,
And bathe my ſcorch'd limbs in their purling pleaſures.
Or ſhoot me up into the higher region,
Where treaſures of delicious ſnow are nouriſh'd,
And banquets of ſweet hail !

King

King John.

PRINCE HENRY.

How fares your majefty?

JOHN.

Poifon'd — ill fare! dead! forfook! caft off!
And none of you will bid the winter come,
To thruft his icy fingers in my maw;
Nor let my kingdom's rivers take their courfe
Through my burn'd bofom, nor intreat the North
To make his bleak winds kifs my parched lips,
And comfort me with cold.

In this very interefting fituation thefe great fcholars and polifhed gentlemen make Alphonfo a fatirift, a quibbler, and a toper; for what fhall we fay of his defiring the frier to bring Charity to him, that he may hug her; "for they fay fhe's cold,"

Infinite cold: devotion cannot warm her.

When he calls for drink, he wifhes to have

— All the worthy drunkards of the time,
The experienc'd drunkards! Let me have them all,
And let them drink their worft: I'll make them idiots.

This

This is not the language of a man in extreme pain. There is, in the old play, a
speech of John whilst in his dying agony,
written with no common power, in which
the author displays the real character of
John, and more agreeably to historical information than what we find in Shakspeare
himself; who, perhaps, from superior
judgement, threw into shade some of the
worst of his qualities. The lines are, I
think, worth preserving.

> Methinks I see a catalogue of sin,
> Wrote by a fiend in marble characters;
> The least enough to lose my part in heav'n.
> Methinks the devil whispers in mine ears,
> And tells me 'tis in vain to hope for grace.
> I must be damn'd for Arthur's sudden death:
> I see, I see, a thousand, thousand, men
> Come to accuse me for my wrongs on earth;
> And there is none so merciful a God
> That will forgive the number of my sins.
> How have I liv'd but by another's loss?
> What have I lov'd but wreck of others weal?
> Where have I vow'd, and not infring'd mine oath?
> Where have I done a deed deserving well?
> How, what, when, and where, have I bestow'd a day

That

That tended not to fome notorious ill ?
My life, replete with rage and tyranny,
Craves little pity for fo ftrange a death.
Why did I 'fcape the fury of the French,
And dy'd not by the temper of their fwords ?
Shamelefs my life, and fhamefully it ends ;
Scorn'd by my foes, difdained of my friends.

Black as this portrait is, and ftained
with various guilt, it does not comprehend all the odious qualities of John.
Other princes have been unjuft, perfidious,
perjured, rapacious, and cruel ; but fome
alloy of virtue, fome noble endowments of
the mind, contributed to refcue them from
utter abhorrence and contempt. John's
evil qualities feemed to be unmixed with
any good. His courage partook more of
brutal violence than heroic gallantry. E-
qually unfit for the field and the cabinet,
his meafures for eftablifhing peace, or car-
rying on war, were fo ill-concerted, that
he brought infinite difgrace and inevitable
mifchief on himfelf and his fubjects. Sir
Walter Raleigh, in the preface to his Hiftory,

tory, declares it to be his opinion, that, if all the pictures of the cruelleſt tyrants who ever reigned were loſt, and the true por-trait of Henry VIII. preſerved, they would be all found in him. Sir Walter muſt have read the reign of King John very in-attentively, or he would have better known where to beſtow the hateful preference. Henry had many accompliſhments and ſome virtues : John was deficient in all.

When the barons abſolutely forced him to renew the Great Charter, granted by Henry I. his great-grandfather, a wife and valiant prince ; the anguiſh of John's mind, and his behaviour after ſwearing to per-form what he had ſigned, are not eaſily to be deſcribed. Hollingſhead and Stow both aſſure us, that, on this occaſion, he *cur-ſed the hour he was born, the mother that bore him, and the paps that gave him ſuck ; wiſh-ing that he had received death by violence of ſword or knife, inſtead of natural nouriſhment. He whetted his teeth, and did bite firſt one ſtaff and then another, as he walked, and oft broke the*

the fame into pieces ; with fuch difordered be-
haviour and furious gefture he uttered his grief,
that the noblemen who were prefent well per-
ceived the inclinations of his inward affections.

The great caufe of his uneafinefs fhewed
the depravity of his mind. By figning the
Great Charter he was now become a king
over freemen ; whereas, before, he looked
upon his fubjects as flaves, and treated
them as fuch.

So brutal a character, as King John,
Shakfpeare was forced to cleanfe and qua-
lify, before he durft expofe it to public
view.

Who were the original actors in this
tragedy, it is now impoffible to know. If
conjecture were of any authority, I fhould
fuppofe that Burbage, who ftands fore-
moft, amongft the comedians of that age,
in the lift of Shakfpeare's, Johnfon's, and
Beaumont and Fletcher's, principal characters, was the reprefenter of John. I
fhould give the Baftard Falconbridge to
Taylor, who was the original Hamlet,
Iago,

Iago, and Paris, in the Roman Actor. By the particular marks of a homely or rather ugly form, given to Hubert by the king, and not denied by himfelf, I fhould fufpect fome deformed Sandford * of that age played that part.

J O H N.

A fellow, by the hand of nature mark'd,
Quoted and figned to do a deed of fhame.
—Taking note of thy abhorred afpect, &c.

H U B E R T.

—You have flandered nature in my form;
Which, howfoever rude exteriorly,
Is yet the cover of a fairer mind, &c.

The word *quoted*, occurs feveral times in Shakfpeare, and it is a playhoufe word. The characters who are to be called by the prompter's boy to be ready for the fcene, are quoted by him in the margin of the play.

I fancy, and it is only a fancy, that Ben Johnfon points at this actor in his Poet-after, by the name of Æfop.

C A P-

---

* An actor much commended in Cibber's Apology.

CAPTAIN TUCCA.

Do not bring your Æfop, your politician,
Unlefs you can ram up his mouth with cloves.

POETASTER, Act III.

I fhould not forget to fpeak of Mr. Garrick's excellence in the dying fcene of
John. The agonies of a man expiring in
a delirium were delineated with fuch won-
derful expreffion in his countenance, that
he impreffed uncommon fenfations, mixed
with terror, on the admiring fpectators,
who could not refufe the loudeft tribute
of applaufe to his inimitable action. Every word of the melancholy news, uttered
by Falconbridge, feemed to touch the tender ftrings of life, till they were quite broken, and he expired before the unwelcome tale was finifhed.

On the late revival of this tragedy, I fhould
not forget that Mr. Smith exerted himfelf
in the part of Falconbridge with much fpirit and gallantry, and to the great fatif-
faction of the fpectators.

I   To

To Cibber's vanity we owe the revival of this excellent tragedy, which had lain in obfcurity above one hundred and twenty years.

I think its worth has been rather under-rated. Dr. Johnfon allows that it is varied with a pleafing interchange of incidents and characters. In the order of Shakfpeare's tragedies, I fhould place it immediately after Othello, Macbeth, Lear, Hamlet, Julius Cæfar, and Romeo and Juliet.

King

King Richard II.

CHAPTER VII.

*Reign of Richard divided into three periods.—
Richard II. revived at Covent Garden, in
1738. — The play without a character of
humour or pleasantry.—Challenge of Hereford to Norfolk. — Their characters. —
Honour of the gauntlet.—Richard oblique-
ly accused of murdering his uncle Glofter.
—Truth the great doctrine of chivalry.—
The lie given by Charles V. and retorted by
Francis I.—Ceremony of Chivalry.—Ryan
and Walker.—Lord Rea and Mr. Ramfay.
—Explanation of* waxen coat.—*Conjecture
concerning Richard's preventing the single
combat of Hereford and Norfolk.—Words*
dear, *and* fo far *as to* mine enemy, *explained. — Hereford's character and the
king's. — Converfation of Richard, Charles
II, and Louis* XIV.

THE

THE reign of Richard II. may be divided into three periods : the firſt
confiſted of that which is called, in our
chronicles, the hurling times ; when the
inſurrection of the commons had nearly
diſſolved all government : about the middle of this reign, the nobles annihilated
the power of the crown, and uſurped the
direction of the ſtate : towards the end, the
court and miniſtry gained the aſcendant,
and, by various acts of injuſtice and tyranny, the king was rendered extremely
odious to his people ; when ſuddenly a
bold uſurper ſnatched the opportunity
given him by the general diſcontent of the
people, and mounted the throne without
the leaſt oppoſition. The twenty-two years
of Richard's government form a moſt intereſting period in the Engliſh hiſtory. I
ſhall endeavour to compare the ſeveral characters as drawn by the maſterly hand of
our poet with the authentic teſtimonies of
hiſtory.

Though

Though Shakfpeare has judicioufly confined himfelf to the latter part of Richard's hiftory, and to thofe events which brought on
his depofition and murder ; he has notwithftanding made ufe of many happy hiftorical
incidents preceding that time, and drawn a
variety of characters with ftrength and ve-
racity ; yet, upon the whole, he has been
lefs happy in this than moft of his hiftorical dramas. Though Mr. Steevens and
Mr. Malone have, from the ftationers
books, placed this play to the year 1597,
I am induced, from its many puerilities, to
believe it was a much earlier production.

This play was revived at Covent-Garden in the year 1738 ; and Haynes, the
then printer of the Craftfman, was pro-
fecuted in the Court of King's Bench, for
publifhing a letter, in which were contained many ftrong applications of feveral
paffages in it to the miniftry, and particularly to Sir Robert Walpole.

I 3   Mr.

Mr. Henley, afterwards Earl of Nor-
thington, then a very young barrifter, was
retained in behalf of Haynes. Amongft
other matters, more material for the fervice of his client, he obferved, that Shakfpeare's Richard II. was inferior to moft of
his other tragedies : that, although many
beautiful paffages might be picked out of
it, yet its blemifhes were confiderable : that
it greatly abounded in quibble and play
upon words; and this character is, I believe, not very different from that which
Dr. Johnfon has given of it.

It is worth our obfervation, that Shakfpeare has, in this play, deferted his ufual
cuftom of introducing fcenes of pleafantry
to contraft with fuch as are more fevere and
tragic. Not one gay character is to be
found in the whole compofition ; and the
only part of it which borders upon mirth
is Richard's defcription of Hereford's
courting the loweft clafs of the people.

Act

Act I. Scene II.

BOLINGBROKE.

Now, Thomas Mowbray, do I turn to thee;
Thou art a traitor and a mifcreant.

MOWBRAY.

I do defie him and I fpit at him;
Call him a flanderous coward and a villain.

The ground of this quarrel between the dukes of Hereford and Norfolk is no where afcertained by our hiftorians. It feems to have proceeded from an accidental con-verfation, which they fell into on the road as they travelled from Brentford to London. Amongft other topics, the duke of Norfolk is faid to have made very free with the character of the king and his mode of government, charging him with arbitrary proceedings, and infinuating that it was unfafe to live under fuch an adminiftration as the prefent.

Richard had indeed, according to Hol-lingfhead, fo entirely fubdued all thofe he efteemed his enemies, and was become fo elated and fo very arbitrary, that he threat-

I 4   ened

ened all men with death who fhould prefume to oppofe his royal will and pleafure.
The impreffion which Norfolk's difcourfe
made on the duke of Hereford was in all
probability very different from what the
fpeaker hoped and expected. The ambition of Hereford was regulated by confummate prudence: his great abilities were
as unqueftionable as his high lineage. He
knew that Norfolk had been the king's
principal inftrument in all his bloody and
tyrannical proceedings, and had been employed by him in the murder of the duke
of Glofter, his own and Richard's uncle:
he therefore, in all probability, confidered
this confidential difcourfe as a political
train or engine of ftate, to draw from him
certain expreffions which might be turned
to his deftruction: and it is not unlikely
that Hereford, by the approbation of his
father, John of Gaunt, determined to
be beforehand with him and accufe him to
the king.

BOLINGBROKE.

Pale trembling coward, there I throw my gage.

The glove was always employed as a gage
or earneſt of challenging. Segar, in his
Diſcourſe upon Honour, avers, *That he
who loſeth his gauntlet in fight is more to be
blamed than he who is diſarmed of his poul-
deron*: for the gauntlet armeth the hand,
without which member no fight can be performed; and therefore that part of armour is
commonly ſent in ſign of defiance.*

I D E M.

Further I ſay, and further will maintain,
That he did plot the duke of Gloſter's death,
Suggeſt his ſoon believing adverſaries.

That is, he raiſed the duke many enemies
by his falſe inventions and baſe inſinua-
tions.

I B I D.

——————————Like a traiterous coward,
Sluic'd out his innocent ſoul through ſtreams of blood,
Which blood, like ſacrificing Abel's, cries
To me for juſtice and rough chaſtiſment:

And,

---

* A part of the armour which guards the combatant's
ſhoulder.

And, by the glorious worth of my defcent,
This arm fhall do it, or this life be fpent.

Hereford's bold declaration, to punifh the
man who put to death the duke of Glofter, could not be pleafing to the king,
who knew himfelf guilty of that murder,
by the agency of Norfolk and others. He
faw evidently that he was himfelf ftruck at
by the challenge; and, in the whole fcene,
Shakfpeare has made him an encourager of
Norfolk, whofe fpirits he endeavours to
fupport by a folemn proteftation of his
impartiality.

RICHARD.

He is our fubject, Mowbray; fo art thou.
Free fpeech and fearlefs I to thee allow.

NORFOLK.

Then, Bolingbroke, as low as to thy heart,
Through the falfe paffage to thy throat, thou lieft.

The nobleft leffon of chivalry was a ftrict
injunction to a conformity with truth. To
this the knight was obliged by his oath to
adhere inviolably. The giving the lie was
therefore an ignominy which no man of
that order could bear without the ftrongeft
refentment,

refentment, and by giving or accepting a challenge. The point of honour, in refpect to the lie direct, is ftill maintained and preferved, as a precious remnant of the inftitution. Monarchs, however, can difpenfe even with this ; for, about one hundred and thirty years after this contention between Bolingbroke and Norfolk, Charles V. emperor of Germany, and Francis I. king of France, gave and returned the lie to each other, in terms as bitter and brutal as thofe made ufe of by the two dukes ; and, though the challenge was fent and accepted, yet nothing came of it*.

NORFOLK.

For that my fovereign liege was in my debt
Upon remainder of a dear account
Since laft I went to France to fetch his queen.

By *dear account* I underftand a demand of debt of a private nature, as ftated in the text.

The appeal of Hereford and the anfwer of Norfolk are taken almoft verbatim from Hol-

---

* Robertfon's Life of Charles V.

Hollingfhead's Chronicle. The Parliamentary Hiftory has omitted the charge of
Norfolk's murdering the duke of Glofter.

Scene III. The Lifts at Coventry.

When this play was revived at the theatre
in Covent-garden, above forty years fince,
the ancient ceremony which belonged to the
fingle combat was very accurately obferved,
with all the decorations and arrangements
proper to the appellant and refpondent, the
fpectators and the judges. Amongft the latter, the king was feated in a throne of
ftate. The combatants were dreffed in
complete armour. Two chairs, finely a-
dorned, were placed on oppofite fides of
the lifts : to thefe they retired after each of
them had ftood forth and fpoken. Bolingbroke was acted by Ryan. Walker perfonated Mowbray. His helmet was laced fo
tightly under his chin, that, when he endeavoured to fpeak, nobody could underftand
him ; and this obftacle occafioned a laugh
from the audience : however, this was foon
removed,

removed, and the actor was heard with attention.   In their perfons, drefs, and demeanour, they prefented fomething like an image of the old trial of right by duel.

The laft attempt towards a trial of this kind, in the reign of Charles I. was attended with fome ridiculous circumftances, which may amufe the reader.   Lord Rea accufed one Mr. Ramfay of uttering fome treafonable expreffions.   Ramfay denied the charge, and challenged the accufer to fingle combat, according to the laws of chivalry.   The king wifhed not to revive this dangerous and obfolete cuftom, and defired the judges to ufe all legal methods to prevent the trial coming to an iffue.   Lord Rea, who feems to have had no ftomach for the bufinefs, petitioned the Court of Honour, that he might be permitted to have counfel with him while in the lifts, and a furgeon with his ointments.   He was allowed a feat or pavilion to reft himfelf, and wine for refrefhments.   He was permitted to have, befides, *iron nails, a hammer,*

hammer, a file, fciffars, and a bodkin, with thread and needle. After a few adjournments, the king fuperfeded his commiffion to the conftable and marfhal, and thus ended the laft of thefe abfurd trials.*

BOLINBROKE.

That it may enter Mowbray's waxen coat.

Mr. Steevens has, on this paffage, given a curious defcription of a coat of mail, from fome which he had feen in the Tower. But, with fubmiffion to fo accurate a writer, I beg leave to underftand the words, *waxen coat*, in a very different fenfe. By ufing thefe words, Bolingbroke means to exprefs a high and confident opinion of the goodnefs of his caufe, of his own ftrength and courage, and of the weaknefs and cowardice of his adverfary, As if he had faid, " So little do I fear the power of my antagonift, that his coat of mail will, to my lance, be as penetrable as if it were compofed of wax." The knights who went

forth

---

* Rufhworth, vol. II.

forth to battle were certainly not better
fecured and guarded in their armour than
thofe who fought for life and honour in a
fingle combat. Hiftorians have defcribed
the former as vulnerable only in the face
when a knight lifted up the vifor of his
helmet ; in the fide, at the extremity of
the armour ; when he was knocked down,
after they had pulled off his coat of mail ;
or, in fine, under the arm-pit, when he
lifted up his arm to ftrike. Voltaire, from
whofe General Hiftory I get this information, tells us that Philip Auguftus, king
of France, at the battle of Bouvines, was
knocked off his horfe, and for a long time
furrounded by the enemy ; who gave him
feveral blows, with various weapons, without his being in the leaft wounded : fo that
a knight, completely armed, fcarce ran
any other rifk than being difmounted.

Not one knight, continues this author,
was killed in this battle except William
Longchamp, who died of a blow levelled
through the vifor of his helmet.

R I C H A R D,

RICHARD.

Let them lay by their helmets and their fpears,
And both retire back to their chairs again.

The hindering of this duel was eventually the caufe of the king's depofition and
death; nor can it eafily be conceived upon
what principle of policy he acted.   As
Richard was not of a compaffionate nature,
the death of either, or of both, would not
have hurt his feelings.   In all probability,
the plan of banifhing both dukes was concerted between the king and his favourites,
before the combatants entered the lifts at
Coventry.   The king could not bear the popularity of Hereford, whofe eminent perfonal virtues were a conftant reproach to his
own imbecillity and worthleffnefs.   By banifhing the duke of Norfolk for ever, he got
into his own hands all the duke's patri-
mony, except one thoufand pounds *per
annum* referved for his ufe when abroad.
This unjuft and impolitic fentence, paffed
on the combatants, was confirmed by four
and twenty commiffioners felected from
the

the upper and lower houfes of parliament, who were chofen to fuperintend the com‑ bat.

KING RICHARD
The datelefs limit of thy dear exile.

The word *dear*, in Shakfpeare, has va‑ rious meanings, and very often that which is quite oppofite to the general fenfe of the word. In this place it fignifies, *fatal, ter‑ rible*, or *hateful*. So in Hamlet,

> Would I had met my *deareft* foe in heaven
> Or ever I had feen that day, Horatio!

I remember that Ryan was fo afraid the audience fhould miftake Hamlet's mean‑ ing, that he always repeated the line thus:

> Would I had met my *direft* foe in heaven.

BOLINGBROKE
Norfolk, fo far as to mine enemy.

The meaning of this addrefs, from one implacable foe to another, feems to be this — " Norfolk, the bufinefs of the duel is over: however, though I profefs myfelf your enemy, let me now calmly intreat you, as a man and Chriftian, to difbur‑

then your confcience and confefs your treafon." The expreffion is fimply no more
than, " So far as one enemy may fpeak
to another."

G A U N T.

All places that the eye of heaven vifits
    Are, to a wife man, ports and happy havens.

Thefe lines are evidently borrowed from
Ovid.

Omne, viro forti, folum patria.

Soon after the decifion at Coventry, the
dukes of Hereford and Norfolk went into
banifhment. Upon reading over the paff-
ports of both thefe noblemen, in Rymer,
we fee a ftrong partiality of the king in
thofe granted to Norfolk, and efpecially in
that public act which is called, *De re-
queflu regis ex parte ducis Norfolciæ.* Richard could not do lefs for the man who
feems to have incurred his banifhment
principally for obeying his illegal orders, and
one too whom he had robbed of the greateft
part of his eftate. Norfolk died, fome few
years after his banifhment, at Venice, univerfally hated.

R I C H A R D.

RICHARD.

How he did feem to dive into their hearts,
With humble and familiar courtefy !

In giving this character of Bolingbroke, Richard is juftified by the very words which Shakfpeare puts into the former's mouth when he was king.

Henry IV. act III. fcene between Henry and the prince of Wales.

And then I ftole all courtefy from heav'n,
And dreft myfelf in fuch humility,
That I did pluck allegiance from men's hearts,
Loud fhouts and falutations from their tongues,
Even in the prefence of the crowned king.

Henry then gives his fon a very farcaftic picture of Richard's behaviour.

The fkipping king, he ambled up and down
With fhallow jefters and rafh bavin wits :
Soon kindled, and foon burnt, &c. &c.

Richard's familiar condefcenfion was too general and too undiftinguifhing to be ef-teemed of any worth.   He delighted in mean company and licentious converfation. He bore no refemblance to his father and

K 2   grandfather,

grandfather, but was more like his unhappy great-grandfather Edward II. whom
our old hiftorians term a *chatterer*. Few men
of princely rank underftand the art of converfing with their inferiors in a manner
that is gracefully condefcending ; and, for
want of this, they often degrade themfelves
in the opinion of thofe whofe efteem and
veneration they want the addrefs to acquire.
Henry IV. of France, being exercifed in
war and adverfity from his early youth, and
perpetually mixing with all ranks of people, acquired fuch an eafy freedom of converfation and fo happy a talent of expreffion, that he endeared himfelf to his fubjects as much by his affability as his great
and illuftrious actions. His two grand-
fons, our Charles II. and Louis XIV.
were equally diftinguifhed for excellence in
their different ftyles of converfing. Charles,
who loved company, and had none but men
of wit conftantly about him, was judged
to be equal, if not fuperior, to any of his
companions, for the pertinency, as well as
brilliancy,

brilliancy, of his converfation : his grandfather Henry would fometimes venture to
give a rough, or even a coarfe, repartee;
but Charles maintained his fuperiority by
never uttering any thing that could difpleafe, or occafion an improper reply.   His
wit was that of the well-bred and accomplifhed gentleman.   The grandeur of
Louis's mind appeared in many fudden ef-
fufions of bons mots.   When a court-lady
laughed at the Marfhal de Brifac, and loudly declared fhe never faw fo ugly a man in
her life, Louis replied " Madam, I differ
from you very much ;   I think him a very
handfome man, for to him I owe many
glorious victories."   When his grandfon
Philip fet out for Madrid to affume the
government of Spain, " Remember, grandfon, faid Louis, there are now no Pyre-
nean mountains," the ufual boundary of
France and Spain.

K 3   Act

Act II. Scene I.

Y O R K.

——Report of fashions in proud Italy,
Whose manners still our tardy apish nation
Limps after in base imitation.

Italy, in our author's time, gave the ton
of fashion, as France does now, to all Europe. The invectives of Roger Ascham,
who in nine days saw more wickedness
committed in Italy than in several months in
our great metropolis, are ridiculed, with some
shew of reason, by Baretti : but when the
same man assures us, from his own knowledge, that the English youth, who returned from their travels in that country to
their own, were generally abandoned in
principle and dissolute in morals, I cannot
help believing him ; but what shall we say
too if Bayle, in the article of Castellan,
great almoner to Francis I. and who travelled to Rome sometime before Roger
Ascham was in Italy, should confirm all
Ascham had said ? Bayle gives the following extract from the life of that prelate

by

by Gallandus. " I remember that when he
was defcribing the wanton lufts, avarice,
and rapacioufnefs, of the Roman pontiffs,
and their contempt of religion ; the pride,
luxury, and lazinefs, of the cardinals;
their riotous feaftings, and other vices,
which he had obferved in the court of
Rome; he would be fo moved with indignation, that, not only the colour of his
face, but the very motions and geftures of
his body, were changed." Bayle's Dict.
Vol. II. p. 371. Lord Chefterfield feems
to have been more anxious concerning the
morals of Mr. Stanhope when at Rome
than in any other part of Europe.

GAUNT.

Againft infection and the hand of war.

Dr. Johnfon thinks that, by *infection*, the
author means that iflanders were fecure by
fituation from war and peftilence: not
furely from the latter, if they had any in-
tercourfe by trade with foreign nations.
In this rhapfodical defcription of England

by Gaunt, the poet means, I think, to include a particular and exclufive kind of moral
happinefs. Though we are not exempted
from warlike invafions, we are fecure from
the contamination of fuch ill habits and
vices as are familiar to Italy and other
parts of the continent. It is a remarkable
obfervation of Machiavel, " That Italy,
France, and Spain, are able to debauch
the morals of all mankind befide."

G A U N T.

A thoufand flatterers fit within thy crown.

Thy fole merit is having poffeffion of
the crown; and that is the charm which
attracts thy flatterers, who with their al-
lurements deceive thee to thy ruin.

R I C H A R D.

Thou a lunatic lean-witted fool, &c.

The fcene between the dying Gaunt and
the king is not borrowed from any chronicle, it is the author's own invention; this
great mafter of Nature takes advantage
from Gaunt's recent injury in the banifhment of his fon and his own defperate
ficknefs,

ficknefs, to give a keennefs to his reproaches which no man in a fedate and unruffled hour of health would have ventured to utter.

GAUNT.

My brother Glofter, plain well-fpeaking man,
May be a precedent and witnefs' good,
That thou refpect'ft not fpilling Edward's blood.

As the death of the duke of Glofter was eventually the caufe of Richard's misfortune more than any thing elfe, I fhall be indulged in fpeaking a little more at large concerning the quarrel between Richard and the duke, which ended fo fatally to them both. Shakfpeare, by calling Glofter a plain-fpoken man, feems to glance at the very words, which occafioned, perhaps, more than any overt act, the refolution of the king to get rid of him at all events.

Richard had been prevailed upon, for a fmall fum of money, to reftore the town of Breft to the duke of Bretagne. The furrendering a fea-port of fuch confequence to the French was generally blamed. The
duke

duke of Glofter was fo particularly difpleafed, that he reproached his nephew for
it in very bitter and taunting terms — " It
would become you better, fir, to gain fome
important place by your prowefs, faid
Glofter, than to furrender to your enemies
that which had been fubdued by the victorious arms of your anceftors." The
king, fays Hollingfhead, bade his uncle
repeat what he had faid. This he complied with, and did not, in the repetition,
foften a word which he had fpoken before.

After all, the duke was certainly a moft
ambitious and turbulent man, whom no
honours, power, or riches, could gra-
tify. His courage in the field, and readi-
nefs to promote any warlike enterprife,
had rendered him exceedingly popular and
the idol of all military men. By this influence he had, nine years before his death,
caufed feveral of the king's minifters to be
publicly executed, and reduced the power
of the crown to a mere fhadow. The infignificant

fignificant character of Richard, who was
neither a foldier nor a politician, gave this
confequence to Glofter; whofe temper was
fo brutal and inflexible, that he refufed to
fpare the life of Sir Simon Burley, though
Richard's queen, called *the good queen Anne*,
folicited this favour feveral hours on her
knees.   Burley had been tutor to the king,
and was in high credit with Edward III.
and his fon the Black Prince.   In fhort,
Richard was in the fame fituation, refpecting the duke of Glofter, as Henry III. of
France was with the duke of Guife; who
was reduced to the neceffity of affaffina-
ting a man who was become too powerful
to be brought to a trial.   But, in both
cafes, the imbecillity of the monarch
brought on the neceffity.

GAUNT.

And thy unkindnefs be like crooked age,
To crop at once a too-long-wither'd flower.

Dr. Johnfon, not liking the word *age* in
the text, propofes *edge* in its ftead: and
Mr. Steevens beftows a very ingenious note

on

on the figure of Time with a fcythe. I
cannot help thinking that the meaning of
the text, as it ftands, is very clear —
" Do thou forget all proximity of blood,
and become a confederate with my prefent
ficknefs and the *many infirmities of old age,*
to deprive me at once of life."

NORTHUMBERLAND.

My liege old Gaunt commends him to you.

There is a fplendid ray of greatnefs, tranf-
mitted from hiftory and tradition, ftill
furrounding the name of John of Gaunt,
and which to this day commands a kind of
awe and reverence. If we examine impartially the character of the duke, we
fhall find that it but ill correfponds with
that celebrity which has attended his memory. I read of no military exploits of
Gaunt which could exalt him either to the
title of great conqueror or brave foldier.
Unlike his father Edward III. or his brother
the Black Prince, he feems to have been
rather a cautious than an enterprifing war-
rior ; and, though no coward, yet he
thought,

thought, with Falstaff, that discretion was no mean part of valour. The boundless ambition which impelled him to struggle for the crown of Castile, and the title of king, which he carried with him to his grave, did not contribute to make him a better subject. He was the great scourge and persecutor of the commons, whom he laboured to reduce to a state of slavery. He thought, with Dr. Mandeville, that teaching the children of the poor to write and read would be the means of rendering them unfit for service; and therefore insisted, with the rest of his brother tyrants, the barons, *that no poor man's son should be permitted to have any instruction by going to school.* I cannot have a doubt that it was chiefly by his advice Richard was persuaded, when young, to pronounce that most disgusting and shocking answer to the petition of the commons, who prayed to be relieved from vassalage, " *That slaves they were, and slaves they should remain.*"

If

If he merited the honour of favouring Wickliffe and his doctrine, we can scarce attribute this conduct to generous motives; he hated the clergy becaufe they were rich and powerful. But no part of his conduct is more liable to cenfure than his neglect of his nephew's education, whom he feems, for no good purpofe, to have fuffered to become the companion of young men whofe manners were diffolute and utterly unfit to train him in that difcipline which is neceffary to form a great prince. The duke of Lancafter was publicly accufed of laying a plot to murder the king and ufurp the crown. The accufer was put into the cuftody of Sir John Holland, but he was found dead in his chamber the very night preceding the day on which he was to appear and make good his charge. Stowe's account of this tranfaction bears hard, I think, upon the duke.

The fcene between Richard and Gaunt, on the revival of this play, was acted with fuch propriety, as gained the approbation

of

of the audience. Mr. Johnson, commonly called *tall Johnson*, being near seven feet
high, the son-in-law of Aaron Hill, and
by him instructed, was properly enough
pitched upon to represent John of Gaunt:
though his conception was not equal to
the animated dialogue of the character, or
his feeling powerful enough for the situation of it, his good understanding and decent deportment rendered him not disagree-
able to the spectators. In this scene too,
Delane, in Richard, drew a good portrait
of a king elated by pride and prosperity,
and possessed with an obstinate and unfeeling disposition.

YORK.

I am the last of noble Edward's sons,
Of whom thy father, prince of Wales, was first;
His face thou hast, for even so look'd he,
Accomplish'd with the number of thy years.

This resemblance of Richard to his father
appears pleasing in poetical description;
but, in fact, though very handsome, the
king was so unlike the Black Prince, that

it

it was infinuated, from that circumftance
and his apparent degeneracy, that he really
was not his fon. If his picture, fays the
Hon. D. Barrington, in his Obfervations
on the ftatutes, which hangs over the pul-
pit in Weftminfter-abbey, be an original,
he certainly had not the complexion of his
father. He proceeds to obferve, that the
refemblance in point of features and complexion is more to be relied on, in proof
of legitimacy, than any hereditary qualities of the mind.

I D E M.

Take Hereford's rights away, and take from time
His charters and his cuftomary rights.
Let not to-morrow then enfue to-day.
Be not thyfelf; for how art thou a king? &c.

David Hume, who feems to eftimate Shakfpeare's beauties by his blemifhes, afferts,*
that, in all his hiftorical plays, there is
fcarce any mention of civil liberty.

Suppofe this fhould be granted; in how
many plays, fince the Reftoration to this

day,

* Vide Hume's Hift. 8vo, vol. VI. p. 192.

day, do we find the fubject of civil rights
either generally difcuffed or occafionally
infifted upon ?   In how many dramas of
the Greek tragedians is it profeffedly or accidentally introduced ?   Tragedy owes its
rife to the paffions ; and though it may involve, as it ought, a topic in which all
mankind are intimately concerned, yet by
experience we find thofe plays, which are
moft fraught with fentiments in favour of
public liberty, are leaft admired and followed.   How often is Cato acted ?   What
is become of Dennis's Liberty afferted ?
But Hume wanted to prove, from Shakfpeare, that, in the reign of Elizabeth, the
common rights of fubjects were no object
of public difcuffion.   But is not the fcene
between Richard and York more interefting
to an audience than all the laboured argu-
ments of political oratory ?   A counfellor of
ftate honeftly tells his prince, that depriving
a fubject of his charters and cuftomary dues
was not only an act of oppreffion and injuf-

tice, but a grofs folecifm: it was undermining the throne on which he fat, and contradicting his own right of fucceffion to the crown!

But York, in the following impaffioned lines, goes farther:

> If you do wrongfully feize Hereford's rights,
> You pluck a thoufand dangers on your head,
> You lofe a thoufand well-difpofed hearts, &c.

Here the fubject tells his prince, that, if he perfifts in his refolution to act with violence and injuftice, the confequence will be the hatred of his people and a civil war. Warm expoftulations of this kind are of the very effence of tragic dialogue; but a train of fentiments upon civil liberty is fitter for a difcourfe than a play. Shakfpeare, though a court poet, has written more fcenes to expofe the tyranny and oppreffion of kings, the pride and rebellion of the nobles, and the turbulent difpofition of the common people, than all the writers of plays put together.

In

In the hiftory of the ftage there is fcarce
any thing more fingular than the fortune
of that perfon who acted the part of York.
This was one Mr. Samuel Stephens, a
button-maker, in Pater-nofter-row. He
had been many years a conftant attendant
at the theatre, and efpecially when Booth
acted a principal part in tragedy. Amongft
his acquaintance he had frequently repeated fpeeches, or favourite portions of
plays, efpecially from Othello. He was
told by his friends that his voice refembled
that of Booth, both in ftrength and me-
lody; and that his imitation of that great
actor's manner was juft, as well as pleafing. He was at length tempted to make
an offer of his abilities to Mr. Rich, who
had juft loft his great tragedian Mr. Quin,
who had left him to engage at Drury-lane-
theatre. In confequence of fome tempo-
rary agreement, Stephens ventured, in
October, 1734, to act his favourite character of Othello. His figure was not unfuitable to the part : his voice was ftrong;

and he had, by clofe auricular attention, acquired fome of Booth's happy cadences. The fpectators were equally furprifed and delighted. During that moft paffionate fcene between the Moor and Iago, in the third act, the pit cried out, " Bravo ! bravo ! *better than Quin ! better than Quin !*" For fix or feven fucceffive nights this man drew after him large audiences. Quin, for a time, it is faid, avoided going to the coffee-houfes he ufually frequented, left he fhould be affronted with the loud praifes of the button-maker.

However, the charm was not wound up fo powerfully as to laft long. Rich, either by miftake or defign, perfuaded the new actor to choofe Polydore, in The Orphan, for his fecond character : than which nothing could have been more illadvifed. Stephens was, in form, bulky ; in the management of his perfon, aukward ; and advanced to near his fortieth year. This act of indifcretion was equally hurtful to the actor and manager. The

ladies

ladies more efpecially were difpleafed with
fuch a mifreprefentation of a young gay
libertine, drefled in a large full-bottom
wig, and, I believe, in red ftockings,
though they had long been laid afide by
the politer part of the town : but Ryan's
predilection for that colour, it is faid, kept
them too long on the ftage. However,
the audience did not forget the pleafure
Stephens had afforded them in Othello :
they forbore, on that account, fhewing
any marks of difpleafure to his Polydore.
To recover the good opinion of the public, he was forced to hide himfelf in his
black vifor. Stephens acted feveral characters, and particularly the duke of
York, with approbation ; but, as he never came up to his firft attempt, he gradually fell in the public efteem. He ended
at laft in an itinerant actor. His laft ftage
was Bath ; where he died, about twenty
years fince, refpected for his general good
behaviour.

CHAP-

CHAPTER VIII.

*Richard goes to Ireland. — Scene of Nor-
thumberland, &c. applied to modern poli-
tics. — War with Spain difliked by Sir Robert Walpole.—His dread of Jacobites, and
dying prognoftication. — Particular lines of
Shakfpeare vehemently applauded on account
of fuppofed refemblance. — Richard marries
an infant. — His great indifcretion. —
Meaning of defpifed arms. — Why Prince
Edward was called the Black Prince. —
York's character. — Shakfpeare's conduct of
his plot. — Refemblance between Richard
and Agamemnon. — Delane's Richard. —
Who was the firft anointed king in Europe.—
Feigned fubmiffion of Hereford, and treachery of Northumberland. — Savage manners of our anceftors. — Fifty challenges in
parliament. — Bifhop of Carlifle's integrity.
— Warburton makes Shakfpeare a Whig.—
Paffive obedience. — Tom Chapman's abfur-
dities and real merit. — Farquhar, Rowe,
Sir Godfrey Kneller, and Hogarth.*

AS foon as Richard, intent upon his
Irifh expedition, had left the ftage, the
author

author introduces a political scene between the earl of Northumberland and the lords Willoughby and Rofs, full of fevere reflections upon the king's mifconduct. The writing is not fingularly good, but it was greatly diftinguifhed by the particular behaviour of the audience, on the revival of this play, who applied almoft every line that was fpoken to the occurrences of the time, and to the meafures and character of the miniftry.

During a long peace of twenty-five years, the people, who feldom know their own happinefs, were eager for a war with Spain. Provocations, it muft be owned, had been given by the court of Madrid. The depredations committed by the Spanifh guard-da-coftas on our merchant-fhips roufed the attention and refentment of the merchants, who addreffed the parliament on the occafion; and the amiable Mr. Glover, then a member of parliament, feconded their petition with an animated fpeech. Sir Robert Walpole dreaded the

confequences of a war with the Spaniards,
and feared it would unite the elder branch
of the houfe of Bourbon in the fame quarrel. He forefaw too that a rebellion in
Scotland would be fomented by the high
Tories and Jacobites in both kingdoms.
He had always entertained a fecret dread
of thofe gentlemen, who affembled in clubs
to toaft the king over the water. Nay,
fome time before his death, which happened in 1744, this great minifter, as I
was then informed by a nobleman, pre-
dicted that the king would be reduced to
the neceffity of fighting for his crown.

The more reluctant Walpole appeared
to fecond the wifhes of the merchants in
commencing hoftilities, the more clamo-
rous the people were for letting loofe the
vengeance of the nation againft the Spaniards. When this tragedy was, after being long forgotten, revived, the cry for
war was at the higheft, and the fpectators
were ready to apply all that was uttered
in the theatre to the tranfactions of the
day

day and to the miniftry. The dialogue of
Northumberland and his friends furnifhed
ample materials for political innuendo and
application. There was in Bridgewater,
who perfonated Northumberland, a moft
grave and folemn manner of delivering a
fentiment, which dwelt fully upon the attentive hearer. When he pronounced the
following words,

> The king is not himfelf, but bafely led
> By flatterers, —

the noife from the clapping of hands and
clattering of fticks was loud and boifterous. And when Rofs faid,

> The earl of Wiltfhire hath the ftate in farm, —

it was immediately applied to Walpole,
with the loudeft fhouts and huzzas I ever
heard. Likewife the following obfervation of Northumberland, that the king's
revenue was not diminifhed by war, was
met, by the audience, with redoubled
fhouts —

War

War hath not wafted it ; for warr'd he hath not.
More hath he fpent in peace than they * in war.

The two following remarkable lines, fpoken by Willoughby and Northumberland, were heard with a dead and refpectful filence : ——

WILLOUGHBY.

The king's grown bankrupt, like a broken man.

NORTHUMBERLAND.

Reproach, and diffolution, hangeth over him.

And now, if Mr. Hume had read over this fcene with attention, he would not have charged Shakfpeare with deferting the civil rights of mankind : for what are the accufations of the fpeakers, in this dialogue, but fo many vindications of the natural and legal claims of the fubject ?

Act II. Scene II. The queen, Bufhy, &c.

BUSHY.

Madam, your majefty is much too fad.

Though Shakfpeare thought it for his purpofe to have a queen in his tragedy, to heighten

---

* His anceftors.

heighten the diftrefs of the fcene, it is certain that Richard, about a year before he was dethroned, married a daughter of France, a child of eight years old : a moft imprudent action, and correfpondent with the reft of his conduct.   He had no iffue by his firft wife, queen Anne; and therefore fhould, in right policy, have married one who could have brought him children.   By wedding a child, he deprived himfelf of the hopes of one great advantage and fupport, at leaft for a confiderable time.   William III. when the parliament obliged him to difmifs his Walloon guards, refented the affront in a moft lively manner, and not without tears.   In the bitternefs of his heart he fwore, that, if he had had a fon, he would not have complied with their requeft.*

Scene III.

Y O R K.

Frighting her pale-fac'd villages with war
And oftentation of defpifed arms.

Defpifed,

---

* Dalrymple's Memoirs.

Defpifed, in this place, means *detefted*, *abhorred*, &c.

I D E M.

Were I but now the lord of fuch hot youth
As when brave Gaunt, thy father, and myfelf,
Refcu'd the Black Prince, that young Mars of men, &c.

This calls to our minds feveral paffages of the Iliad, where old Neftor vaunts, in moft exulting terms, of his great prowefs in his younger years. The renowned prince of Wales, eldeft fon of Edward III. was called the Black Prince from his complexion, not his armour, as is generally fuppofed.

Y O R K.

Well, well, I fee the iffue of thefe arms.

The character of York, as delivered down by hiftorians, is not much to his advantage : he was efteemed a light and capricious man. Shakfpeare, in this fcene, though not in all the reft, conforms to the hiftorical outline of the duke. In this interview with Bolingbroke, he firft threatens, that, if he had power, he would attach the infurgents ; then fays, he will

remain

remain neuter. After that, he invites the
heads of the conspiracy into his castle;
and, upon Lancaster's telling him that he
must go with him to seize the king's mi-
nisters in Bristol-castle, he calmly says,
" It may be ; I will go with you :" and
yet the good man declares, " he is loath
to break his country's laws :" but immediately after complies with the usurper, who
makes him a chief instrument to support
his rebellion.

Act III. Scene the king, Aumerle, bishop
         of Carlisle, &c.

The following lines bear a strong resemblance to Agamemnon's saluting his country's soil, and shedding tears for joy, in Homer's Odyssey, book IV.

R I C H A R D.

Dear earth, I do salute thee with my hand :
As a long parted mother with her child
Plays fondly with her tears, and smiles in meeting,
So weeping, smiling, greet I thee, O earth,
And do thee favour with my royal hands.

Η τοι ὁ μεν χαιρων επεϐησετο πατριδος αιης,
Και κυνει απτομεν@ ἡν πατριδα· πολλα δ' απ' αυτε
Δακρυα θερμα χεοντ' επει ασπασιως ιδε γαιαν.

Weil

Well pleas'd, the king beheld his Argive foil,
And, leaping eagerly upon the ſtrand,
With tears of joy he kiſs'd his native land.

When Philip II. huſband to Queen
Mary, firſt landed in England, he knelt
down on the ground, and as he roſe he drew
his ſword, as if reſolving to conquer the
kingdom.

Shakſpeare has not, I believe, manifeſted
more ſkill in the conduét of his plot than
in this ſcene. The king lands from Ireland with a very few followers : his confidence is equal to his ignorance of his ſituation. He vents his complaints of rebellion in an affeéting addreſs to the Engliſh earth, and, without any apparent
hopes of withſtanding a powerful inva-
der of his kingdom, he idly preſumes,
upon the ſacredneſs of his perſon, that he
ſhall conquer all oppoſition. The author
gradually leads him from confidence to
doubt, from doubt to fear, and from that
to deſpondency. Every incident is managed with the niceſt ſkill. Saliſbury a-
larms

larms him, and Scroope terrifies him into absolute despair. Richard's pathetic reflections on the miserable fate of kings has been justly admired, and was marked by Pope in his edition as a masterly passage.

Delane, who on the revival of this play acted Richard, though he did great justice to several scenes of the character, could not exhibit the tender feelings of the king's distressful situation. His voice was too loudly extended for the desponding and almost effeminate grief of this unhappy prince. Had Barry ever been called upon to represent this part, " he would (in our author's emphatic language) have drowned the stage with tears."

RICHARD.

Not all the water in the rough rude sea
Can wash the balm from an anointed king.

One would imagine that monarchs have been taught to believe that the anointing them with the sacred oil at their coronation was to operate like a miraculous charm, which was to render their perfons facred and inviolable, and their actions fuperior to cenfure. But who was the firft man who went through the anointing ceremony? Pepin of France, a robber and ufurper; a man who deprived his lawful fovereign of his crown, and fhut him in a cloifter. This fuccefsful ruffian was fupported in his treafon by Pope Zachary, who ftood in need of Pepin's affiftance, and who afterwards, with the help of St. Boniface, performed the office of anointing a rebel, king of France, at Rheims.

RICHARD.

Strives Bolingbroke to be as great as we?
Greater he fhall not be: if he ferve God,
We'll ferve him too, and be his fellows fo.

This is the nature of man. In his profperity he forgets all piety to heaven, all focial ties and obligations. Richard, who, while his affairs wore a fmiling afpect, neither reverenced God nor regarded man, is here, by our excellent moralizer, made fo humble as to find no relief in his dif-

trefs

ftrefs equally efficacious with repentance and amendment of life.

RICHARD.

The power, I have, difcharge, and let them go
To ear the land. ———

Mr. Steevens rightly fays, that earing the land is ploughing it. It is properly a Scotch word, and is fpelt *ere*, which is derived from another North-Britifh word, *erde*, the earth.*

Scene III.

Our author purfues the thread of hiftory very clofely, and has given proper colours to the feigned fubmiffion of Hereford and the treachery of Northumberland. The king, deferted by the greateft part of his followers, retired to the Ifle of Anglefea ; where he purpofed to embark for Ireland or France, there to wait fome opportunity of returning to England : but the ufurper, alarmed at this ftep, fent Northumberland to deceive him with falfe promifes of

---

* Gloffary to Gawin Douglas's Virgil.

loyalty and fubmiffion. The earl, by folemn proteftations and fhameful perjury, made himfelf mafter of the king's perfon, and carried him to Flint-caftle. The interview between the king and his coufin of Lancafter was more rough and auftere, on the part of the duke, than the poet has reprefented it. He told the king, in plain terms, that, his fubjects being diffatisfied with his government, he was come to affift him to govern better. The king anfwered humbly : " Dear coufin, fince that is your pleafure, it is ours alfo." To mortify the king on a very tender point, during the whole of his journey from Flint-caftle to London, he was, befides being mounted on a very fhabby horfe, not fuffered to change his apparel. No prince in Europe had fo rich a wardrobe as Richard, or delighted fo much in fplendid and coftly dreffes.

Act IV. Scene I. The parliament-houfe.

A ftronger and truer picture of the favage manners of our anceftors cannot be

delineated

delineated than in this illiberal fcene between the prime nobility of the land.   A
glove is thrown down by one nobleman
with terms of fcorn and reproach, and accepted by another with words of brutality and
fiercenefs.   The prefence of the duke of
Lancafter, mafter of the kingdom and pretender to the throne, could not awe the
difputants into refpect and filence.   Mr.
Hume fays that no lefs than fifty challenges were given and accepted at this
meeting of the parliament.

BOLINGBROKE.

In God's name then I'll afcend the throne.

BISHOP OF CARLISLE.

Marry, God forbid !

Thomas Merks, bifhop of Carlifle, (a
name which ought to be revered to la-
teft pofterity,) was, in that great con-
courfe of the clergy and laity affembled on
this occafion, the only man who had the
honefty and courage to fpeak in the defence of his unhappy fovereign, and a-
gainft the violence and ufurpation of Bo-

M 2   lingbroke.

lingbroke.   His fpeech was long, and is
quoted from Sir John Hayward, in the
Parliamentary Hiftory.   It contains a re-
trofpective view of all kinds of government; and the bifhop's argument is ftrength-
ened from fcripture authority.

I D E M.

And fhall the figure of God's majefty,
His captain, fteward, deputy elect,
Anointed, crowned, planted many years,
Be judg'd by fubject and inferior breath ?

In vain does Dr. Warburton ftrive to make
Shakfpeare a Whig in principle, long before the limits between prerogative and
privilege were determined.   The political
and religious creeds in Queen Elizabeth's
reign were equally favourable to the abfolute power of the prince; and I have often wondered that Lord Bolingbroke fhould
affert, that the doctrine of paffive obedience lay undifcovered, in fome old homily,
till the times of James I.   All the Chronicles of Hollingfhead, Hall, Grafton,
Stowe, and Fabian, breathe the fame non-
                                    refifting

refifting fpirit ; nor do I know that any Englifh divine oppofed it, till our incomparable Hooker, in his Ecclefiaftical Polity, with an irrefiftible force of argument, demolifhed that infamous pofition on which is founded

Th'enormous faith of millions made for one.

Tom Chapman, a moft excellent actor in various parts, but efpecially in all Shakfpeare's clowns, in petulant would-be-wits, fops and fantaftics, and many other abfurd humorous characters, infifted upon reprefenting what nature never defigned him for, — a grave tragic character. The bifhop of Carlifle was a delicious morfel, which he would not fuffer to efcape him. No man was ever more eager for preferment than Chapman for the *os rotundum* of tragic elocution. Rich, it was obferved, took delight in thwarting the inclinations of his actors. How Chapman could prevail upon him to let him indulge himfelf in his abfurd humour, I cannot guefs; unlefs he

M 3 flattered

flattered the manager's vanity by fubmit-
ting to be taught by him : for this was a
failing as weakly peculiar in Rich as the
love of reciting tragedy was in Chapman.
In truth, there was nothing more diffo-
nant and unharmonious than his fpeaking, or rather bellowing, the bifhop's ha-
rangue. He was endured in his difcords,
on account of his many excellences in comedy. But fo fond was he of what he did
not underftand, that, although the firft
actor in his own proper walk, he would
condefcend to folicit earneftly for any inferior part in tragedy. It was hopelefs, he
knew, to contend for the character of
Richard III. however, he folaced himfelf
in the fhort part of Treffell, in the fame
play; in which he inhumanly murdered
a moft pathetic defcription of Prince Edward's death by the hand of the duke of
Glofter. At his own theatre of Richmond, where he had the double claim of
manager and principal performer, he exerted his power, to the deftruction of his

own

own property, as well as of all propriety.
Inftead of Tom in The Confcious Lovers,
(in which part he was fure to give infinite
pleafure,) he would needs affume the fine
gentleman, in the perfon of young Bevil.
As to the comedy of The Bufy Body, he
declared that Marplot, in which he excited as much good laughter as ever fhook
a merry audience, was not his proper part,
and therefore infifted upon making himfelf
of no confequence, by acting Sir George
Airy.   At Richmond, too, he ftrutted in
the robes of King Richard III. to empty
benches.   Nothing but his being deferted
by the fpectators could reftore him to his fen-
fes.   However, Tom Chapman has had many to keep him company in his ridiculous
paffion. —— Did not Farquhar think himfelf a good actor, and excite the commiferation of his friends, when he murdered
his own Sir Harry Wildair on the Dublin
ftage ?   Did not the tragic Rowe write
The Biter, a comedy ; and was he not the
only perfon of the audience that laughed

M 4   during

during the acting of it ? Did not Sir Godfrey Kneller fwear to Mr. Gay, that, inftead of ftudying the art of painting, he ought to have been bred a foldier, becaufe he had a martial mien ? And did not Hogarth prefer his lamentable Sigifmunda to his Marriage a la Mode ?

CHAPTER

CHAPTER IX.

A king refigning his crown before his people.—
Shakfpeare inferior to himfelf. — Interview
in the Tower between Richard and Lan-
cafter. — Richard's folly in upbraiding the
infringement of oaths.—Oaths made only for
fubjects. — Univerfity of Oxford contradict-
ing its own doctrine. — Character of Nor-
thumberland.—The family of Percy. — The
actor who prefented to Richard a looking-
glafs.—Richard's houfehold. — Their profu-
fion and profligacy. — Meaning of the word
purveyor. — A member of parliament con-
demned to be hanged.—Saved by the clergy.—
Aumerle ftigmatized.— Hallam an imitator
of Wilks. — Michael Stoppelaer, an honeft
blunderer.—Story of Stoppelaer and Rich.

Scene continues. Re-enter York with
Richard.

WE cannot fuppofe a more awful and
affecting tranfaction, than a prince
brought before his fubjects, compelled to deprive

prive himself of his royalty, and to refign his crown to the popular claimant, his near relation. This is a fubject worthy the genius of Shakfpeare ; and yet, it muft be confeffed, he has fallen infinitely fhort of his ufual powers to excite that tumult of paffion which the action merited : he was ever too fond of quibble and conceit ; but here he has indulged himfelf beyond his ufual predilection for them ; and I cannot help thinking, from this circumftance alone, that Richard II, was written and acted much earlier than the date in the ftationers books of 1597. However, if it fhould happen to be as it is recorded, the author made the public ample amends by producing, the year following, one of the moft perfect of all his pieces, The firft Part of King Henry IV. However Shakfpeare might think proper to heighten the fcene by introducing Richard before the parliament to renounce his right to the crown, in fact it was not fo. The poet has worked up the whole from what paffed in the tower between the

deputies

deputies of the parliament, Lancafter and Richard. The deputation confifted of the chief nobility and commons, with the archbifhop of York at their head; who, after being introduced to the captive king, put him in mind of his voluntary offer to refign the crown in the prefence of the archbifhop of Canterbury and the earl of Northumberland : Richard acknowledged his promife, and defired to have an interview with his fucceffor. After fome converfation between him and Lancafter, the king, with an air of cheerfulnefs, called for the act of refignation, which he read over diftinctly, and folemnly confirmed it by an oath; he then conftituted the archbifhop of York and the bifhop of Hereford his procurators to fignify his intention to parliament, and drawing the royal fignet from his own finger, he put it on that of the duke of Lancafter; faying, at the fame time, that he could wifh all his people fhould know, that, if it were in his power, the duke fhould fucceed him to the crown of England.

RICHARD.

RICHARD.

There fhouldft thou find one heinous article,
Containing the depofing of a king,
And cracking the ftrong warrant of an oath.

In vain does the prince accufe the fubject
of infringing his oath of obedience, who
has himfelf broken through the moft folemn of all obligations, the oath taken at
his coronation. Richard thought, with
King John and other arbitrary monarchs,
that oaths were only framed for fubjects:
but it is furely abfurd to imagine that millions fhould be bound by folemn ties
to obey one man, and that he fhould be
fubject to no other reftriction than his own
will and pleafure. To fay that the gofpel
exacts the fame fubmiffion to a Nero as a
Titus, to a Richard II. as a George II. is
to libel that religion which profeffes to
fpeak peace and good-will to man, and
which certainly never intended to leave
mankind worfe than it found them. But
indeed the doctrine of paffive obedience
and non-refiftance has been ever found a
wifp of ftraw, in this country, whenever
princes

princes have trampled upon law, juftice, and humanity. The famous univerfity of Oxford, at a time when it was fuppofed their immunities were in no danger, fo-lemnly enforced unlimited obedience to the king ; but, when the privileges of that learned community were attacked by the hand of power, they fupported the inva-der of the kingdom, who profeffed him-felf a friend to the laws and the conftitu-tion, with all their influence.

NORTHUMBERLAND.

My lord, difpatch ; read over thefe articles.

The family of Percy, one of the nobleft and beft allied of any in the kingdom, were, for their great hofpitality and their military atchievements, defervedly in high eftimation with the people of England. However, it muft be confeffed, that, for many centuries, the hiftory of the peerage furnifhes us ample matter of contention between this noble family and the crown, which always ended much to the diminu-tion of that fplendor which a contrary
conduct

conduct would have reflected on that illuftrious houfe. The earl of Northumberland, in the play of Richard II. is
drawn, by the pen of Shakfpeare, as a moft
cruel and unremitting perfecutor of Richard; nor has he given the leaft hint for
a conduct fo apparently reprehenfible,
though hiftory could have furnifhed him
with a very plaufible, if not a reafonable
one.

When Richard fet out for the Irifh
wars, having formed a jealoufy of the earl
of Northumberland, more from a con-
fcioufnefs of his own imbecillity than any
real caufe of diftruft, he fummoned the
earl to attend him at Briftol, and to pafs
over with him to Ireland. Northumberland offered the king many excufes for
his not being able to comply with his
commands; but more particularly one,
with which the king was well acquainted,
— the bad faith of the Scots; intimating
that they would in all probability invade
England, fhould they find the army removed

moved from the borders. The infatua-
ted king, not fatisfied with this anfwer,
ordered the earl and all his adherents to be
proclaimed traitors.

Enter one with a glafs.

The perfon who, about forty-five years
fince, was employed to bring in a mirror
to Richard,* is now, by the general voice,
allowed to be the firft comedian of the
age. He was then indeed a very young
actor, and has gradually rifen to that degree of eftimation which he now defervedly
enjoys.

RICHARD.

———————— Was this the face
That every day, under his houfehold roof,
Did keep ten thoufand men ? ————

This is a fact which hiftory has delivered
down to us. It bears the fhew of great
humanity and the moft extended benevolence, and therefore merits a ferious difcuffion. From what fource of wealth
could

———————————————

* Mr. Yates.

could fo vaft a multitude be maintained? If from the revenues of the crown, the greatnefs of the expenditure muft have contributed to leffen their value : and accordingly we find that Gaunt charges the king, in the fecond act, with letting his lands to farm, and being not the king, but the landlord, of England. To fupply this wafte of the crown lands, it was neceffary for the king to make frequent applications to the lords and commons ; and indeed none of our Plantagenet princes gained from their fubjects more ample parliamentary fupplies than Richard. But the charge of maintaining fo large a houfe-hold, and fuch a number of officers dependent upon it, was one of the great enormities of this oppreffive reign. Immoderate exactions, which were occafioned by the king's purveyors, whofe office it was to procure provifion for the king and houfehold whenever they removed from one place to another, were of the moft intolerable nature. It is obferved, in our

law-

law-books, that the word *purveyor*, about this period of our hiftory, was become fo odious, that, by a ftatute, it was changed to *acateur*, or purchafer. But the court or houfehold of Richard was branded on more accounts than one. The luxury, diffipation, and debauchery, of the courtiers, male and female, are recorded and cenfured by all our hiftorians. In Richard's time, the houfe of commons, having for fome time been feparated from the lords,* began to feel their ftrength and importance. A certain member of that houfe, apprized of the profligate conduct of the courtiers, and their uncontrouled wafte of the public money, made a motion to enquire into the abufes in the king's houfehold. Richard, hearing of this unexpected attack upon his royal œ-

Vol. I.　　　N　　　conomy,

---

* The feparation of the two orders of men was a happinefs which the people of Scotland never experienced ; and this prevented their partaking of that democratic part of government to which they had an undoubted claim.

conomy, went immediately to the houfe
of peers, and complained to the lords of
the grofs affront put upon him by a com-
moner. They, in compliance with the
king's intimation, took up the bufinefs
with great eagernefs, and immediately ordered the author of the motion to be
hanged. Very luckily for the offender,
he happened to be a churchman ; and, the
archbifhops and bifhops falling on their
knees and intreating for him, his life was
faved.

A U M E R L E.

> You holy churchmen, is there no plot
> To rid the realm of this pernicious blot.

The character of Aumerle is, above all
the noblemen of his time, ftigmatized by
Hume, for bafenefs, treachery, and cruelty.

The perfon who acted Aumerle, was
one Mr. Adam Hallam, who, by an imitation of the action of Wilks, efpecially in
a certain peculiar cuftom of pulling down
his ruffles and rolling his ftockings, joined
to a good degree of diligence, fo far gained
upon

upon Rich's want of difcernment, that he hired him for feven years at a very large falary. When the term of his engagement was expired, his employer difmiffed him, and for the greateft part of his remaining life he was an itinerant actor. Hallam, about fix and thirty years fince, tranflated The Beggar's Opera into French, which was reprefented in the little theatre in the Haymarket with fome fuccefs. He alfo invented the armour and other decorations, preparatory to the fingle combat between the dukes of Hereford and Norfolk. Hallam died a kind of penfioner to the managers, who were the immediate fucceffors of Rich, to whofe family he was, I think, related.

ABBOT OF WESTMINSTER.

Before I fpeak my mind herein,
You fhall not only take the facrament, &c.

The perfonæ dramatis of this play are fo numerous, that the manager was reduced to the neceffity of employing honeft

Michael

Michael Stoppelaer, of blundering memory, in the part of a dignified clergyman,
the abbot of Weſtminſter, to which he was
by no means equal ; for Stoppelaer's action and behaviour, added to an accidental
hoarſeneſs, ſet the ſpectators in a loud
laugh. Honeſt Mich was remarkable for
ſinging a Scotch or Iriſh ſong, particularly
Arrah my Judy and *Corn-Riggs are bonny.*
He was ſomething of a ſcholar too, and
educated at Trinity-College, Dublin. He
ſang, not *unpleaſingly*, to a tune which
I have forgotten, Horace's Ode of *Integer*
vitæ, ſceleriſque purus, &c. It was Mich's
faculty to utter abſurd ſpeeches and diſagreeable truths, without any deſign to
give offence. I ſhall quote one anecdote,
which will give the reader an idea of his
character. Rich was talking to ſome of
the actors, when Stoppelaer was preſent,
concerning the diſproportioned agreement
he had made with Hallam, who acted Aumerle, Stoppelaer ſhook his head and ſaid,
Upon my ſoul, Sir, he got on the blind ſide of

you

you there. Rich, apprehenfive of hearing fomething more offenfive, left the company: fomebody prefent obferved that Stoppelear's fpeech was exceedingly improper, and really affronting, becaufe every body knew that Mr. Rich had a great blemifh in one of his eyes.—" Upon my word, faid Mich, *I never heard of it before, and I will go immediately and afk his pardon.*"

N 3   CHAP-

CHAPTER X.

Scene between Richard and his queen.—Some excellent lines.—Mrs. Horton, the actress, her great beauty.—Playing with strollers at Windsor.—Juba and Lord Malpas.—Mrs. Horton's address to ill-natured critics.— Her merit in acting.—Her love of coquetry. — Fine description of Bolingbroke and Richard. — His tyrannical conduct to the citizens of London. — Kings of England pillagers of London. — Richard and his groom.—Nat Clarke.—Anecdote of Rich.— Shakspeare differs from historians in the account of Richard's death.—Reflections upon it.—Sad consequences of Henry's usurpation.

Act V.

Queen and Richard.

THE scene between Richard and the queen is not written in Shakspeare's happiest style; the play upon words and exuberant extension of sentiments are justly reprehended

reprehended by the critics. However, fome part of it muft be exempted from cenfure, and particularly this thought of Richard.

> ———I am fworn brother, fweet,
> To grim neceffity, and he and I
> Will keep a league with death.

Likewife his advice to the queen, to tell his melancholy tale, by a winter's fire,

> ————————To good old folks,
> And fend the hearers weeping to their beds,

is affecting. Colley Cibber has judicioufly borrowed and applied it to the ftory of Henry VI. in his Richard III.

The queen was perfonated by Mrs. Horton; one of the moft beautiful women that ever trod the ftage. She was married, when very young, to a mufician, who was infenfible to her charms, and treated her, as it has been faid, very brutally. The firft notice that was taken of her was at Windfor, in the fummer of 1713 ; where fhe acted Marcia, in Cato, in a company

of

of miferable ftrollers, who were drawn there on account of Queen Anne's making it the place of her refidence feveral months in the year. Cato and his fenate met with little refpeдt from the audience ; and poor Juba was fo truly an objeдt of ridicule, that, when he cried out, in a tranfport of joy, on hearing Marcia's confeffion of her paffion for him, " What do I hear ?" my Lord Malpas, wilfully miftaking the aдtor, loudly faid, from behind the fcenes, *Upon my word, fir, I do not know : I think you had better be any where elfe :* and this joke, I believe, put an end to the play. However, Mrs. Horton was fo fuperior in merit to the reft, and fo attraдtive in her perfon, that fhe was foon after very powerfully recommended to the managers of Drury-lane Theatre, who engaged her at a moderate falary. Her chief merit confifted in giving fprightlinefs to gay coquets, fuch as Belinda in the Old Batchelor, and Millamant in the Way of the World ; in which laft charaдter fhe was faid to have
excelled

excelled Mrs. Oldfield.   Upon   Mrs.
Younger's quitting Drury-lane for a more
advantageous income at Lincoln's-inn-
fields, fhe was called upon by Wilks to act
the part of Phillis in the Confcious Lovers.   Younger had given the public fo
much entertainment in that part, that
Mrs. Horton met with very uncandid treatment from the audience ; who fo far forgot what was due to merit and the handfomeft woman on the ftage, that they endeavoured to difcourage her by frequent
hiffing.   She bore this treatment with pa-
tience for fome time.   At laft, fhe advanced to the front of the ftage, and boldly
addreffed the pit : " Gentlemen, what do you
mean ? what difpleafes you ; my acting or
my perfon ?"   This fhow of fpirit recovered the fpectators into good humour,
and they cried out, as with one voice,
" No, no, Mrs. Horton ; we are not difpleafed : go on, go on."   As fhe advanced
in life,   though fhe ftill retained great
beauty of features, fhe grew corpulent ;
                                                 and,

and, by ftriving to preferve the appearance
of a fine fhape, fhe laced herfelf fo tight
that the upper part of her figure bore no
proportion to the reft of her body.

For many years fhe was a favourite actrefs in tragedy and comedy, and commanded a large income : but the natural
and eafy dialogue of Pritchard fo captiva-
ted the public, that poor Horton was foon
deprived of that influence which fhe had
poffeffed, and was ftripped of her characters one by one.   At laft fhe became fo
low in credit with the public, that Rich,
out of compaffion, offered to employ her
at the reduced falary of 4l. per week.
This fhe refufed, in a fit of ill-timed refentment, and could never perfuade him
to make a fecond offer.   Mr. Garrick and
Mr. Lacy, by giving her a part of a benefit annually, made fome addition to a fmall
annuity fhe enjoyed.   Her beauty was fo
remarkable in the early part of life, that
few young men could fee her without
having a tendreffe for her, which fhe never

ver difcouraged; for, indeed, fhe was fo
true a coquet, that a compliment to her
charms, from the meaneft perfon in the theatre, was acceptable, and always returned
with a fmile or tap with her fan. On the verge
of threefcore fhe dreffed like a girl of twenty,
and kept fimpering and ogling to the laft,
and if features, preferved even at that cold
age, could juftify her weaknefs, fhe certainly
was pardonable; for, of all the women I
ever faw, fhe had the greateft pretence to
vanity. A nobleman, fome few years before her death, offered her a very large fettlement to live with him, which fhe ge-
neroufly reje６ted. Her fole paffion was to
be admired. She died about the year 1756.

Scene II. York and his duchefs.

Y O R K.

As in a theatre the eyes of men,
After a well-grac'd ａctor leaves the ftage,
Are idly bent on him who enters next.

This pathetic defcription of Richard's
entry into London, finely contrafted with
that

that of Bolingbroke, has been univerfally admired; Mr. Dryden declares that he knows nothing equal to it in ancient dramatic poetry, and, I believe, we may defy the moderns to pattern it.

I D E M.

——————— Mens eyes did fcowl
On Richard : no man cry'd, God fave him !
No joyful tongue gave him his welcome home,
But duft was thrown upon his facred head !

Richard's reception in London could not be very different from the poet's defcription of it*. Some citizens were brutal enough to propofe to his rival the putting

---

* Stowe has added a circumftance in Lancafter's behaviour on this occafion, which is not to be found, I think, in any other writer.

" When the duke came within two miles of the city, he caufed the hoft to ftay, and then faid to the commons of the city, ' My mafters, behold here your king, confider well what you will do with him.'— They anfwered, ' He fhould be fent to Weftminfter :' whereupon he was delivered unto them, and they led him to Weftminfter, and from thence by water to the tower of London."

ting him to immediate death. And, though no man of humanity can forbear refenting with indignation the bafe propofal of thefe wretches, it muft be confeffed that Richard merited little favour from the Londoners. He had given them great and almoft unpardonable provocation. For the offences of a few members of the corporation he had deprived the city of London of its privileges, and imprifoned the chief magiftrate and others next to him in office. In his whole conduct in this affair he manifefted a mean and cruel difpofition. When the king, upon the city's humble fubmiffion, was reconciled to the citizens, he accepted, from the mayor, aldermen, and principal inhabitants, a grand entertainment, at which he and all his court were prefent. The prefents given to Richard, his queen, and courtiers, were eftimated at ten thoufand pounds, which, at that time, amounted to an immenfe fum. On this occafion, to win the good-will of Richard, the city difplayed all its grandeur, and no expence

was

was fpared to fhew their profound refpect to royalty. But, notwithftanding the king expreffed himfelf to be highly pleafed with his reception, and received the magnificent gifts prefented to him with complacency, he fined the city of London in the fum of ten thoufand pounds. This exorbitant penalty and outrageous act of power, when a contrary conduct was expected, exafperated the citizens, and they never forgave the king.

The kings of England, it muft be obferved, from King John to James I. feemed to have confidered the city of London as a place which they might fafely pillage whenever impelled by their neceffities. To gain the good-will of that fhamelefs fpendthrift, Henry III. who had the folly to declare, *that it was more charity to beftow money upon him than on the meaneft beggar*, London was obliged to pay down the fum of 20,000l. and James I. we are informed by Camden, without fo much as pretending any right or claim except his

immediate

immediate wants, demanded alſo of the
Londoners 20,000 l.   The citizens, although they knew his weakneſs and deſpiſed his power, yet with great conde-
ſcenſion made him an offer of half the
ſum ; which James prudently accepted.
Quarrels between the court and the city
of London have never produced any real
advantage to the crown.   To affect a contempt for a reſpectable body of men, who
contribute ſo largely to the revenue, is
ſomething more than ridiculous.

Act V. Scene V.   Richard and a groom.

G R O O M.

Oh ! how it yearn'd my heart when I beheld
In London ſtreets ————————
When Bolingbroke rode on roan Barbary ;
That horſe, which thou ſo often haſt beſtrid,
That horſe, that I ſo carefully have dreſs'd.

This is one of thoſe ſcenes which diſgrace
the tragedy of a great king, and gives to
me   convincing proof, that Shakſpeare,
after writing this play, and not finding it
much reliſhed by the audience, took no
                                                        ſuitable

fuitable pains to correct and improve it. However, the groom fpeaks much in character; for he feems more anxious about the horfe, *which he had fo carefully dreffed,* than concerned for the misfortunes of his mafter. One of our Chronicles relates, that, when Richard was firft delivered into the power of Lancafter, a favourite greyhound of his abandoned his mafter, and fawned upon the conqueror, who feemed much pleafed with the omen.

To fill up the account of the actors in this play when laft revived, I fhall juft mention fome particulars relating to Nat Clarke, who acted the groom. He was a man fitted by nature to reprefent underparts. Clarke was the original Filch in the Beggar's Opera; and, though I greatly admire Mrs. Wilfon's adroitnefs in it, yet I think his meagre countenance and fhambling figure were much better adapted to the character of a pickpocket than a female's delicate perfon. Nat was the chronicle of the theatre : he knew the whole

hiftory

hiftory of the players, and made himfelf
acceptable to bufy enquirers after theatrical matters by communicating to them
many a laughable anecdote. His chief
employment (on account of his refembling Rich in fize and figure) was that of
an under-harlequin, to relieve his mafter
in fuch fituations of the pantomime as
were leaft interefting. Nat was happy
when the audience, from fimilarity of form,
were furprifed into a clap by miftaking the
man for the mafter. The fubftitute was
fo like the original, that Rich one night
paid feverely for the refemblance. One of
the actors, having had fome words with
Clarke during the reprefentation of a pantomime, waited till he fhould find an opportunity to fhew his refentment. Unluckily Rich threw himfelf in the way of
the angry perfon, as he came off the ftage,
and received fuch a blow of the fift, on his
ftomach, as for fome time deprived him
of the power to breathe. The man, per-
ceiving his miftake, implored the mana-

ger's pardon; protefting, upon his honour, he thought that he had ftruck Nat
Clarke. " And pray, faid Rich, what
terrible provocation could Clarke give, to
merit fuch a violent blow?"

Some few years before his death, Clarke
retired to Hammerfmith; where he lived
at eafe, and treated his vifitors with good
ale and much hiftory.

R I C H A R D.

Mount, mount, my foul! thy feat is up on high;
Whilft my grofs flefh finks downward here to die.

Though Shakfpeare has followed the hiftorian who makes Sir Pierce of Exon and
his accomplices the murderers of Richard,
yet the greateft number of writers, on this
period of our hiftory, affert that he was
ftarved to death. His dead body was produced to the public in a fhell, with his
face uncovered. His fucceffor attended
his funeral, with diffembled grief, and followed him to that place which his ambition had marked out for him.

By

By whatever means this unhappy prince was fent out of the world, it cannot be doubted that all methods were put in practice, by thofe to whom he was entrufted, to make life as burdenfome to him as poffible. Power ufurped is ever fufpicious, arbitrary, and cruel. By various modes of brutal unkindnefs, ftudied neglect, and outrageous infult, it was no difficult matter to render him weary of his exiftence, and to make him wifh for repofe, where only it was to be had, in the grave. They might abridge his diet, difturb his fleep, and be artful in finding out methods to diftrefs and torment him whofe caufe no man durft efpoufe. The meffengers of his death they knew would be entertained with a glad welcome by their employers.

We may collect, from Shakfpeare and the Chronicles, that Richard, in his perfon, was extremely handfome; in his younger years he gave evident proofs of ability, more particularly in his fuppreffing, by an act of perfonal courage and prefence

O 2   of

of mind, at the age of fixteen, the dangerous infurrection of Wat Tyler and Jack Straw. His greateft enemies were his three ambitious uncles, the dukes of Lancafter, York, and Glofter, who purpofely fuffered his mind to be uncultivated with princely virtues, and his morals to be corrupted by vicious companions. They took no care to have him trained in the art military, the only great and fhining accomplifhment of the age.

During the time of the feudal fyftem, the prince fupported his power by military prowefs. Without this, he could not guard himfelf againft the incroachments of his barons, who, in their own diftricts, were fo many arbitrary defpots. The firft and third Edward, by perpetual wars on the continent and their own perfonal courage, kept their peers conftantly in employ, and preferved a reverence for their perfons. By their wars with France, the rapacity of their followers was in fome meafure glutted. All wars with France, till

that

that which raged in 1782, were the dear
delight of the Englifh nation, and ufhered
in fometimes with bonfires and other tokens of public rejoicing.

Richard was fond of fine clothes, of pomps,
fhows, and ceremonies. The fpirit of chivalry, that fpur to noble actions, fuperior in
fome refpects to the Greek and Roman military inftitutions, which had been revived
by his father and grandfather, he feemed
not to have cherifhed, except in the mock
reprefentation of it in tilts and tournaments. He wifhed to gain popularity;
but his converfation was too trifling, and
too often proftituted, to gain upon the affections of the people. Dr. Henry attributes many focial virtues to this prince,
and amongft the reft his fidelity to friendfhip; but that virtue, which is praife-
worthy in a private man, often degenerates
in princes to a moft pernicious vice. Grofs
partiality to a few fubjects is inconfiftent
with the good of the whole community.
With Richard and his minifters it was an

O 3   eftablifhed

eſtabliſhed maxim, ' Be true to me, and I
will be faithful to you ;' — nay, ſays Lord
Bolingbroke, he was ſo very weak, that his
favourites prevailed upon him to bind
himſelf to them by an oath. He was undone at laſt by his great confidence in his
own importance : he weakly imagined,
that the inſulted, the injured, and the op-
preſſed, would be tied down by ſuch oaths
as he wantonly impoſed upon them. Acts
of parliament were heaped upon acts, to
eſtabliſh laws, which were in their intention unſalutary, and conſequently odious.
Hiſtory can ſcarcely furniſh ſuch an inſtance of a monarch being ſo ſuddenly a-
bandoned by all his ſubjects. There was,
in this unhappy man, one diſagreeable
quality, which contributed not a little to
his downfal : he had an imperious and inſolent manner of ſpeaking, on important
occaſions, to perſons who, from their of-
fices in the ſtate, claimed a right to give
him advice, and ought to have been liſten-
ed to with attention. When the lords and
commons,

commons, in parliament affembled, fent a deputation to him, to inform him, that it was neceffary for the good of the ftate he fhould remove from their employments his treafurer and chancellor, he bade them meddle for the future with no fuch thing ; adding, ' *That he would not, for them, or at their pleafure, remove the meaneft fcullion in his kitchen.*' Of Richard II. it may with truth be faid, that he had all the bad qualities of his great-grandfather, Edward II. without any mixture of his good ones.

Notwithftanding the depofition of Richard was univerfally approved at that time, the confequence of Lancafter's ufurpation, who fet afide the right heir to the crown, defcended from Lionel, duke of Clarence, proved more fatal to the kingdom than even the weak and arbitrary conduct of the depofed king. Shakfpeare has three plays (the three parts of Henry VI.) which include a period that exhibits nothing but the flaughter of princes and fubjects.— Within the fpace of thirty-fix years, twelve

fet

fet battles were fought in England, concerning the fucceffion to the crown, by
Englifhmen only; more than fourfcore
princes of the blood royal were flain by
each other's fwords.   Nay, the hand of
death did not ftop till it had actually extin-
guifhed all the male heirs of each line*.

---

* Parliamentary Hiftory.

King

King Henry IV. Firſt Part.

CHAPTER XI.

What rank the Firſt Part of Henry IV. holds in the opinion of the critics.— Its remarkable excellences. — Falſtaff and his rivals.— The poet's intention in advancing the king's ſickneſs. — Cruſades.—Thirſty entrance of the ſoil explained.—Shakſpeare and Voltaire. —Earl of Worceſter.—Thieves of the day's beauty, why ſo called.— Sir John Oldcaſtle. —Sir John Falſtaff. — Gib cat.— A laugh indulged. — Foote's ſerenade of cats. — Cat Harris. — The original performer of Falſtaff, Lowin.— Cartwright, Lacy.—Henry's jealouſy of the houſe of March. — Ranſom of priſoners. — Speeches of Hotſpur and Eteocles. — Amyot and Gaſcoigne. — Burbage.— Tayler. — Hart. — Winterſhal. — Booth's Hotſpur commended. — Anecdote of Giffard and Booth.—Garrick's Hotſpur.

IN the opinion of Dr. Warburton, and I believe of all the beſt critics, the Firſt Part of Henry IV. is, of all our author's plays, the moſt excellent; not indeed for power of invention, for ſcenes of paſſion, or even variety of incident or ſituation; but for delineation of character, propriety of ſentiment, and dignity of expreſſion.

The King, the Prince of Wales, and Hotſpur, are admirable portraits. The two firſt are faithful reſemblances taken from hiſtory; and the variation of humour, and heightening of paſſion, given to the latter, render him an intereſting dramatic perſonage.

As for Falſtaff, of whoſe character no man can ſay too much, and every man will be almoſt afraid to ſay any thing, from an apprehenſion of his not being able to treat ſo fertile a ſubject as it deſerves; he, in the confeſſion of all men, is the great maſter-piece of our inimitable writer, and of all dramatic poetry. Shakſpeare had gi-

ven

ven ſeveral ſketches of humourous characters, as if to try his abilities, before he introduced to the public this theatrical prodi-
gy, which then aſtoniſhed Ben Jonſon, the
great poet of humour, and has bidden
defiance to all ſucceeding attempts to rival it.
What name too deſpicable can we give to
thoſe wretched imitations of the fat knight,
the Tucca of Jonſon's Poetaſter, and the
Cacofogo of Fletcher? Above fifty years
ſince, it was traditionary, among the comedians, that Cacofogo was the intended rival of Falſtaff, whom he reſembles in nothing but in bulk and cowardice. And,
as to Tucca, I ſubmit to the reader, whether that part be not a fruitleſs attempt of
ſurly Ben to meaſure ſwords with his maſter.

Act I.   Scene I.

K I N G.

So ſhaken as we are, ſo wan with care!

The action of this play begins early
in the reign of Henry IV. and before
he

he had been afflicted with any dangerous
and lingering diftemper : at leaft, hiftory
takes no notice of his being difeafed before
the battle of Shrewfbury.

Shakfpeare thought it would beft anfwer
his purpofe to reprefent the king labouring with ficknefs, and refolving on his
recovery to vifit the Holy Land, in conformity to his prior declaration in the preceding play of Richard, to expiate the
murder of his fovereign.

All our hiftorians agree in this purpofed
expedition of Henry, which, on a clofe examination, feems not to be very well founded in probability. The crufades, at the
beginning of the fifteenth century, had
almoft entirely ceafed. The paffion of
Chriftian princes to recover Jerufalem from
the infidels was then almoft expiring,
from the ill fuccefs of many great and
powerful adventurers, and from a perfect
knowledge of the crafty defigns of the court
of Rome, to involve monarchs in foreign
wars, that the fovereign pontiffs might

reap

reap advantages by their abſence from their dominions. Beſides, Henry was too ſagacious to leave his kingdom with a title ſo doubtful as his was. If ſo weak and worthleſs a man as Prince John could, in the abſence of his brother Richard at Jeruſalem, excite ſuch diſorders as to make it neceſſary for that king to quicken his return to England, what had not Henry Bolingbroke to apprehend from one who had a fairer title to the crown than himſelf ? The expedition to the Holy Land ſeems to have been a feint; perhaps, indeed, at ſome times, when, in ſpite of worldly grandeur, his conſcience roſe with ſome violence upon him, a tranſient thought of expiating his guilt, by this univerſal panacea for all crimes, might come acroſs his mind, but, in all probability, without any fixed purpoſe or vigorous reſolution.

I D E M.

No more the thirſty entrance of this ſoil
Shall daub her lips with her own childrens blood.

This

This paffage is very difficult : Dr. John-fon and Mr. Steevens have, with great in-genuity, endeavoured to explain it, but, I think, without fuccefs. The *entrance* of the foil is, I believe, an unneceffary ad-junct; and means, I think, the foil or land itfelf. The epithet *thirfty* is employed to concur with the verb *daub.* The whole is a periphrafis, fignifying, no longer fhall Englifh ground be ftained with the blood of its inhabitants.

I D E M.

> To chafe thofe pagans in thofe holy fields,
> Over whofe acres walk'd thofe bleffed feet,
> Which, fourteen hundred years ago, were nail'd,
> For our advantage, to the holy crofs.

The circumftance of our Saviour's tread-ing the foil of Jerufalem, and dying there for all mankind, is finely and pathetically defcribed by Voltaire in his Zaïre, and employed as a convincing argument to re-claim an apoftate to the true faith :

> E'en in the place where thou betray'ft thy God,
> He dy'd, my child, to fave thee ! Turn thine eyes
> and fee,

For

For thou art near his holy ſepulchre !
Thou canſt not move a ſtep *but where he trod !*
Thou trembleſt !————————

      HILL's ZARA. Act II.

The pleaſure of walking over that ground
which had been trodden by Chriſt and his
apoſtles, was, no doubt, one great in-
ducement to many Chriſtians to aſſume
the croſs and fight againſt the infidels.
Nor can this be deemed a meer act of ſu-
perſtition : for, if our learned travellers can
feel an enthuſiaſtic delight in walking over
thoſe parts of Rome, where the Scipio's,
Pompeys, and Brutus's, formerly trod,
Chriſtians may, with the ſame or ſuperior
ardour, viſit thoſe places which our Saviour
and his apoſtles were known to frequent.

    W E S T M O R E L A N D.
——————— In the very heat
And pride of their contention.————

That is, during the fury of the battle, when
both ſides ſeemed to be equally matched.

     I D E M.

This is his uncle's teaching. This is Worceſter,
Malevolent to you in all aſpects.——

       Thomas

Thomas Percy, earl of Worcefter, is charged, by our old Chronicles, with exciting his brother and nephew to rebellion, from motives of peculiar rancour to the king. This our author, who read thofe hiftories with great attention, has, in feveral parts of this play, fufficiently marked.

Scene II. Prince and Falftaff.

FALSTAFF.

Let not us, that are fquires of the night's body,
Be called thieves of the day's beauty.

The *day's beauty* is the fun ; confequently Falftaff intreats that he and his affociates may not be termed robbers in open day. He rather wifhes to be diftinguifhed by the honourable title of Diana's forefters, minions of the moon, &c. This fuits with Falftaff's courage, who would much rather rob by night than in the face of the fun like a daring highwayman.

PRINCE HENRY.

As the honey of Hybla, my old lad of the caftle !

I have

I have read with attention, more than once, the ſeveral notes of Dr. Farmer and Mr. Steevens, in which they labour to exculpate Shakſpeare from having ever introduced Sir John Oldcaſtle in his play of Henry IV. Fuller, who wrote about twenty years after our author's death, and ſeems to have been no ſuperficial inquirer into matters in which the reputation of families was concerned, abſolutely fixes the charge upon Shakſpeare, and I cannot help thinking that the apology in the epilogue, to the ſecond part of this dramatic hiſtory, " *For Oldcaſtle died a martyr, and this is not the man*," is ſomewhat aukward, if Shakſpeare had not himſelf given ſome offence reſpecting Oldcaſtle.

Sir John Oldcaſtle, commonly called the martyr, whom Henry V. ſacrificed to the clergy, becauſe they aſſiſted him with their purſes in his expedition againſt the crown of France, was, in all probability, a man of a lively and gay humour ; and the clergy, whom he had provoked, might, in revenge, reprefent him to the populace as a light and lewd fellow, a drunkard and a profane jefter. This would furnifh an opportunity to the poets of the times to prefent him on the ftage in no favourable light. But, though this fatirical abufe of Oldcaftle might be permitted during the times of popery, yet, when his character became better known in the days of Queen Elizabeth, fuch freedoms would give offence. I think it is poffible that Shakfpeare might at firft have inadvertently fallen into this error, and have laid hold on Sir John Oldcaftle as a proper fubject of buffoonery and mirth. I fhall have occafion, in the courfe of thefe obfervations, to fay more on this fubject.

FALSTAFF.

A gib cat or a lugg'd bear.

Amongft a great number of very excellent remarks, which are plentifully ftrewed in the editions of Shakfpeare by Johnfon and Steevens, we muft not be furprifed

fed if we find fome that will occafionally raife our mirth, and fuch as we may fafely pronounce unworthy of their writers. In the laft edition of the Variorum Shakfpeare, we have no lefs than four grave notes on the meaning of the word *gib*. Two reverend gentlemen, Dr. Percy and Mr. Warton, befides Mr. Steevens and Mr. Tollet, have laboured hard to explain what furely was very generally underftood: that a gib cat is one that is gelt, or caftrated, might have been told in four or five lines. Mr. Warton prefents us with many authorities from Caxton, from the Romant of the Rofe, &c. to prove that Gilbert and Tib, were ancient names given to he-cats. But how came the critics to forget the authority of Shakfpeare himfelf in Romeo and Juliet, where Mercutio calls Tibbald *rat-catcher and king of cats*, from his name *Tybalt ?*

———Tybalt, you rat-catcher,
Good king of cats, nothing but one of your nine lives.

P 2   Thefe

Thefe curious notes might have been clofed with a duetto, fung by Dr. Defaguliers, to that good-natured gentleman, Frederick, prince of Wales, (who dearly loved the bagatelle,) between a he and a fhe-cat. The prince often confeffed that the doctor underftood cat-language better than any man in England.

When Foote firft opened the theatre in the Haymarket, amongft other projects, he propofed to entertain the public with an imitation of cat-mufic; for this purpofe, he engaged a man famous for his fkill in mimicking the mewing of cats. This perfon was called Cat Harris. He not attending the rehearfal of this odd concert, Foote defired Shuter would endeavour to find him out, and bring him with him. Shuter was directed to fome court in the Minories, where this extraordinary mufician lived. But, not knowing the houfe, Shuter began a *cat-folo*. Upon this, the other looked out of the window, and anfwered him with a cantata of the fame fort —

fort.—" Come along, ſays Shuter, I want
no better information that you are the
man :—Mr. Foote ſtays for us :—we cannot begin the cat-opera without you !"

The original performer of Falſtaff was,
doubtleſs, that excellent comedian W.
Lowin ; the praiſe and boaſt of his time
for variety of comic parts. In Downes's
Roſcius Anglicanus, we have the name of
Cartwright for Falſtaff's repreſentative, ſoon
after the Reſtoration. Little is ſaid of this
player by any ſtage-hiſtorian. We find
his name in the Rehearſal, in which he
ſpoke Bayes's prologue, I think, and acted
one of the Majeſties of Brentford. It is
ſomewhere ſaid that he was a bookſeller.
Lacy, a favourite actor of Charles II. who
had him drawn in three different characters, ſtill to be ſeen at Hampton Court,
ſucceeded Cartwright in Falſtaff. Langbaine ſpeaks of him as the moſt perfect comic player of his time. Cibber, I fancy,
had never ſeen him ; for the name of Lacy
is not mentioned in his apology. He was

P 3

one

one of the recruits which the king's company picked up foon after the Reftoration. I can find no trace of his having acted before the civil wars. He wrote three plays, in which, I believe, his own action was the principal recommendation. He died about the year 1683.

The prince of Wales was reprefented originally, if we may be allowed to guefs, by Burbage, who was tall and thin. I fhall defer what I have to fay farther of the prince and Falftaff till their next fcene.

Scene III.   King, Northumberland, Hotfpur, Worcefter, ' &c.

K I N G.

The moody *frontier* of a fervant brow.

Dr. Warburton propofes to read *front-let*. Mr. Stcevens fays the word *frontlet* does not fignify forehead :—not in its original fenfe, it is granted : but furely in its applied and metaphorical. He did not recollect that, in a parallel paffage, Lear fays to Goneril,

Now,

Now, daughter, what means that frontlet on?

Shall we buy treason and indent with fears?

It may be asked, Who are the fellers of this treason?—The Percy family: though they had not, indeed, according to Mr. Steevens, forfeited their lives and estates, the king plainly insinuates that they were the abettors and partisans of Mortimer, and encouragers of his traiterous practices. Henry's anger is principally owing to his hatred and jealousy of Mortimer, whose title to the crown was much clearer than his own. In such dread did he hold the house of March, that he would not permit any of the family to be named in parliament.

Revolted Mortimer!

These two words should be spoken loudly and vehemently, from a sudden impulse of passion, which the impetuous Hotspur

P 4　　　　could

could not reftrain. Upon the king's turning quickly on him with a look of anger
and refentment, he immediately foftens the
tone of his voice to a low and fubmiffive
cadence.

KING.

Send us your prifoners, or you fhall hear of it!

In the time of the feudal fyftem, one
great motive to incite the barons to ferve in
war, was the treafure they acquired by the
ranfom of the prifoners they took in battle.
A war with France was, to the nobility of
this kingdom, for that reafon, a very de-
firable event.

Sir William Manny, in the French wars
during the reign of Edward III. is faid by
hiftorians to have gained immenfe treafures
by the prifoners he captured in war. For
this reafon, Henry's conduct, in demanding
all Hotfpur's prifoners, appears to be very
unjuft.

By the ancient laws of Norway, the prifoner, and every thing he had about him,
belonged

belonged to the captor; except the gold in his purſe, which was reſerved for the king*.

H O T S P U R.

As this ingrate, this canker'd Bolingbroke.

Cankered Bolingbroke was a term which Mr. Addiſon, in converſation, applied to Henry St. John, Lord Bolingbroke; with what propriety I do not ſee. That this great ſtateſman was ardent both in his friendſhips and enmities is to be learned from his letters and his general conduct; but that he harboured a rancorous and cankered diſpoſition I cannot perſuade myſelf. Addiſon, however benevolent in his writings, was not free from that leaven of party which often ſours the beſt minds.

I D E M.

By heavens ! methinks it were an eaſy leap
To pluck bright honour from the pale-fac'd moon,
Or dive into the bottom of the deep,
Where fathom-line did never touch the ground,
And pluck up drowned honour by the locks ;

So

---

* Speculum regale.

So he that did redeem her thence might wear,
Without co-rival, all her dignities.

This fally of Hotfpur Dr. Warburton has ftamped with the epithets of heroic and fublime ; and, to juftify Shakfpeare, has quoted Euripides. Dr. Johnfon has critically defended this rapturous explofion of a hot and fiery difpofition, which is certainly not quite fimilar to the fpeech of Eteocles in the Phœniffæ of Euripides, nor can it be termed allegorical. The learned Mr. Woodhull, in a note to his tranflation of that tragedy, has given this fpeech of Eteocles, as verfified by Amyot, from an extract of Plutarch's treatife on Fraternal Love ; and another tranflation from Gafcoigne's works, publifhed in 1575. It muft be owned that the lively Frenchman, in fpirit and elegance, excels the Englifhman.

Je monterois en l'étoilé féjour
Du clair foleil, où commence le jour ;
Et je defcendrois deffous la terre baffe ;
Si je pouvois acquérir par l'audace
Le roiaume fouverain des dieux.

Gafcoigne

Gaſcoigne rather creeps than ſoars :

> If I could rule or reign in heav'n above,
> And eke command in depth of darkſome hell,
> No toil, no travail, ſhould my ſprites abaſh,
> To take the way unto my reſtleſs will, —
> To climb aloft, or down for to deſcend.

IDEM.

> By heavens, he ſhall not have a ſcot of them.

In our author's time this was a prover-bial expreſſion, meaning — he ſhall not have the moſt worthleſs thing I have*.

IDEM.

> Oh ! let the hours be ſhort,
> Till fields, and blows, and groans, applaud our ſport.

This ſpirited exclamation of Hotſpur reſembles a ſpeech of Eteocles, in the Septem contra Thebas of Æſchylus :

> Μη νυν, εαν θνησκοντας η τετρωμενας
> Πυθησθε, κωκυτοισιν αρπαλιζετε·
> Τϑτω γαρ Αρης βοσκεται φονω βροτων.

> If haply now your eyes behold the dead
> Or wounded, burſt not forth in loud laments ;
> For blood and carnage are the food of war.

POTTER.

The action of this ſcene is very anima-ting and important. The jealouſy, ſuſ-picion,

---

* Fuller.

picion, and diftruft, of Henry, are finely contrafted with the high fpirit and daring impetuofity of Hotfpur; Agamemnon and Achilles are not more ftrongly delineated, nor their paffions more highly coloured, by Homer, than thefe characters of Shakfpeare. The conduct of the fcene is truly dramatic, from the beginning to the clofe of it.

I have fuppofed, and I believe with probability, that Burbage originally acted the Prince of Wales; and am of opinion we may give Hotfpur to Taylor, the original Hamlet. If Taylor was, as we may conjecture from what the Queen fays of him in the fencing-fcene between Hamlet and Laertes, ' fat, and fcant of breath,' we cannot fuppofe him fit for the tall and flender Harry. After the Reftoration, Hart reprefented Hotfpur, Burt the Prince of Wales, and Winterfhul the King. The excellence of Hart is univerfally acknowledged; of Burt we can only tranfcribe what Downs has recorded. He

ranks

ranks him in the liſt of good actors, with
Shotterel and Cartwright, but without any
diſcriminating marks. That he was not a
man of ſuperior merit we may gather from
his being obliged to reſign the part of O-
thello to Hart, who had formerly acted
Caſſio when Burt played the principal character. Winterſhul was, in the opinion
of the beſt critics, a very judicious actor in
comedy and tragedy, and an excellent
teacher of the art he profeſſed. He was ſo
celebrated for the part of Cokes, in Ben
Jonſon's Bartholomew-Fair, that the public preferred him even to Nokes in that
character. Winterſhul is mentioned with
honour in the notes on the Rehearſal; he
died in July, 1679.

Betterton's Hotſpur is celebrated by
Cibber amongſt his moſt capital exhibitions, and by Sir Richard Steele in the
Tatler. But the verſatility of Betterton's
genius was never more conſpicuous than in
his reſigning the choleric Hotſpur, in his
declining years, and aſſuming the humour
and

and gaiety of Falftaff, in which he is faid to have been full as acceptable to the public as in the former. Powel was, I believe, his fucceffor in Hotfpur. With the happy advantages of perfon, voice, and gefture, this comedian muft have given a ftriking refemblance of a young, gallant, and brave, foldier. But Powel's intemperance rendered him often unequal to himfelf; and he fo far at laft impaired his abilities, that his parts were often fupplied by players of inferior merit.

Booth's Hotfpur was, in the opinion of the critics who faw him in the character, one of the moft perfect exhibitions of the ftage. His ftrong, yet harmonious, pipe, reached the higheft note of exclamatory rage without hurting the mufic of its tone. His gefture was ever in union with his utterance, and his eye conftantly combined with both to give a correfpondent force to the paffion. His tread in this part was quick, yet fignificant, accompanied with princely grandeur. — When Giffard, late manager of the theatre

in

in Goodman's Fields, — an actor much favoured by Wilks, on account of paying
him that moſt pleaſing of all flattery, an i-
mitation of his manner of acting, — was,
through the intereſt of his great exemplar,
favoured with a benefit, and permitted to
act that night the Prince of Wales; Booth,
who entertained too great a contempt for
Wilks in tragedy, and of conſequence ſtill
more deſpiſed his humble imitator, declared, without any ceremony, that he would
that night ' let off an Iriſh actor.' The
theatre was extremely crouded, both in the
front and on the ſtage. I have heard Mr.
Lacy, the late manager, Mr. Victor, and
others, who were preſent, declare, that
they never ſaw ſo animated a performance,
and attended with ſuch loud and repeated
plaudits from all parts of the theatre, as
Booth's Hotſpur. Giffard, who was juſt
arrived from Dublin theatre, honeſtly
owned that he was ſtruck with aſtoniſhment, and heartily joined in the general
approbation. When rouſed by accidental

jealoufy or humour, Booth always excelled himfelf.

In acting Othello once, to a fmall audience, Booth threw fuch a languor into feveral fcenes of the part, which was faid to be his mafter-piece, that nobody could difcern their favourite and admired actor. But, in the third act, as if roufed from a lethargy to the moft animating vigour, he difplayed fuch uncommon fire and force, that the players and the audience feemed to be equally electrified by this fudden exertion of his poweis. When, at the end of the act, the players retired into the green-room, Cibber, who acted Iago, faid to him, ' Prythee, Barton, what was the charm that infpired you fo all on a fudden ?' — ' Why, Colley, I faw, by chance, an Oxford-man in the pit, whofe judgement I revere more than that of a whole audience.'

In the agreement between Quin and Garrick, in 1746, to affift each other with their mutual fkill in feveral felect plays, Quin laid his hand upon Henry IV. and
called

called upon Garrick to give him his aſſiſtance, by exerting his talents in Hotſpur :
' For you know, David, Falſtaff is ſo
weighty, that he cannot do without a le-
ver.' The other complied, though I believe with ſome reluctance ; for he knew
that the portion of Hotſpur, which beſt
ſuited his animated manner of ſpeaking,
would be exhauſted in the firſt ſcene of the
part. The old comedian, by this manœuvre, ſurpriſed the caution of the young
actor.

The perſon of Garrick was not formed
to give a juſt idea of the gallant and noble
Hotſpur. The mechanic, or bulky, part
was wanting ; nor could the fine flexibility
of his voice entirely conquer the high rant
and continued rage of the enthuſiaſtic war-
rior. He had not then acquired that
complete knowledge of modulation which
he was afterwards taught by more experience. During the acting of this play,
he was ſeized with a cold and hoarſeneſs ; and, after acting Hotſpur about five

nights with applaufe, though not with that univerfal approbation which generally attended his performance, he fell fick, and was confined to his chamber fix or feven weeks. This happened about the latter end of February; nor did he make his appearance on the ftage till he acted Ranger, in the Sufpicious Hufband, for his benefit, in April following.

His drefs in Hotfpur was objected to: a laced frock and a Ramilie wig were thought too infignificant for the character.

During his illnefs, as much concern was expreffed by the public, for his recovery, as if he had been a prince of the blood greatly honoured and beloved. The door of his lodgings was every day crouded with fervants, who came from perfons of the firft rank, and indeed of all ranks, to enquire after his health. Mrs. Oldfield happened to be in fome danger in a Gravefend-boat: and, when the reft of the paffengers lamented their approaching fate, fhe, with a confcious dignity, told them, their

deaths

deaths would be only a private loſs ;—' But I am a public concern.' The indiſpoſition of Garrick might, more ſeriouſly, be termed ſuch.

Barry's Hotſpur, from his noble figure, rapid and animated expreſſion, and lively action, was pleaſing and reſpectable : but there is a military pride, and camp-humour, if I may be indulged in the expreſſion, to which Barry was a ſtranger. For the ſame reaſon, Mr. Smith's repreſentation of this part, though well marked with fire, impetuoſity, and dignified deportment, is ſomewhat defective.

C H A P-

CHAPTER XII.

Pitiful ambition to gain applause. — Gorbellied knaves.— *Lady Percy and Brutus.* —
A green-room quarrel. — *Five authorities
for* rivo.—*Mr. Steevens justified.*— *Clement
Marot and the weavers.* — Strapado *ex-
plained, from Tom Coriat.*— *Improvement on
Shakspeare.* — *Falstaff's superior wit.* —
Foote and Garrick.— *A mock-representation
of the Prince and King.* — *Extract from
Cambyses.* — *An account of* sack.— *Bristol
milk.* — *Wine of the ancients.*— *Betterton's
Falstaff.* — *A Dublin paviour an excellent
actor.*—*History of Falstaff.*— *Booth, Mills,
Quin, Berry, Harper.*—*Henderson.*

Act II.

The Carriers.

FIRST CARRIER.

Out of all *cess.*

THE word *cess* is, I believe, derived
from *census*, a tax.

SECOND

SECOND CARRIER.

Lend thee my lantern !
Marry ! I'll fee thee *hang'd* fir ſt.

From the pitiful ambition of pleaſing the upper gallery, and getting their hands, the actor of the Carrier too often alters the word *hang'd* to *damn'd*.

Enter Chamberlain.

Chamberlain was a kind of upper ſervant, formerly belonging to inns on the road, who attended and waited on travellers as the chambermaids do now. Their office, I believe, extended to the care of every thing belonging to coaches and carriages, which is at preſent the buſineſs of the book-keeper.

GADSHILL.

I am joined with no foot-land-rakers.

Such, I believe, as Falſtaff termed, in a preceding ſcene,

Thieves of the day's beauty.

Q 3   IDEM.

I D E M.

Such as can hold in.

This is certainly very obfcure. I think
Mr. Steevens's ' Such as can curb our old
father antic the law' is nearer the author's
fenfe than Mr. Tollet's explanation. By
hold in is underftood *hold faft*. ' Such affociates have I,' fays Gadfhill, ' as can
maintain their robberies, and will not part
with their booty.'

F A L S T A F F.

Hang ye, gorbellied knaves.

Not content with explaining the word
gorbellied by fat and corpulent, which, I
believe, every reader of Shakfpeare under-
ftands without inftruction, Mr. Steevens
not only refers us to Bifhop Kennet's Pa-
rochial Antiquities, but lugs in three or
four authorities from old plays. Thus is
the margin fometimes enlarged to very little
purpofe.

Scene

Scene III. Hotſpur, ſolus.

HOTSPUR.

Have I not all their letters to meet me in arms by the ninth of next month?

This ſcene was neceſſary, to acquaint the audience with the progreſs of the inſurrection projected by the Percys in the laſt ſcene of the firſt act.

LADY PERCY.

O my good lord ! why are you thus alone ? ~~
Why haſt thou loſt the freſh blood in thy cheeks ;
And giv'n my treaſures and my rights of thee
To thick-ey'd muſing and curs'd melancholy ?

Lady Percy's ſpeech is an excellent comment upon Brutus's deſcription of the mind of man when labouring with the impreſſion of a conſpiracy:

Between the acting of a dreadful thing
And the firſt motion, all the interim
Is like a phantaſm or a hideous dream.

Small matters, they ſay, often ſerve as preludes to mighty quarrels. In the year 1746, this play was acted at the theatre in

Drury-

Drury-lane. Barry was the Hotfpur; a
very beautiful and accomplifhed actrefs
condefcended, in order to give ftrength to
the play, to act the trifling character of
Lady Percy; Berry was the Falftaff. The
houfe was far from crouded; for the public
could no more bear to fee another Falftaff,
while Quin was on the ftage, than they
would now flock to fee a new Shylock, as long
as Macklin continues to have ftrength fit
to reprefent ' *the Jew which Shakfpeare
drew.*'

A very celebrated comic actrefs triumphed in the barrennefs of the pit and
boxes; fhe threw out fome expreffions a-
gainft the confequence of the Lady Percy.
This produced a very cool, but cutting,
anfwer from the other; who reminded the
former of her playing, very lately, to a
much thinner audience, one of her favourite parts. And now, the ladies not
being able to reftrain themfelves within the
bounds of cool converfation, a moft terrible
fray enfued. I do not believe that they went

fo

ſo far as pulling of caps, but their altercation would not have diſgraced the females of Billingſgate. While the two great actreſſes were thus entertaining each other in one part of the green-room, the admirer of Lady Percy, an old gentleman who afterwards bequeathed her a conſiderable fortune, and the brother of the comic lady, were more ſeriouſly employed. The cicifbeo ſtruck the other with his cane: thus provoked, he very calmly laid hold of the old man's jaw. ' Let go my jaw, you villain !' and ' Throw down your cane, ſir !' were repeatedly echoed by the combatants. —— Barry, who was afraid leſt the audience ſhould hear full as much of the quarrel as of the play, ruſhed into the green-room, and put an end to the battle. The print-ſellers laid hold of this diſpute, and publiſhed a priꞓt called ' The Green-room Scuffle.'

Prince

Prince Henry and Poins.

PRINCE HENRY.

I am now of all humours that have shewed themselves humours since the old days of goodman Adam.

This is the genuine language of a young man whose body is vigorous and mind active; who, having more spirits than he knows what to do with, and not being engaged by noble exercises or generous pursuits, spends his hours in idleness and frolic.

Rivo. Here we have five authorities, from old plays, to justify Shakspeare's use of the word *rivo.*

PRINCE HENRY.

Pitiful-hearted Titan! who melted at the tale of the sun.

It is impossible to make sense of this passage as it now stands; Mr. Steevens's restoration from the old copy, which plainly refers to the story of Phaeton prevailing on Titan to give him the management of his

his chariot for a day, is, I think, extremely happy.

FALSTAFF.

I would I were a weaver; I could ſing all manner of
ſongs.

It is a common expreſſion this day, in
Scotland, to ſay ' pſalm-ſinging weavers.'
Clement Marot, who is juſtly eſteemed the
firſt poet of his time, and who died in
1544, tranſlated the pſalms into French
metre. It was not uncommon to ſet them
to muſic and ſing them at the court of
Francis I. The Proteſtants of Calvin's
perſuaſion had many of them ſet to various tunes, and ſang them in their
churches. Thoſe, who were exiled on the
repeal of the ediſt of Nantz, ſang them in
all the countries where they were received :
in England, Holland, and ſeveral parts
of Germany.

IDEM.

Were I at the ſtrapado, I would not tell you on
compulſion.

The

The punifhment of the *ftrapado*, as put in practice at Venice in the days of Shak-fpeare, is thus defcribed by Tom Coriat:

" The offender, having his hands bound behind him, is conveyed into a rope that hangeth by a pulley; after which he is raifed up by two feveral fwings, where he fuftaineth fo great torment, that his joints are for a time loofed and pulled afunder; befides which, abundance of blood is gathered into his hands and face. And, for the time he is in the torture, his hands and face look as red as blood."

FALSTAFF.

By the Lord, I knew you as well as he that made you.

The players have, from time immemorial, fubftituted in this place fomething of their own, which, I believe, the fevereft critic will not only pardon, but confefs that it heightens the mirth of the fcene, and gives a ftronger colour to the high-fea-

foned

ſoned impudence of the fat knight. While
the Prince and Poins are teazing Falſtaff
to give a plain anſwer to the proofs they
produce of his cowardice, he is buſy in
hatching up a laugh, in the diſcharge
of which he breaks out into this unexpected interrogation : —— ' What ! do
you think I did not know you ? By the
Lord, I knew you as well as he that made
you.'

It is confeſſed, by all the world, that
there is an uncommon force and verſatility
in the mirth of Falſtaff which is ſuperior
to all that dramatic poetry has hitherto invented. Prince Henry's converſation is
not without wit, and abounds in eaſy
pleaſantry and a gay turn : but the Prince
ſtands not in need of that ready power of
repartee, that impenetrable ſhield of inven-
tive audacity, and that ability to ſhift his
ground continually to ward off the blows,
to which the lies of Falſtaff inceſſantly ex-
poſe him. The jolly knight is never in a
ſtate of humiliation ; he generally riſes

ſuperior

fuperior to attack, and gets the laugh on his fide in fpite of truth and conviction. It was by this kind of invincible courage in converfation, as well as the quicknefs of his conception and brilliancy of his fancy, that Foote, without the help of Jack Falftaff's lies, was enabled to rife up and win the field when his opponents imagined he was laid flat and conquered outright. Garrick had a great fhare of wit, as well as fine animal fpirits; but a fmart blow of a repartee would filence him for the evening. If fuffered to take the lead, he was highly entertaining; but he could not bear interruption.

I D E M.

You muft to the court in the morning.

This is a preparation for the enfuing pathetic fcene between the King and Prince.

P R I N C E   H E N R Y.

Do thou ftand for my father, and examine me upon the particulars of my life.

The

The following mock-repreſentation of
an interview between the Prince and his father is generally left out on the ſtage, as
an incumbrance to the action. It has
been occaſionally revived, but never produced the effect which the admirers of
Shakſpeare expected. It is certainly managed with great art, and larded with wit
and humour ; but it is not heightened with
incident, nor ſtuffed with that high jocu-
larity which throws an audience into fits
of laughter.

F A L S T A F F.

And I will do it in King Cambyſes' vein.

Shakſpeare ridicules, in this paſſage, an
old play, of one Thomas Preſton, called
' A lamentable Tragedy, mixed full with
Mirth, containing the Life of Cambyſes,
King of Perſia.'

A taſte of this author's poetry will afford
a ſpecimen of the miſerable traſh our anceſtors were forced to ſwallow down. ——
Tragi-comedy was then the taſte of the
nation,

nation, as it continues to be now, for the excellency of Shakfpeare's genius has fix-ed it upon us. Nor is it very ftrange, when we fee the politeft people in Europe obliged to tack a diverting petite piece to make a tragedy palatable to the audience. The Spaniards, too, will not be fatisfied without a dafh of buffoonry added to their more ferious pieces.

Extract from Cambyfes.

My council grave and fapient,
    With lords of legal train,
Attentive ears towards us bend,
    And hear what fhall be fain :
So you, likewife, my valiant knight,
    Whofe manly acts doth fly,
By bruit of fame, the founding trump
    Doth pierce the azure fky.

The laft editors have quoted a line or two of this curious piece; I thought a lit-tle larger fample would do juftice to the genius of Mafter Prefton. Mr. Steevens relates, that Queen Elizabeth was fo well pleafed with his acting a part before her

at

at the univerſity of Cambridge, that ſhe ſettled 20l. per annum on Preſton; and this, he ſays, was little more than 1s. per diem. In thoſe days of ſtrict œconomy, 20l. was a conſiderable penſion: I queſtion if Ro-ger Aſcham's ſtipend was more than twice that ſum, who was the queen's preceptor in the learned languages.

F A L S T A F F.

If ſack and ſugar be a fault.

At this diſtance of time, it is not an eaſy matter to determine what ſort of wine this ſack was, of which our anceſtors were ſo fond. By the knight's mixing it with ſu-gar, it can ſcarcely anſwer Dr. Johnſon's definition, who calls it ' a ſweet wine chief-ly brought from the Canaries.' Minſhew derives the word *ſack* from *ſeccare, propter magnam ſeccandi humores facultatem:* to this derivation Falſtaff would himſelf have no objection. Skinner thinks the word *ſack* takes its name from the Spaniſh *ſecco, dry,* having a rough and ſharp quality. The

conjecture

conjecture of Mandelſo is, that *ſack* is derived from *Xeque*, a city of Mauritania,
and thence tranſplanted into Spain. After
all, the ſame learned Dr. Skinner calls
ſherry *ſherry-ſack*, a well-known wine,
derived from *Xeres*, formerly Eſcuris, in
the province of Andaluſia. Falſtaff himſelf, in his profuſe commendations of
ſherry, terms it ' a good ſherris-ſack,' as
if there were two ſorts of ſack, and he gave
the preference to the ſherris. Blount, in
his Gloſſography, ſays, ' that ſherris-ſack
is ſo called from Xeres, a ſea-town of Cor-
duba, in Spain, where that kind of ſherris
is made.'

That the ſack, of which our anceſtors
drank, had a tartneſs in it, ſeems evident
from their mixing ſugar with it. All
wine-merchants, as well as old topers, are
agreed, that at preſent we have none of
that excellent ſherry which was drunk ſo
plentifully about forty or fifty years ſince,
and which was called *Briſtol milk*, from a
common practice of the inhabitants of that
city,

city, who generouſly preſented ſtrangers
with a glaſs of that pleaſant wine.

The liquor, which Homer pours out ſo
abundantly, is old wine, and yet he calls
it ηδυς, *dulcis*.

Οινοιο παλαιϛ ηδυποτοιϛ.

Odyss. Lib. II.

It cannot be ſuppoſed that old wine could
really be ſweet wine, becauſe age gives it a
tartneſs. It is obſerved, by a French critic, that the word ηδυς, or *dulcis*, ſhould be
tranſlated *pleaſant*, or *agreeable*; becauſe,
ſays he, that ſharpneſs, which was the
conſequence of wine's being kept long,
ſeemed to be a quality very agreeable to the
ancients. *Hiſt. crit. de la République des
Lettres*, tom. I. p. 240.

For ſome time after the union of the king's
and duke of York's companies of comedians,
Betterton, with general approbation, acted
Hotſpur; a character which, according to
the laws eſtabliſhed then by the lord-chamberlain, he was not permitted to attempt

R 2　　　　　during

during the time Hart continued to act; the play of Henry IV. Firſt Part, being aſſigned to the king's company. Towards the decline of his life, Betterton relinquiſhed Hotſpur to try his abilities in Falſtaff; and, in this change of character, his powers of pleaſing did not forſake him; being a perfect maſter of his profeſſion, he wore the ſock with as much eaſe and grace as the buſkin. With the greateſt ſtock of merit, this conſummate comedian poſſeſſed an equal ſhare of modeſty. He was ever open to advice, and refuſed it from no man who offered it.

In the beginning of this, or the end of the laſt, century, Ben Jonſon, the actor, took a trip to Dublin, where his great merit gained him much applauſe with conſiderable profit.

There he ſaw a comic actor whom he much admired, one Baker, a maſter-paviour of Dublin. He excelled in Sir Epicure Mammon in the Alchemiſt, in the Spaniſh Frier, and more eſpecially in Falſtaff.

ſtaff. Baker would ſtudy his parts while
ſurveying his workmen in the ſtreets.
This practice was once the occaſion of a
very whimſical adventure. Two of his
men, who had been lately hired from Cheſ-
ter and were ſtrangers to their new maſter's cuſtom, obſerving one day his countenance and geſtures, while talking to himſelf, imagined that he was ſeized with
madneſs. He, on taking notice of their
attention, bade them mind their buſineſs.
They obeyed, — but ſtill kept a watchful eye on him, who was rehearſing to
himſelf the part of Falſtaff. He was in
that ſcene where the knight ſurveys the
dead body of Sir Walter Blunt,—and ſaying, *Who have we here, Sir Walter Blunt?*
There's honour for you! Upon this, the fellows laid hold of their maſter, and, by the
help of the by-ſtanders, tied him hand and
foot, and, in ſpite of his reſiſtance, carried
him home with a great mob at his heels*.

R 3   Jonſon

---

* Chetwood's Hiſtory of the Stage.

Jonfon communicated to Betterton this actor's manner of perfonating Falftaff, which he not only approved, but adopted; and frankly owned that the paviour's drawing of Sir John was more charaċteriftical than his own.

George Powell, who was malicious enough to envy this great actor, and weak enough to think himfelf capable of fupplying his place, during the life of Betterton aċted Falftaff in his particular manner; and, to take all advantages, he mimicked him in thofe acute pains of the gout which fometimes furprifed him in the time of aċtion.

Since the death of Betterton, in April, 1710, many comedians of Drury-lane Theatre have tried their fkill in Falftaff; but moft of them with very indifferent fuccefs. By the particular command of Queen Anne, Booth ventured to put on the habit of Falftaff, for *one night only*. That he did not venture a fecond attempt might be owing either to a confcious deficiency to

assume

affume Falftaff's humour, or a predilection
for Hotfpur in the fame play. The elder
Mills would likewife try his fkill in comic
archery, and handled, for a few nights,
this bow of Ulyffes. But, alas, in vain!
His fober gravity could not reach the
inimitable mirth of this ftage-prodigy.
Harper's fat figure, full voice, round face,
and honeft laugh, rather than his intelligence, fixed him at laft in the jolly knight's
eafy chair.

The company of comedians which began to act under the management of John
Rich, from a patent of Charles II. in
1715, though confifting of fome good old
players, from recruits picked up from all
parts of the country, and the difcontents of
Drury-lane, were, for a long time, unable to
cope with the eftablifhed comedians of the
laft-mentioned theatre. Lincoln's-inn Fields
houfe was finely decorated. The fcenes were
new. The ftage was more extended than that
of the rival theatre, and fuperbly adorned with looking-glafs on both fides of
the ftage; a circumftance, which Quin

R 4   faid

faid was an excellent trap to catch actresses who admired their persons more than their profession of acting. But, when the novelty was worn away, the audiences forsook the new company for their old friends at Drury-lane.

The first play acted at Lincoln's-inn Fields, which fixed the attention of the public, was The merry Wives of Windsor. This comedy was so perfectly played in all its parts, that the critics in acting universally celebrated the merit of the performers*. The characters were so well adapted to the abilities of the actors, that no play had been represented with equal skill and propriety at that theatre.

The great applause Quin gained in this, the feeblest portrait of Falstaff, encouraged

him

---

* Falstaff, Quin ; Ford, Ryan; Page, Ogden ; Sir Hugh Evans, Hippesley; Justice Shallow, Boheme ; Slender, Christopher Bullock; Host of the Garter, old Bullock ; Dr. Caius, Egleton ; Mrs. Ford, Mrs. Seymour; Mrs. Page, Mrs. Bullock ; Mrs. Quickly, Mrs. Egleton.

him to venture on the moſt high-feaſoned
part of the character, in The Firſt Part of
Henry IV. Of this large compound of lies,
bragging and exhauſtleſs fund of wit and
humour, Quin poſſeſſed the oſtenſible or
mechanical part in an eminent degree.
In perſon he was tall and bulky: his voice
ſtrong and pleaſing: his countenance manly, and his eye piercing and expreſſive.
In ſcenes, where ſatire and ſarcaſm were
poignant, he greatly excelled; particularly in The Witty Triumph over Bardolph's carbuncles, and the fooleries of the
hoſteſs. In the whole part he was animated, though not equally happy. His ſu-
percilious brow, in ſpite of aſſumed gaiety,
ſometimes unmaſked the ſurlineſs of his
diſpoſition; however, he was, notwithſtanding ſome faults, eſteemed the moſt
intelligent and judicious Falſtaff ſince the
days of Betterton. Berry, who ſucceeded
Quin at Drury-lane, was neither exact in
his outline nor warm in his colouring.
He was, indeed, the Falſtaff of a beer-
houſe;

houfe; while the *other* was the dignified Prefident, were the choiceft viands and the beft liquors were to be had. Love, who came next in order at Drury-lane, wanted not a good fhare of vis comica, and laughed with eafe and gaiety. To pafs by Ned Shuter's exhibition of this favourite part would be unpardonable. What Ned wanted in judgement he fupplied by archnefs and drollery. He enjoyed the effects of his roguery with a chuckle of his own compounding, and rolled his full eye, when detected, with a moft laughable effect. Woodward and Yates put on Falftaff's habit for one night only. Their refpect for the judgement of the audience prevented their affuming the boldnefs of the character. I think their diffidence was greater than their deficiencies. Thefe excellent comic actors might, by repeated practice, have reached the mark which they modeftly defpaired to hit.

The prefent age has, in my opinion, produced a Falftaff who has more of the pleafant

pleafant and gay features of the character than any actor I have yet feen. I know very well that fome of the furviving companions of Quin will pronounce it theatrical treafon to fuppofe that it was poffible for this character to furvive their departed friend. But Nature is not fo niggardly in her productions. The rifing generation may fee new Garricks, Barrys, Cibbers, and Quins. While I am writing this, a great and admirable genius has ftruck the world with admiration. — Mrs. Siddons is the lawful fucceffor of our moft perfect actreffes. Much is faid of old fchools and new fchools in acting : this lady is the great ornament of Nature's fchool, which will eternally be the fame.—But to return to my fubject.

Henderfon had many difficulties to conquer before he could bring Falftaff within his grapple : neither in perfon, voice, nor countenance, did he feem qualified for the part. By the affiftance of a moft excellent judgement

judgement he has contrived to fupply all
deficiencies. In the impudent dignity, if
I may be allowed the expreffion, of the
character, Quin greatly excelled all competitors. In the frolickfome, gay, and
humorous, fituations of Falftaff, Henderfon is fuperior to every man.

From his figure, and other out-
ward accomplifhments, Falftaff feems to
have courted Quin to embrace him; while
Henderfon was obliged to force him into
his fervice. Quin's fupercilious manner
was of ufe to him in fcenes where he wifhed to overawe his companions into compliance with his humour. Henderfon's
gay levity was beft fuited to midnight pleafure and riotous mirth.

The mafter-action of Quin was the
detection of his cowardice by the prince
and Poins, in the fecond Act; and though,
In this, Henderfon fhews much art and
true humour, yet his foliloquy in defcribing his ragamuffin regiment, and his enjoying

joying the miſuſe of the king's preſs-mo-
ney, are ſo truly excellent, that they are
not inferior to any comic repreſentation
of the ſtage.

CHAPTER

CHAPTER XIII.

*Mortimer, Hotfpur, and Owen Glendower.
— The fcene between them generally omitted in reprefentation. — Meaning of the
word* lewd.—*Courtefy from heaven.—Mr.
Steevens and Mr. Malone. — Robe pontifical.*—Favours in a bloody mafk *explained.
—Curious extract from Hollingfhead.—Obfervation on the interview between the king
and prince.——Wilks, his excellence in the
prince of Wales. — Mr. Lewis and Mr.
Palmer.* — The infide of a church,—A
brewer's horfe,—-Artificial nofes,—-Stew'd
prunes,—*and the word* quailing, *explained.
—Nimblenefs of Prince Henry. — Accurate
account of the oftrich.—Death of Hotfpur.
—Falftaff and Hotfpur.—The difficulty of
raifing a dead body on a living fhoulder.—
Henderfon and Smith.*

Act

Act III. Scene I. Hotſpur, Worceſter, Mortimer, Glendower.

THIS Interview of the principal conſpi-
rators has been often preſented to
the public, but could not preſerve a per-
manent ſtation on the ſtage. It ſeems of
great uſe in the œconomy of the play, to
unfold the progreſs of the rebellion, and to
diſplay the paſſions and intereſts of the ſeveral perſons concerned in it. By the am-
putation of this ſcene, Hotſpur's part appeared to be ſo maimed, that Mr. Garrick
inſiſted on its being revived. However,
after the firſt or ſecond night's acting,
finding that it produced no effect, he con-
ſented to omit it. If I remember right,
Colley Cibber formerly played Owen Glendower. The necromantic forgeries and
vain boaſtings of the Welchman are
well contraſted with the blunt humour and
contemptuous diſdain of Hotſpur.

Scene

Scene II. King and Prince of Wales.

K I N G.

To punifh my miftreadings!

In this, and the former part of the
fpeech, where Henry fpeaks of the dif-
pleafing fervice he had done, Shakfpeare,
I believe, alludes to his depofing and murdering of Richard II. The poet, agrea-
bly to hiftory, makes him keep his great
offences to his fovereign conftantly in
mind; and Henry's continual compunction
and remorfe leffens our hatred to the ufurper.

I D E M.

————Such lewd, fuch mean, attempts!

The word *lewd* has, in Shakfpeare, various meanings; fuch as *impudent*, *illiberal*,
licencious, and *wanton*. Verftegan proves
that it originally fignified *ignorant*; here,
as Mr. Steevens obferves, it ftands for *licencious*.

I D E M.

And then I ftole all courtefy from heaven.

Mr.

Mr. Steevens has juſtified Dr Warburton, who fays our poet in this alludes to
the ſtory of Prometheus ſtealing fire from
heaven, by producing a parallel paſſage
from Maſſinger's Duke of Florence, which
proves this author underſtood it in that
ſenſe, by uſing the very words of Shakſpeare.
But Mr. Malone denies that Shakſpeare
dreamt in the leaſt of the fable of Prometheus, and infiſts that Henry means that
he robbed heaven of its worſhip, as he did
his fellow-ſubjects of their allegiance.

This is certainly more than the author
intended. Courtefy for devotion is ſurely
ſomewhat ſtrained. The progreſs, from
courtefy to humility, is natural e-
nough ; that Prometheus's ſtealing fire
from heaven was not unfamiliar to Shakſpeare, can be proved from a ſimilar expreſſion in Othello.

 ——But once put out thy light,
Thou cunning'ſt pattern of excelling Nature,
I know not where is that *Promethean* heat
That can thy light relumine!

     OTHELLO, Act V.

I D E M.

My prefence, like a robe pontifical.

Such as popes, patriarchs, and archbi-
ſhops, wear only at high maſs.

Lord Bolingbroke on being once preſent
at high maſs, in the church of Notre
Dame in Paris, was ſo greatly delighted
with the high ceremony and ſolemn muſic,
that he declared, if he had been king of
France, he would alſo have officiated as
pontiff.

PRINCE OF WALES.

Stain my favours in a bloody maſk!

This is to be underſtood in the ſame
ſenſe as the following paſſage relating to
the ſame prince of Wales in Richard II.
Act V. of whom, it is ſaid, that he declared,

———He would unto the ſtews,
And from the common'ſt creature pluck a glove,
And wear it as a favour, and with that
He would unhorſe the luſtieſt challenger.

This admirable ſcene between King Henry and his ſon owes its origin to a very
extraordinary

extraordinary and pathetic interview of theſe great perſonages, which happened about a year before the death of the king. Shakſpeare does not always obſerve the order of time, but frequently ſelects ſituations and events to ſuit his own plan. The particulars are thus recorded by Hollingſhead and Stowe.

" That Henry, Prince of Wales, being informed, that certain ill-minded perſons had not only ſpread abroad very ill reports of him, but had endeavoured to ſow diſſention between the king, his father, and himſelf; he wrote public letters to clear his reputation; and, to free himſelf the better from ſuch aſperſions, on the 29th of June, 1412, he came to the court with certain noblemen and others his friends. — He was dreſſed in a gown of blue ſattin, full of ſmall eyelets, at every hole the needle hanging by a ſilk thread. About his arm he wore a hound's collar ſet full of SS of gold. The court was then at Weſtminſter. The retinue of the prince, in obe-

dience

dience to his commands, would advance
no farther than the fire-place, though frequently requefted by the lords in waiting.
The prince himfelf, accompanied with
fome of the king's houfehold, was admitted
to his royal father; who, in the prefence
of three or four perfons, commanded him
to tell the caufe of his coming to him.

" The prince, kneeling down before his
father, faid, — Moft redoubted and fovereign lord and father, I am at this time
come to your prefence as your liegeman
and your natural fon, in all things to be
at your commandment; and, whereas I
underftand you have in fufpicion my de-
meanor againft your grace, you know very
well, that, if I knew any man in this
realm of whom you fhould ftand in fear,
my duty were to punifh that perfon,
thereby to remove that grief from your
heart; then how much more ought I fuffer death to eafe your grace of that grief
which you have of me, being your natural
fon and liegeman; and to that end I have
                                        made

made myſelf ready, by confeſſing and receiving the ſacrament; and therefore I
beſeech you, moſt redoubted lord and dear
father, for the honour of God, to eaſe
your heart of all ſuch ſuſpicion you have of
me, and to diſpatch me here with this ſame
dagger, (and withal delivered to the king
his dagger in all humble reverence, adding
farther, that his life was not ſo dear to
him that he wiſhed to live one day with his
diſpleaſure;) and, therefore, in thus rid-
ding me out of life, and yourſelf from all
ſuſpicion, here, in preſence of theſe lords,
and before God, at the day of the general
judgement, I faithfully proteſt clearly to
forgive you.

" The king, herewith moved, caſt from
him the dagger, and, embracing the
prince, kiſſed him; and, with ſhedding
tears, confeſſed that indeed he had him
partly in ſuſpicion, though now, as he
perceived, not with juſt cauſe; and from
thenceforth no report ſhould have him in

S 3 miſtruſt,

miftruft; and this he promifed from his honour."

In this fcene, between the King and Prince, Shakfpeare has not ufed one harfh or obfcure word; the language is clear, flowing, and majeftic, well adapted to character. Though it is little more than a fine picture of ftill life, not blended with pity or terror, the great ingredients of tragic paffion, by the admirable fkill of the writer it is rendered abundantly interefting and affecting.

I have already obferved that Winterfhul, who firft acted the King after the Reftoration, was a comedian of merit. Cibber draws a mafterly picture of Kynafton's behaviour in this fcene, to which I muft refer the reader.

The elder Mills wanted dignity of deportment neceffary to reprefent the grandeur and majefty of the character, which were eminently fupplied by Boheme. —— Havard was decent, but without fpirit; Benfley is chiefly deficient in perfon. —

The

The Prince of Wales by Wilks was one of the moſt perfect exhibitions of the theatre. Wilks threw aſide the libertine gaiety of Hal, when he aſſumed the princely deportment of Henry. At the Boar's Head he was lively and frolicſome; in the reconciliation with his father, his penitence was gracefully becoming, and his reſolution of amendment manly and affecting. In his challenge of Hotſpur, his defiance was equally gallant and modeſt. In his combat with that nobleman, his fire was tempered with moderation, and his reflections on the death of the great rebel, generous and pathetic. The Hotſpur of Booth, though a noble portrait of courage, humour, and gallantry, was not ſuperior to the Prince of Wales by Wilks. It is no diſgrace to Mr. Lewis and Mr. Palmer, who are both actors of great merit, and deſerve much commendation in their ſeveral repreſentations of Prince Henry, to be inferior to the accompliſhed Wilks.

S 4 FALSTAFF.

FALSTAFF.

And I have not forgotten the infide of a church I am
a pepper-corn, a brewer's horfe! The infide of a
church!

It requires no fagacity to fee that the *infide of a church* is not one of his vile com-
parifons, as Prince Henry termed the
knight's fimiles in a former fcene; it is
certainly a repetition of his confeffing that
he was utterly unacquainted with any
place of devotion. — I believe, in the days
of Shakfpeare, brewers horfes did not re-
femble thofe of our days; they were probably poor jades, worn out with fervice;
and therefore the comparifon of the fat
Falftaff with a lean Rofinante is not fo i-
dle. In the reign of Henry IV. the bufinefs of brewing was carried on by females.*
Whether the men chiefly employed themfelves, in Queen Elizabeth's reign, in the
occupation of brewing, I know not.

HOSTESS.

* Henry's Hiftory of Great-Britain.

H O S T E S S.

You owe me money, Sir John ; and now you pick a quarrel to beguile me of it.

This is a good preparative for the arreſt of Falſtaff in the Second Part of Henry IV.

F A L S T A F F.

Let him coin his noſe.

In Shakſpeare's time, a large carbuncled noſe was a richer joke than it is now, as may appear from this ſarcaſtical deſcription of one by Falſtaff. For ſuch characters as the Jew of Malta and Bardolph, the actors made uſe of artificial noſes*.

I D E M.

There is no more faith in thee than in a *ſtewed prune*.

To explain at full what is meant by *ſtewed prunes*, Mr. Steevens has given no leſs than fourteen authorities from old books and plays. I would recommend to that gentleman to be content with one half of

---

* Vide Mr. Read's note on a paſſage in the Jew of Malta.

of these quotations; which, with Dr. Farmer's account of the price of a stewed prune, will, I think, satisfy every reasonable man.

Act IV. Scene I.

H O T S P U R.

There is no quailing now.

The word *quailing* is very expressive, and taken from the nature of the *quail;* which of all birds is one of the most timorous as well as lascivious.

" The Arabs, says Dr. Shaw, do not spring game with dogs; but, shading themselves with a piece of canvas stretched upon two reeds into the shade of a door, they walk through avenues where they expect to find it. The canvas is usually spotted, or painted with the figure of a leopard; and, a little below the top, there is one or more holes, for the fowler to look through and see what passes before him. Quails, and such-like birds as do not feed in flocks, will, upon sight of the canvas, *stand still and look astonished.*

aſtoniſhed.   This gives the ſportſman an opportunity of coming very near them; and then, reſting the canvas upon the ground, and directing the muzzle of his piece through one of the holes, knocks down ſometimes a whole covey of them."

Shaw's Travels.

.With the Egyptians, the quail was an emblem of impiety; the voice of that bird was ſuppoſed to be diſpleaſing to the gods.

Scene IV.

WORCESTER.

We of the offering ſide.

That is, we who make propoſals for alteration of government, and offer new terms to the people: ſuch as a king with a juſter title to the crown than he has whom we call uſurper; and many other new articles to gain the public favour and aſſiſtance.

HOTSPUR.

HOTSPUR.

The nimble-footed mad-cap Prince of Wales.

Shakſpeare rarely beſtows his epithets at random, ſays Mr. Steevens. Mr. Bowle had made an obſervation ſomething like this upon a ſimilar paſſage in the ſecond act of this play. But, although I am willing to grant his highneſs was as ſwift-footed as Achilles, yet I hope I ſhall be excuſed from giving credit to what is quoted gravely from an hiſtorian : for, if Hal himſelf would not believe that Hotſpur could ' ride up a hill perpendicular, and kill a ſparrow flying,'— neither will I ſubſcribe to a writer who tells us, that ' Henry Prince of Wales, and his companions, would run after a ſtag, and take him, without hounds, or any weapon whatſoever.'

VERNON.

All plum'd like eſtridges.

The beſt and moſt accurate account we have of the oſtrich is to be found in Dr. Shaw's

Shaw's Travels, which is indeed a good commentary on feveral verfes of the 39th chapter of Job. As that learned writer's defcription is taken from his own perfonal knowledge, I fhall quote a paffage relating to the uncommon fwiftnefs and beauty of the oftrich.

" When any of thefe birds are furprifed, by coming fuddenly upon them, whilft they are feeding in fome valley, or behind fome rocky or fmall eminence in the deferts, they will not ftay to be curioufly viewed and examined ; neither are the Arabs dex-trous enough to overtake them, though they are mounted upon their jinfes, or horfes of family. *They, when they raife themfelves up for flight, laugh at the horfe and his rider.** They afford him an opportuni-ty only of admiring, at a diftance, the ex-traordinary agility, and the ftatelinefs like-wife, of their motions ; the richnefs of
their

---

* Job, ch. xxxix. verfe 18.

their plumage, and the great propriety there was of afcribing to them *an expanded quivering wing*.* Nothing certainly can be more beautiful and entertaining than fuch a fight: the wings, by their repeated, though unwearied, vibrations, equally ferving them for fails and oars; whilft their feet, no lefs affifting in conveying them out of fight, are no lefs infenfible of fatigue." Shaw's Travels into Africa.

HOTSPUR.

Tafk'd the whole ftate.

Tafked is a word, in the old Chronicles, for *taxed*.

IDEM.

———————— To feek out
This head of fafety. ————————

So Worcefter, in the laft fcene of the firft act:

And it is no little reafon bids us fpeed,
To fave our heads by raifing of a head.

Act

———————————————

* Verfe 13.

Act V. Scene II.

PRINCE HENRY.

Heaven forbid a ſhallow ſcratch ſhould drive
The Prince of Wales from ſuch a field as this.

Henry was preſent, though then very young, being ſcarcely fifteen years of age, at the battle of Shrewſbury ; where he fought bravely, and was wounded : he would not leave the field of battle, though earneſtly intreated by ſeveral of the nobility.

I D E M.

And now two paces of the vileſt earth
Is room enough. ——

—— *Mors ſola fatetur*
Quantula ſint hominum corpuſcula.——

JUVENAL, Sat. X.

The King, according to Hall, who is copied by Hollingſhead, fought very ſtoutly, and killed, with his own hand, thirty-ſix of the rebels. Though the ſame authors expreſs themſelves ſomewhat obſcurely,

fcurely, yet we may gather from the con-
text that Percy was flain by the Prince of
Wales. Stowe fays, that Hotfpur, run-
ning forward amongft the thickeft of the
enemy, was flain.

FALSTAFF.

Therefore, firrah, with a new wound in your thigh,
&c.

A man of genius has taken pains to refcue the character of Falftaff from the
charge of cowardice; * not confidering,
that, if the knight is proved to be a man
of courage, half the mirth he raifes is
quite loft and mifplaced. The Prince and
Poins obtained, by their contrivance, fuch
evident proofs of his daftardly fpirit, that
the whole mirth, in the admired fcene of
his detected tergiverfation, depends upon
it. Old Jack is fo fairly hunted down, by
the plain tale and keen reproaches of the
Prince, that he is reduced to the neceffity
of

---

* Effay on the Character of Falftaff.

of excufing his want of courage, by attri-
buting his fear to inftinct : but, if any
proof of his timidity be yet wanting, we
have, in this fcene, fuch as bids defiance to all queftion ; for Falftaff, not
fatisfied with feeing the dead body of Percy before him, to make all fure, wounds
the corpfe in the thigh. Nobody, I believe,
is angry that he afterwards fwears he killed him. I cannot think the author of the
Effay on the Character of Falftaff intended any thing more, by his argument, than
to convince the public that he was very
competent to fupport any hypothefis by
brilliancy of wit and plaufibility of argument.

I D E M.

I'll follow, as they fay, for the hope of reward !

No joke ever raifed fuch loud and repeated mirth, in the galleries, as Sir John's
labour in getting the body of Hotfpur on
his back. If Hotfpur and Falftaff had
been on ill terms, or any quarrel had taken
place between them, the hero, if he was

fo inclined, could have teazed the fat knight in fuch a manner as to have given him no little vexation. How Booth and Harper managed this pantomimic fcene is not very eafy to tell. Booth's weight and roundnefs of figure would render the bulky Harper's lifting him on his back worfe than walking a hundred yards on uneven ground. Quin had little or no difficulty in perching Garrick upon his fhoulders, who looked like a dwarf on the back of a giant. But, oh! how he tugged and toiled to raife Barry from the ground! As they were rivals, and fometimes jarred, we may, without breach of charity, fuppofe, that Hotfpur fometimes enjoyed the fweat of Falftaff. If the dead man was not friendly to the living, he might have made the weighing him up an Herculean labour.

At length this upper-gallery merriment was done away by the difficulties which Henderfon encountered in getting Smith on his fhoulders. So much time was con-
fumed

fumed in this pick-a-pack business, that the spectators grew tired, or rather disgusted. It was thought best, for the future, that some of Falstaff's ragamuffins should bear off the dead body.

Scene the last.

KING.

Ill-spirited Worcester, did we not send grace,
Pardon, and love, to all of you !———

This reproof of Worcester's malignity is agreeable to historical fact.

King

King Henry IV. Second Part.

CHAPTER XIV.

Second Part of Henry IV. *owing to the Success of the firſt.—When regiſtered.—Shakſpeare's age. — Ben Jonſon. — Rumour. — Dr. Johnſon's diſtribution of certain lines. — Mandrake explained. — Walkers in St. Paul's.—All ſingle combatants give the lie.— Remark on the word* old. *— The original actor of Falſtaff. — Hunt Counter.—Single wit. — Boman the actor. — Text reſtored.—Quean and Queller. — Fuſtilarian. — Cards eaten by a gameſter. — Propoſed alteration of the text. — Lady Percy and Northumberland. — Piſtol and Theophilus Cibber. — Stage Mutineers. — Overſight of the author.—Death of Glendower.*

THE

THE fuccefs of the Firſt Part of Henry IV. muſt have been uncommon, for it appears, from Mr. Malone's Chronnological feries of our author's plays, that it was entered into the Stationers books in the beginning of the year 1598, entitled the Hiſtory of Henry IV. The writer did not, at that time, perhaps, forefee that he ſhould be encouraged to continue the ſtory. However, the Second Part of Henry IV. was regiſtered, in the fame books, in the beginning of the year 1599. Shakfpeare was not more than thirty-four years old when thefe admirable productions of his genius were exhibited. If I could poffibly envy the pleafure which the audiences enjoyed in old times, it would be for that inconceivable delight which intelligent auditors muſt have felt at the firſt acting of Shakfpeare's nobleſt dramas. Methinks I fee and hear the tumultuous joy and thundering applaufe which the unparallelled character

T 3 of

of Falftaff muft have afforded at his firft reprefentation! A character, fo fuperior to the conception of the brighteft fancy, muft have ftruck them with aftonifhment! To have feen Ben Jonfon, with an affumed countenance of gaiety, and with envy in his heart, join the groupe of laughers and applauders, muft have added to the pleafure of our author's real friends and admirers.

The Prologue.

Rumour is fo eafy and plain *a ftop,*
——— The wavering multitude
Can play upon it.

Rumour is here compared to a mufical inftrument. So Hamlet, in fhewing a flute to Guilderftern:

Can you play upon this pipe?
Why, 'tis as eafy as lying.
Look you, thefe *are the ftops.*

Act I. Scene I.

NORTHUMBERLAND.

——— Every minute now
Should be the father of fome ftratagem.

That

That is, fhould bring forth fome great event.

I D E M.

———————— Ha ! —— Again ! —
Said he young Harry Percy's fpur was cold ?

Northumberland, by the word *again*, calls upon Travers to repeat what the man on horfeback faid of Harry Percy.

I D E M.

So looks the ftrond, whereon th'imperious flood
Hath left a witnefs'd ufurpation.

The mind's diftrefs, when ftrongly pictured on the countenance, is finely expreffed by Otway, in his Venice Preferved.

Then, Jaffier, fhouldft thou not wear
Thofe *feals of woe* upon thy face.

N O R T H U M B E R L A N D.

Yet, for all this, fay not that Percy's dead !

Dr. Johnfon would give this line to Bardolph : however, he does not offer to alter the text, but candidly propofes a mode of diftributing the parts of the fpeech, which he thinks belong to feveral interlocutors.

T 4

cutors.   I cannot fee any advantage to be
gained by it.   Grief is talkative, and can
bear no interruption.   Cibber, in adapt-
ing this fcene to the circumftance of Prince
Edward's murder, in the tragedy of Richard III. has given this line to King
Henry, the father of Edward, and has
thereby rendered the fcene more affecting.
Morton is, I think, too much overwhelmed with the weight of his unhappy
tidings to reafon fo conclufively and coolly
as in the lines which Dr. Johnfon gives to
him.   Lord Bardolph very properly breaks
filence, by faying,

I cannot think, my lord, your fon is dead.

Great part of this fcene between Northumberland and Travers is not unfkilfully wo-
ven into the firft act of Cibber's alteration
of Richard III. and applied to Henry VI.'s
lamentation for the murder of his fon.
The celebrated imprecation of Northumberland, fo defervedly praifed by Addifon
and Dr. Johnfon, Cibber would not lofe ;
he

he tranfplanted feveral lines of it into his
fourth act, and with the remainder he
clofed the dying fpeech of Richard.

Scene II. Falftaff and Page.

F A L S T A F F.
Thou whorefon mandrake.

Mandrake is an herb of a narcotic and
cold quality; efpecially the root, which is
large and fhaped like thofe of parfnip,
carrot, white briony, &c. and, in old
times, has been applied to deaden pain in
parts to be opened or cut off. Its roots
are fometimes forked; which made the
fruitful heads of antiquity fancy they were
like the legs or thighs of man, and de-
rive its Greek name, *quafi* Andragora,
*quod inter eradicandum ejulatur et humanam
refert vocem.* Pythagoras calls it Anthro-
pomorphus; Columella, Semihomo; Al-
bertus de Mandragora, Drufius de Mon-
ftris, Kircherus de Magia Paraftatica,
Pliny, (Nat. Hift.) and others, have run
into the fame conceit. The ancients believed

lieved it grew only at places of execution, out of the urine and fat of the dead; that, in eradication, it fhrieked; and that it brought calamity on fuch as pulled or dug it up: to prevent which difafters, Pliny gives directions at large to be obferved in pulling it.

Cunning impoftors have confirmed thefe errors, by choofing forked roots out of it, and carving, in fome, the generative parts of men; in others, thofe of women; and putting into fmall holes, made in proper places, the grains of millet, barley, or the like, and fetting them in a moift place till they grew and fent forth blades; which, when dried, look like hair. For the dif-covery of thefe cheats, we are beholden to Matthioli, Crollius, Sir Thomas Brown, and others. *Murphy's Lucian, note to Ti-mon Mifanthropos.*

Machiavel wrote a diverting, but very licencious, comedy, called Mandragora.

I D E M.

To bear a gentleman in hand.

To

To bear a gentleman in hand fignifies not only keeping him in expectation, but alfo with the farther defign not to comply with the gentleman's requeft.

I D E M.

I bought him in Paul's.

That is, *I picked him up there.* That St. Paul's Church-yard was, till the latter end of Queen Anne's reign, a common refort for all forts of people we find from Pope's Effay on Criticifm :

Nor is Paul's church more free than Paul's Church-yard.

In Shakfpeare's time, it was not only a place for idle people, cheats, and knights of the poft, but for politicians, courtiers, and others, who met there to hear court and city news, and difcufs political matters. This information Ofborne gives us, who was himfelf an ambulator in St. Paul's.

I D E M.

You lie in your throat if you fay I am any other.

The lie direct preceded, or accompanied, all challenges from the combatants, with fand bags, to kings and emperors, who
fought

fought armed at all points. Francis I. king of France, and Charles V. emperor of Germany, gave and returned the lie to each other with equal brutality.

FALSTAFF.

Very well, my lord, very well.

Mr. Theobald's remark that the word *old*, in the quarto edition, placed before this fpeech, refers to the word *Oldcaſtle*, cannot eaſily be refuted. Mr. Steevens's obſervation that *old* might ſtand for the beginning of an actor's ſurname is not very ſolid. The actor of Falſtaff was un‐doubtedly Lowin. On looking over the ſeveral liſts of actors names fixed to the editions of Shakſpeare, Ben Jonſon, and Beaumont and Fletcher, there is not one which begins with *Old*.

IDEM.

———You hunt counter.

With fubmiſſion to Dr. Johnſon and Mr. Steevens, I think Falſtaff by *hunt counter* alludes to the buſineſs of Tipſtaff, who, by the judges warrants, conveys of‐fenders

fenders to fafe cuftody. The chief juftice
talks of punifhing Falftaff by the heels;
and, if he had put his threat into execution, the officer then prefent with him
muft have been employed in that fervice.
The head of the law, in this fcene, does
not appear in the character of a private
gentleman, but dreffed in his robes of office, and, confequently, with proper atten-
dants to commit delinquents to prifon.

CHIEF JUSTICE.
Your wit is fingle.

I am always diffident of my opinion when I cannot affent to the judgement of two fuch eminent critics as Dr.
Johnfon and Mr. Steevens. The firft fuppofes that, by *fingle wit*, Shakfpeare means
that which is unfafhionable; and the
latter, that Falftaff had more fat than wit.
The chief juftice, in my opinion, intends
to reproach him with being folely mafter
of that wit which promoted diffipation,
licencioufnefs, and debauchery. That his
ideas and practice were perfectly conformable,

mable, he was become fo habituated to
loofe difcourfe and a profligate mode of
living, that he could not reform. In
fhort, fays the chief juftice, your wit is
confined to one fubject, you are a perfect
ftranger to reafoning on any topic, except
that which is connected with luxury, and
leads to the tavern or the bawdy-houfe.

The character of the chief juftice, in
this play, is that of grave dignity, and of
authority tempered with lenity. It was
rendered important, many years fince, by
Mr. Boman, the contemporary of Betterton; who maintained the ferious deportment of the judge with the graceful eafe of
the gentleman.

Scene III. Archbifhop of York, Haftings,
Mowbray, and Lord Bardolph.

HASTINGS.
——————— It never yet did hurt
To lay down likelihoods and forms of hope.

LORD BARDOLPH.
Yes, in this prefent quality of war,
Indeed of inftant action.

Mr.

Mr. Pope altered the reading of the two laſt lines thus :

> Yes, if this preſent quality of war
> Impede the inſtant act.

Which, ſays Dr. Johnſon, was ſilently embraced by Theobald, Sir T. Hanmer, and Dr. Warburton. But Dr. Johnſon, with diffidence, propoſes to read :

> Yes, in this preſent quality of war,
> Indeed of inſtant action.

Mr. Steevens thinks *impel* might be the word ; and Mr. Tollet ſuppoſes *inſtanced* might be admitted. I ſhall offer a very ſlight alteration, which may poſſibly re-ſtore the genuine reading :

> Yes, in this preſent quality of war,
> *In deed* of inſtant action.

By diſſolving the adverb, *indeed*, into the prepoſition *in* and the ſubſtantive *deed*, ſenſe is made of the paſſage, without any violence to the text. " It certainly (ſays Lord Bardolph) is hurtful to build upon fortuitous hopes, if by them we are tempted into action unprepared."

Act

Act II. Hoſtefs and officers.

HOSTESS.

I am undone by his going.

If Falſtaff goes to the wars without paying me his debt, I ſhall be ruined.

FALSTAFF.

Throw the quean into the kennel.

Quean is a word ſeldom uſed now. It
means, in general acceptation, a woman
lewd in her perſon, and vociferous in her
diſcourſe. Originally, ſays Verſtegan, it
ſignified a barren old cow.

HOSTESS.

Thou art a man queller.

The word *queller* was formerly written
cweller, and ſignified a troubler or tor-
mentor. Anciently, ſays Verſtegan, it
ſometimes meant a hangman.

FALSTAFF.

Away, you ſcullion! you rampallian! you fuſtilarian! I'll tickle your cataſtrophe!

This is certainly addreſſed to the hoſteſs.
Scullion is plain enough. Rampallian,
Mr.

Mr. Steevens fays, is an old rampant prof-
titute; and, we may add, perhaps, a
dealer in fuch goods. Fuftilarian is a
bitter farcafm, fignifying, from the word
fufty, that fhe was ftale and mufty. The
lady, in Gay's comedy of the Diftreffed
Wife, calls her own and her hufband's relations *old fufties*. As to *I'll tickle your ca-*
taftrophe, if we confider the fpeaker, and
to whom it was fpoken, the meaning
may be eafily gueffed.

FALSTAFF.

My lord, I will not undergo this fneap.

Mr. Pope has explained a *fneap* to be a rebuke. But Mr. Steevens, not content
with this, has (befides referring us to
Ray's Proverbs) produced no lefs than
three authorities to prove the fame thing;
for, what is to *check*, but to rebuke? *Sneap*
has, by lofing a letter, been changed into
fnap.——

HOSTESS.

I hope you will come to fupper.

Here this foolifh woman is cajoled by the knight to increafe her debt by pawning her plate,—and this is very eafily accounted for, by refolving her behaviour into the power of cuftom. The hoftefs could not endure the melancholy thoughts of having her rooms unoccupied by her old guefts, Falftaff and his companions.

Scene II. Prince and Poins.

POINS.

I will fteep this letter in fack, and make him eat it.

Mr. Steevens quotes the ftory of an apparitor who was obliged to eat a citation, wax and all, by the famous Robert Green. Modern times can produce nothing like this, except the contrivance of a noted gamefter, who, being determined at all events to win a pretty large fum of money, refolved to deftroy the evidence of a card againft him ; and, calling for two flices of bread and butter, and clapping the obnoxious witnefs between them, he fairly devoured it, and won the game.

PRINCE

PRINCE HENRY.

From a god to a bull ! a heavy defcenfion !

The word *heavy* feems to convey no appofite meaning. I fhould imagine Shakfpeare wrote *heavenly* defcenfion, and the
words which follow feem to juftify this
reading,—*It was 'Jove's cafe*. It was a defcent from heaven by Jupiter himfelf.
*From a prince to a 'prentice, a low transfor-
mation,* feems to be contrafted with the former metamorphofis.

Scene III. Northumberland, Lady Percy, &c.

LADY PERCY.

For thofe, who could fpeak low and tardily,
Would turn their own perfections to abufe
To feem like him.

This is the general practice of inferior
minds, to catch at, and imitate, the defects
of great fpirits, becaufe eafily attained,
rather than emulate their noble and generous qualities. This admirable fpeech of
Lady Percy, in which fhe endeavours to
U 2 diffuade

diffuade Northumberland from joining the
revolters, by putting him in mind of Hotfpur's fate, concludes with a moſt beautiful picture.

> Had my ſweet Harry had but half their numbers,
> To-day might I, hanging on Hotſpur's neck,
> Have talk'd of Monmouth's grave!

>   NORTHUMBERLAND.
> I will refolve for Scotland.

Notwithſtanding the Earl of Northumberland had been pardoned by the king,
foon after the battle of Shrewſbury, his
reſtleſs mind perſiſting in acts of rebellion,
he determined to join Archbiſhop Scroope,
but was prevented by forces ſent againſt
him, which apprehending he could not
reſiſt, he fled to Scotland; whence, after fome little ſtay, he retired to Wales
with Lord Bardolph. From Wales they
marched into Yorkſhire, and raiſed an army; but were oppoſed by the king's forces.
Northumberland was killed in the battle
of Bramham-more, and Lord Bardolph
died of the wounds he received there.

Scene

Scene IV.   Falſtaff and Doll.

F A L S T A F F.

A tame cheater, he.

By a very good note of Mr. Steevens on
this paſſage, in which he quotes Mihil
Mumchance, the gameſters were called
cheaters, and the dice *cheters*. I ſuppoſe
cheters were falſe dice, which in more
modern times are called *the doctors*.

P I S T O L.

Sweet knight, I kiſs thy neif.

Neif is the Scotch word, at this day, for
fiſt.

F A L S T A F F.

A raſcally ſlave ! to brave me !

This ſcene preſents us with a new character —— Piſtol ! a coward, who talks
big enough to frighten away fear. He
is an excellent portrait of the ſword
and buckler men, or bravoes, of Queen
Beſs's days, who were ready to ſhew
courage where no oppoſition would be
made.   Theſe were the bullies in the
houſes of entertainment of our author's
time.

time. Piftol is a hero, where fuch as Bardolph,
Nym, and Peto, are the underlings. He
feems to be an obvious character; and yet
it muft be owned that no actor, however
well inftructed and judicious, has gained
great applaufe in the reprefentation of the
burlefque and boifterous humour of Piftol fince it was played by Theophilus Cibber. He affumed a peculiar kind of falfe
fpirit, and uncommon bluftering, with
fuch turgid action, and long unmeafurable
ftrides, that it was impoffible not to laugh
at fo extravagant a figure, with fuch loud
and grotefque vociferation. He became fo
famous for his action in this part, that he
acquired the name of Piftol, at firft as a
mark rather of merit, but finally as a term
of ridicule. He was drawn in that character by Hogarth, with feveral other comedians who revolted from the patentees
of Drury-lane in 1733, and was brought
on the Covent-garden ftage. He was not
ill reprefented by Afton a fon of the famous Tony Afton, in a farce called The

Stage

Stage Mutineers, in 1734.*   The. Cibber
acted Piſtol when young, and Colley Cibber, his father, took unuſual pains to in-
ſtruct him.

U 4   C H A P-

---

* The firſt eight lines of the prologue to this forgotten piece have ſomething in them like humour :

Britons attend !——Infpir'd, the poet ſings
The fall of empires and the fate of kings !
Empires, by too much policy o'erthrown ;
And kings, expelled from kingdoms—not their own.
He ſings no fables, but domeſtic jars,
Heroic dudgeons, and theatric wars :
Wars without armies, battles without blool,
For ſeas of paſteboard, and for realms of wood.

CHAPTER XV.

*Mistake of Shakspeare.—Death of Glendower.—
Shallow and Silence.—Mr. Steevens.—Proof
that Falstaff was originally Sir John Old-
castle.—Sir Dagonet.—A fool not fit to represent one. — Justice Shallow. — John of
Ghent and the great Duke of Marlborough.
—Falstaff and Shallow. —— Ben Jonson
the actor. — Colley Cibber's art.—His admirable acting. — Treachery not stigma-
tized. — Who first beheaded prelates and
burned heretics. — Miracles put to flight.
—Falstaff's opinion of the effects of wine.—
Fish diet. — Falstaff and Hippocrates.—
Strabo, Diodorus Siculus, Aristotle, and
Dr. Falconer. — Duke of Clarence.—Cru-
sade to Jerusalem. — King Henry's character.—Actors of King Henry and Prince
of Wales.*

Act

Act III.   Scene, king, &c.

K I N G.

Though then, Heav'n knows, I had no such intent.

SHAKSPEARE forgets that, before this interview between Richard and Northumberland, Henry had laid claim to the crown, and was proclaimed king.

W A R W I C K.

———————————— I have receiv'd
A certain instance that Glendower is dead.

Instance for *information.*   Glendower was pardoned, at the request of David Holbeck, Esq. by the king ; but, being driven to great straits, and reduced to wander from place to place, he perished for mere want.*

Scene II.   Shallow, Silence.

S H A L L O W.
How does your fair daughter ?

S I L E N C E.
Alas ! a black ouzle.

My

* Stowe.

My daughter is fo far from being fair, as
you term her, that fhe is of a very dark
complection.

S H A L L O W.

And page to Thomas Mowbray, Duke of Norfolk.

In a note on this paffage, Mr. Reed brings
fome obfervations, from a poem of J.
Weever, and a pamphlet called The Travel-
ling Jew, which tend to prove that Shakfpeare altered the name of Oldcaftle to Falftaff. Mr. Steevens, as if the honour of
Shakfpeare were mightily concerned in this
matter, fets himfelf with great vigour to
oppofe thefe proofs, and thinks it very
ftrange that, becaufe Shakfpeare borrowed
a fingle circumftance from the Life of the
real Oldcaftle, and imparted it to the ficti-
tious Falftaff, it fhould be inferred that
the name of the former fhould be a cover
to the vices of the latter. But is it true
that there is but one circumftance common
to both knights? The contrary can, without much difficulty, be proved. That

Sir

Sir John Oldcaftle, before the acceffion of Henry V. to the crown, was much about his perfon, nay, one of his domeftics, we learn from the Life of that king, written in Latin by T. Livius. — *Erant namque, per id temporis, milites duo equeftris ordinis, Joannes Oldcaftle, (qui ante coronationem regis ab ipfo, propter has opiniones, dimiffus fuerat, et ab ejus famulatu penitus abjectus,) et Joannes Acton.*

That Sir John Oldcaftle had been guilty of many and great irregularities, we have his own confeffion, in thefe words, recorded in Bale's Chronicle of his Life. " And with that he kneeled down on the pavement, holding up his hands towards heaven, and faid, ' *I fhrive* * *me here unto thee, my eternal living God, that, in my frail youth, I offended the Lord moft grievoufly, in pride, wrath, and gluttony, in covetoufnefs and lechery ; many men have I hurt in mine anger, and done many other horrible fins.*"

Oldcaftle

---

* Confefs,

Oldcaſtle was extremely hateful to the clergy on many accounts : not content with cenſuring the doctrine, they preached, with unbounded freedom, he endeavoured to prove that they were become an order of men totally unneceſſary, and a burden to the ſtate. By reproaching them with their grandeur and magnificence, he plainly manifeſted that he would greatly leſſen, if not entirely deprive, them of their revenues. He ſeems to have had, at leaſt, full as much zeal as knowledge. When ſummoned before the heads of the church, he treated them with an aſperity of language which no body of men would tolerate.

He told them at his trial, ' *That they never followed Chriſt ſince the venom was ſhed in the church.*' When the archbiſhop of Canterbury aſked him what he meant by that venom. He replied, ' *Your poſſeſſions and lordſhips:*' he went on to ſay ' *That Chriſt was poor and forgave. The pope is rich and a cruel manſlayer. Rome is the very neſt*

neſt of Antichriſt, and of that neſt came all his diſciples ; of whom, prelates, prieſts, and monks, are the body, and theſe ſhaven friers the tail, which cover his moſt filthy part.'

Can we doubt that the clergy would embrace every opportunity to encourage ſuch repreſentations of Oldcaſtle's character as would tend to make him an objeċt of ſcorn and ridicule ?   I am convinced that Oldcaſtle was made the jack-pudding in all the common interludes of public exhibition.   He was a liar, a glutton, a profane ſwearer, and a coward ; in ſhort, any thing that might render him odious to the common people.

That Shakſpeare found him ſuch, it is reaſonable to imagine, and that he adopted the name of Oldcaſtle in his firſt ſketch of the ſcenes of licencious gaiety between the prince of Wales and the fat knight.

When the Reformation was eſtabliſhed, in the reign of Queen Elizabeth, the Proteſtants claimed Oldcaſtle as a proto-martyr in their cauſe ; conſequently, all repreſentations

prefentations of him in a ludicrous light on the ftage became offenfive to ferious people : and hence we may conclude, that, though Shakfpeare had inadvertently been furprifed into the ufe of Oldcaftle's name, he foon relinquifhed it, by giving one lefs offenfive to his favourite character.

MOULDY.
You fhall have forty, fir.

You fhall have an equal fum to what Bull-calf has offered; four Harry, ten fhillings, or forty fhillings.

FALSTAFF.
For you, Mouldy, ftay at home till you are paft fervice.

This is the fecond time Sir John has mif-ufed the king's prefs-money *damnably*, as he terms it. Modern times will furnifh many inftances of fuccefsful imitators of Jack Falftaff; of men who have, as fhame-fully and with equal impunity, robbed the king and the people of their money.

SHALLOW.
I was then Sir Dagonet in the play.

I be-

I believe Sir Arthur Addle, in the comedy of Sir Solomon Single, was taken from Sir Dagonet.

I do not entirely agree with Mr. Malone, that Shallow's acting Sir Dagonet was a proof of his folly; for he that performs the fool well is not a fool.

FALSTAFF.

He beat his own name.

John of Ghent, or Gaunt, was so named from Ghent, the place of his birth. But Ghent is pronounced as the French word *gans*, gloves. To this pun, I think, Falstaff alludes, and not to Shallow's being gaunt or lean. *The truffing him and his whole apparel into an ell-skin* seems to favour my conjecture. This sort of quibble was applied to the great Duke of Marlborough; who, at the close of the campaign in 1709, and on the eve of winter, having besieged and taken the same city of Ghent, the news-writers quaintly said, his Grace declared he could not at that time of the year cross the water without

Ghent,

Ghent, or *gloves*, to keep him warm. —
Vide Annals of Queen Anne.

In this fcene Shakfpeare exerts his power
to fupport an equal comic vein with his
dialogue in the firft part of this hiftory.
It cannot be denied that, however rich the
humour is in the former play, he fhews
little or no inferiority in this. Falftaff
and Shallow form an admirable contraft:
the barrennefs of the country-fquire fets
off the fecundity of the knight. They are
both egregious liars; and, though Falftaff's inventions are more fruitful in matter and brighter in fancy, the lies of Shallow, though of a colder complexion, entertain from their charaƈteriftic formation.

That Kempe aƈted Shallow originally, the
diligence of Mr. Malone, I think, has proved.
I do not fee any authority to fuppofe that
the fecond part of Henry IV. was revived,
immediately after the Reftoration, nor till
about the middle or latter end of Queen
Anne's

Anne's reign, when Dogget perſonated Shallow.

When John Rich, Eſq. opened his theatre in Lincoln's-inn-fields, in 1715, Booth, Wilks, and Cibber, the managers of Drury-lane, ſolicitous to retain in their ſervice comedians of merit, paid a particular reſpect to B. Johnſon the actor, and gave him, beſides an addition to his income, ſuch parts of Dogget (who had taken his leave of them) as were of moſt conſequence and beſt adapted to his manner. Amongſt the reſt was the part of Juſtice Shallow. But Colley Cibber took ſuch a fancy to the merry, ignorant, and fooliſh, old rake, that, upon Jonſon's ſudden illneſs, he made himſelf maſter of the part, and performed it ſo much to the ſatisfaction of the public, that he retained it as long as he remained upon the ſtage. Cibber, in his Apology, whether from real or affected modeſty, alledges that he was, in moſt of his characters, no more than a cloſe imitator of all ſuch players as had formerly reprefented them. This was the cafe in his Fondlewife; in which he copied fo exactly the tone of voice, manner, and drefs, of Dogget, that the audience, he fays, at firft believed him to be that celebrated comedian.

Whether he was a copy or an original in Shallow, it is certain that no audience was ever more fixed in deep attention, at his firft appearance, or more fhaken with laughter in the progrefs of the fcene, than at Colley Cibber's exhibition of this ridiculous juftice of peace. Some years after he had left the ftage, he acted Shallow for his fon's benefit. I believe in 1737, when Quin was the Falftaff, and Milward the king. Whether it was owing to the pleafure the fpectators felt on feeing their old friend return to them again, *though for that night only*, after an abfence of fome years, I know not; but, furely, no actor or audience were better pleafed with each other. His manner was fo perfectly fimple, his look fo vacant, when he queftioned his

Coufin

Coufin Silence about the price of ewes,
and lamented, in the fame breath, with
filly furprife, the death of Old Double,
that it will be impoffible for any furviving
fpectator not to fmile at the remembrance
of it. The want of ideas occafions Shallow to repeat almoft every thing he fays.
Cibber's tranfition from afking the price of
bullocks, to trite, but grave, reflections
on mortality, was fo natural, and attended with fuch an unmeaning roll of his
fmall pigs-eyes, accompanied with an important utterance of tick! tick! tick! not
much louder than the balance of a watch's
pendulum, that I queftion if any actor
was ever fuperior in the conception or
expreffion of fuch folemn infignificancy.

Jonfon, a year or two after Cibber had
left the ftage, and, when he was between
feventy and eighty, undertook the part of
Shallow; and though the old hound had loft
almoft all his teeth, he was ftill fo ftaunch,
that he feized his game and held it faft.

It

It is true that, however chafte he was in his colouring and correct in his drawing, he wanted the high finifhing and warm tints of Colley Cibber ; yet his acting was fuch as we may defpair to fee excelled, if equalled : for, though that excellent comedian, Mr. Yates, has often given great pleafure in Shallow, I cannot think that he is fo abfolutely juft, in the delineation of the part, as Ben Jonfon. Mr. Parfons has, of late years, played Shallow with that happy mirth and glee which is fure to captivate an audience : for who can be grave when Parfons either looks or fpeaks?

Whether Jonfon confidered his being deprived of Shallow, for almoft twenty years, as a manager's trick, or difhoneft manœuvre of Colley Cibber, is not known ; but the old man never fpoke of him with any complacency.

Act IV.   Scene, Archbifhop of York, &c.

The interview of the infurgents, and the Earl of Weftmoreland and Duke of Lancafter,

caſter, with their armies in ſight, was never repreſented with any warm tokens of
approbation from the auditors, who always
diſmiſſed it with indifference ; and, indeed,
it appeared generally dull and unintereſt-
ing ; but, whether this was owing to deficiency in the acting, or the frittering of
the ſcene by the prompter, or any other
cauſe, it is not eaſy to be decided. Perhaps we may with juſtice attribute the
cold behaviour of the ſpectators to the
ſcene itſelf, which, however ſkilfully written, is not calculated to excite the paſſions
or to raiſe applauſe.

LANCASTER.
Some guard theſe traitors to the block of death.

This maſterpiece of infamous treachery
and breach of compact, as related by our
poet, is taken pretty exactly from Hollingſhead and Stowe, though it is differently related by Hall, who makes the account
much more honourable to the royaliſts.
He ſays the apprehending the biſhop and
his confederates was an action of ſurpriſe.
However, all later hiſtorians copy the two

X 3   firſt

firft Chronicles, and, what is very furprifing, this perfidious breach of faith paffes
without cenfure of any writer from Hollingfhead to Hume. Our author is furely to blame for not marking this tranfaction with a proper ftigma: he might have
done it in very forcible terms from the
mouth of the archbifhop of York or Lord
Mowbray, who ftrenuoufly oppofed the
proffered treaty.

The archbifhop of York, fays Hall, requefted the executioner, when at the block,
to cut off his head with five ftrokes, in remembrance of the five wounds of Chrift.
In confequence of this, it was reported,
that, when the king fat at dinner, he received five ftrokes by an invifible hand,
and was inftantly feized with a leprofy:
but this, fays Hall, in great wrath, was a
manifeft lie. However, the fuperftitious
people believed the archbifhop was a faint,
and many miracles, like thofe of Abbé
Paris, were wrought at his grave, till
Henry, by his authority, frightened away
the people and the miracles at the fame time.

Scroope

Scroope was the firſt biſhop in England
that ſuffered death for treaſon or any other
crime ; Henry was the firſt of our kings
who burned heretics and beheaded prelates,

Scene III.

F A L S T A F F.

A man cannot make him laugh : but that's no mar-
vel ; he drinks no wine. Thin drinks do ſo over-cool
the blood, and making many fiſh-meals, that they fall
into ą kind of male green-ſickneſs ; and, when they
marry, they get wenches.

What Shakſpeare ſays ludicrouſly of thin
potations, or water-drinking, is confirmed
by no leſs authority than that of Hippocrates himſelf, in his Treatiſe on Diet,
lib. 1. ſect. 20. It has likewiſe been proved,
that, in the Eaſt-Indies, where they drink
no wine, the number of the women ex-
ceeds that of the men conſiderably.

As to fiſh-diet, the common opinion is
againſt Falſtaff ; for it is by many ſuppoſed to be of a prolific nature. This was
hinted by Arbuthnot in his Treatiſe on
Diet, and ſuggeſted by Monteſquieu in his
Spirit of Laws. Haller and Dr. Reynold

X 4   Foſter

Foster are of a different opinion. However, as far as filence on the fubject may
be allowed to fpeak for the jolly knight's
opinion, the ancient hiftorians are on his
fide : for neither Strabo, Diodorus Siculus, nor Arrian,* (all of whom have defcribed feveral nations living on fifh-diet,)
have mentioned this quality belonging to
it, or obferved that fuch countries were
more than commonly populous. There is
another quality charged upon fifh, which
is ftill more remarkable. Whether the authority of Diodorus Siculus be fo weighty
as to gain any credit, I muft leave to the
reader : but he declares that conftant ea-
ters of fifh are endued with a remarkable apathy, or infenfibility, not only to the
fentiments of the mind, but alfo to fome
of the natural appetites.

I D E M.

Skill in the weapon is nothing without fack. A good
fherris fack hath a twofold operation in it : it afcends
me into the brain, and dries me all the foolifh and dull
vapours.

With

---

* Falconer on folid food.

With Falftaff, wine is the promoter of
courage and every good quality of the
mind.

Athenæus, fays Dr. Falconer, makes
an obfervation fimilar to this. It is true ;
and I could quote many Greek verfes to
prove it : but the doctor knows there
are fo many precepts from various poets,
and other writers, quoted by the fame author, againft the immoderate ufe of
wine, that Falftaff's followers would lofe
more than they got by the authority of
Athenæus. After this long note on fifh
and wine, I hope the reader will pardon
a quotation from Ariftotle's Problems ;
in which that philofopher gives an accurate defcription of the progrefs of
wine, and the effects of its immoderate
ufe.

' When a fober, moderate, and filent
man drinks wine in a quantity more liberal than ordinary, it has the effect of che-
rifhing and roufing his fpirits and genius,
and rendering him more communicative :

if

if taken ftill more freely, he becomes talkative, eloquent, and confident of his abilities: if taken in ftill larger quantities, it
renders him bold and daring, and defirous
to exert himfelf in action: if he perfift in
a more plentiful dofe, it makes him petulant and contumelious. The next ftep
renders him mad and outrageous, Should
he proceed ftill farther, he becomes ftupid
and fenfelefs.' Ariftot. Probl. fect. 30.

Scene IV.   King, Warwick, Clarence,
Glofter.

KING.

Nothing but well to thee, Thomas of Clarence.

The king's recommending to the Duke of
Clarence a particular obfervance of his brother the Prince of Wales, and affuring
him of the prince's affection for him, is
grounded upon a converfation between the
king and prince, recorded by Stowe; in
which the former puts the latter on his
guard

guard againſt the machinations of Clarence. The uſe which Shakſpeare makes
of this hiſtorical incident every reader will
ſee and approve.

I D E M.
Towards fronting peril and oppos'd decay.

That is, to deſperate adventures and aſ-
ſured deſtruction.

C L A R E N C E.
The river hath thrice flow'd; no ebb between!

The ſhort reign of this king was ſignalized by many ſad diſaſters. Beſides this
extraordinary flow of the flood, which
Mr. Stevens authenticates, a moſt de-
ſtructive plague depopulated the whole
kingdom. In London no leſs than thirty
thouſand were deſtroyed by it ; and the
king, endeavouring to retire by water to
Eſſex, very narrowly eſcaped being taken
by ſome armed veſſels from France.

The much-admired interview, between
the King and the Prince of Wales, owes
its beauty principally to ſituation and character.

racter. The taking away the crown by
the prince produces a moſt pathetic dialogue; ſuch perhaps as no writer, except
Shakſpeare, could draw from ſo ſlender an
incident. Where the heart ſpeaks, no ornament of words is neceſſary : the more
plain and ſimple the diction, the more affecting it will be. Such is the ſcene, though
ſtill more intereſting, between Queen Katharine and Griffith, in the fourth act of
Henry VIII. where that princeſs takes
leave of the world, with a noble grandeur
of mind, in expreſſions the moſt feeling,
and at the ſame time the moſt familiar and
unadorned.

The great expiation of ſin, in the days
of Henry, was eſteemed to be a cruſade to
the Holy Land; and, though I once imagined he was not ſincere in his intention
of undertaking the expedition, yet I know
not whether motives religious and political
might not have co-operated to urge him to
it. He certainly made great preparations for it, and it is as certain that
                                            his

his fon, Henry V. as a proof of his piety, on his death-bed declared, that if he had recovered from his illnefs, it was his firm refolution to refcue, if poffible, the Holy Land from the infidels. This paffion of delivering the Holy Sepulchre was fo predominant for a long time, that the Countefs of Richmond, mother of Henry VII. declared, if the Chriftian princes would undertake a crufade, fhe would herfelf turn laundrefs and wafh their linen for them.

If it were poffible that any thing could reconcile us to an ufurper and the murderer of his fovereign, it muft be the deep remorfe and fincere compunction which the offender feels for crimes fo atrocious. Had Henry been the next heir to the crown, his wickednefs would not have been lefs; but the people would not have fuffered from infurrections in favour of Roger Mortimer, the rightful fucceffor by birth. This circumftance rendered his whole reign one continued fcene of tumult,

battle.

battle, and bloodfhed ; and involved his
pofterity and the kingdom in the longeft
and moft fanguinary war that ever afflicted
a nation. However he may have been
cried up by the clergy for his piety in per-
fecuting the followers of Wickliffe, and being the firft king of England who burned
heretics, it is well known that he and his
father John of Gaunt, (who were the great
patrons of Wicliffe,) when they underftood
that the clergy poffeffed almoft half the revenues of the kingdom, declared that they
would clip their wings ; or ufed words to that
purpofe. But the king ftood in need of the
clergy as much as they did of him. Henry's
conftant jealoufy and fear of lofing the crown
may be forgiven ; for that was a juft part
of his punifhment for feifing it : but his
cruelty, in fhedding torrents of blood to
maintain the crown, can only be juftified
by the tyrant's law, neceffity; a neceffity
which he had impofed on himfelf.

Almoft all the actors, who have for
more than thefe laft fifty years reprefented
this

this pathetic fcene of the king and his fon,
have been fortunate in engaging the attention and raifing the affections of their
auditors. Booth, who played the king,
and Wilkes, who acted the prince, were
highly accomplifhed, and underftood dignity and grace of action and deportment,
with all the tender paffions of the heart,
in a fuperior degree. The elder Mills, in
the king, and his fon, an imitator of
Wilks's manner, in the prince, followed
almoft immediately thefe confummate actors; and though they were by no means
equal to them, were above mediocrity, e-
fpecially the father in Henry, which happened to be the laft part this worthy man
appeared in. He was taken ill a few days
after he had acted it, and died, I believe,
in November, 1736. His name was announced in the bills for Macbeth, but
Quin was obliged to fupply his place. I
faw him hurrying to the playhoufe between
five and fix in the evening. Milward, the
fucceffor of Mills in Henry, was, in pathos,

thos, greatly his fuperior. His countenance was finely expreffive of grief, and the plaintive tones of his voice were admirably adapted to the languor of a dying perfon, and to the fpeech of an offended yet affectionate parent. Garrick's figure did not affift him in the perfonating of this character, but the forcible expreffion of his countenance and his energy of utterance made ample amends for defect of perfon. To defcribe the anguifh, mixed with terror, which he feemed to feel when he caft up his eyes to heaven, and pronounced thefe words,

How I came by the crown, O God, forgive me!

would call for the pencil of a Raphael or a Reynolds.

Though Garrick, from a mean jealoufy, a paffion which conftantly preyed on his mind, denied to Powel the merit of underftanding the pathos of this celebrated fcene, the audience thought far otherwife, and, by their tears and applaufe, juftified the action of that very pleafing tragedian.

In

In the laſt lingering ſtage of life, when worn by complicated diſtemper, and tormented with afflicting pains of the gout, the ſick and emaciated Barry undertook to repreſent the dying ſcenes of Henry. In perſon, if we conſult hiſtory, he was better adapted to the part than any of his predeceſſors; for almoſt all the princes of the Plantagenet line were remarkable for procerity : but that was but a trifling requiſite in this great actor. The fatherly reproofs and earneſt admonitions, from the conſequence imparted by Barry's pleaſing manner, as well as noble figure, acquired authority and importance. His feelings were, perhaps, heightened by the anxiety of his mind in the declining ſtate of his health, and the frequent pains of his cruel diſtemper. From his ſetting ſun, which emitted a warm though glimmering ray, ſpectators might form a judgement what Barry had been in his meridian glory.

CHAPTER XVI.

*Retrospect on Lowin, and several other come-
dians, who lived during the civil war.*

BEFORE I take my leave of Henry IV.
I cannot forbear reflecting, with
some concern, upon the fate of honest
Jack Falstaff; I mean John Lowin, the
original actor of this inimitable character;
and his constant friend and fellow-labourer,
Joseph Taylor, the first actor of Hamlet.

When the civil wars shut the doors of
the theatres, many of the comedians, who
had youth, spirit, and vigour of body,
took up arms in the defence of their royal
master. When they could no longer serve
him by the profession of acting, they boldly
vindicated his cause in the field. Those,
who were too far advanced in age to give
martial proofs of their attachment to royalty, were reduced to the alternative of
starving or engaging in some employment

to

to ſupport their wants. Lowin and Taylor were, in the fatal æra of our civil diſ-
ſenſions, got beyond their grand climac-
teric: for Taylor had acted Hamlet almoſt forty-five years before that time, and
Lowin had, for at leaſt forty-two years,
delighted the public in Falſtaff.

The fanatical zeal of the Nonconformiſts
could bear no exhibitions or ſhows but
their own: all ſtage-plays theſe religioniſts
looked upon as profane; and devoted the
actors, whom they denominated the children of Satan, to perdition. That tedious
writer, William Prynne, in his Hiſtrio-
maſtix, had, with as much folly as brutality, involved the king and queen in
the guilt of encouraging, by their preſence,
the Satanical diverſions of the theatre. To
read and amuſe himſelf with the writings of
Shakſpeare, the great Milton moſt ſhame-
fully charged upon Charles as a crime:
though Milton himſelf was a profeſſed admirer of our great bard. Such is the ma-
lignant ſpirit of party! and ſo little able

are

are the nobleſt minds to reſiſt its influence!

During the firſt years of the unnatural
conteſt between the king and parliament,
the players were not unwelcome gueſts to
thoſe towns and cities which eſpouſed the
royal cauſe: but, in London, where bigotry and oppoſition to the king were triumphant, they experienced nothing but
perſecution. A few of the nobility, indeed, who loved the amuſements of the
ſtage, encouraged the players to act in their
houſes privately: but the watchful eye of
furious zealots prevented all public exhibitions; except, as the author of Hiſtoria
Hiſtrionica aſſerts, now and then ſuch as
were given with great caution and privacy.
Some time before the beheading of the unhappy Charles, a company of comedians
was formed out of the wreck of ſeveral,
who played at the Cockpit three or four
times: but, while they were acting Fletcher's Bloody Brother, the ſoldiers, ruſhing
in, put an end to the play, and carried
the

the actors to Hatton-houfe, at that time a fort of prifon for royal delinquents; where they were confined two or three days, and, after being ftripped of their ftage-apparel, were difcharged. In this tragedy, Lowin acted Aubrey, and Taylor Rollo.

The governing powers, however they might exert themfelves to fupprefs ftage-plays by violence, did not, by any formal act of ftate, prohibit their reprefentation till October, 1647, and the February following; when the Long Parliament iffued two ordinances, by which all ftage-plays and interludes were abfolutely forbidden, under very fevere penalties.

Much about this time, as far as I can collect from the little that has been handed down to us of thefe eminent men, Lowin kept the Three Pigeons at Brentford, where he was attended by Jofeph Taylor; but, whether as friend, affiftant, or partner, cannot be determined. Here they lingered out an uncomfortable exiftence, with fcarce any other means of

Y 3   fupport

fupport than thofe which they obtained
from the friends of royalty and the old
lovers of the drama, who now and then
paid them a vifit, and left them marks of
their bounty. Upon thefe occafions Lowin
and Taylor gave their vifitors a tafte of
their quality. The firft roufed up the
fpirit and humour of Falftaff. Again the
fat old rogue fwore that he knew the prince
and Poins as well as he that made them.
Hamlet, too, raifed the vifionary terrors
of the Ghoft, and filled his felect auditors
with terror and amazement! To entertain their guefts, we muft fuppofe they
affumed various perfonages, and alter-
nately excited merriment and grief. How
often were thefe honeft fellows furprifed
into a belief of the good news that the
king and parliament had come to a treaty!
that peace would be reftored, and the king
return to his capital in triumph! How
would their countenances then be lighted up
with joy, the glafs cheerfully circulate,
and

and the meeting be difmiffed with *The king fhall enjoy his own again!*

Their honeft friend and affociate, Goff, the actor of womens parts at Black-friers and the Globe, was the ufual jackall to fummon the fcattered comedians together, that they might exhibit at Holland-houfe, or fome nobleman's feat, within a few miles of the capital.* The want of fine clothes, and the proper ornaments of a theatre, was excufed by their noble employers; for the perfeverance of their furious perfecutors, and the violence and rapacity of the foldiers, had rendered it hazardous to wear any coftly garments. Painted cloth ferved as a good fubftitute to rich habits and royal trains.

In thefe diftracted times what became of thofe comedians who had reprefented queens, princeffes, and other females, in Shakfpeare's, Ben Jonfon's, Beaumont and Fletcher's, and Maffinger's, plays, at this

Y 4   diftance

---

* Hiftoria Hiftrionica.

distance of time cannot be learned;
for no hiftorical trace of them is to be
found. The two moft celebrated of
thefe performers, were John Thomfon
and John Hunnieman. The laft was the
author of a play, with the name of which
I fhould be glad to enrich the dramatic catalogue, but I cannot learn whether it was
a tragedy, a comedy, or a mixture of
both. From a copy of verfes, to the author, by Sir Afton Cockaine, we are informed that this dramatic piece was much
approved by the public : as Sir Afton's e-
piftle contains the only information of
Hunnieman's authorfhip, I fhall tranfcribe
it as a theatrical curiofity :

To Mr. John Hunnieman.

On, hopeful youth, and let thy happy ftrain
Redeem the glory of the ftage again ;
Leffen the lofs of Shakfpeare's death, by thy
Succefsful pen and fortunate phantafy.
He did not only write but act, and fo
Thou doft not only act, but writeft too.
Between you there no difference appears,
But what may be made up with equal years,

This

This is my fuffrage, and I fcorn my pen
Should crown the heads of undeferving men.

Great muſt have been the loſs of this play to the public, if Hunnieman was a rival of Shakſpeare, as is fuggeſted by Sir Aſton.

Of all the players, mentioned in any narrative relative to the Engliſh ſtage, Eylæard Swanſton, the fucceſſor of Burbage in the character of Othello, was the only one who profeſſed himſelf a Preſbyterian, and an avowed friend of the parliament, in oppoſition to the royal cauſe. I will not go ſo far as Charles II. who told a nobleman that Preſbyterianiſm *was a religion not fit for a gentleman*; but I much doubt whether Swanſton's zeal did not abridge his charity. —— A convert is often a narrow-minded bigot, and poor Lowin, Taylor, and the reſt of his old friends, could not expect, from one of Calamy's congregation, any kind retroſpect of friendſhip.*

But

* The author of Hiſtoria Hiſtrionica ſays, Swanſton took up the trade of a jeweller. I ſhould imagine that he had been originally bred one, and left jewelling for the ſtage.

But the only man, who triumphed over the wild fanaticifm and cruel hypocrify of the times, was that excellent comedian Robert Cox, whofe name I do not fee in any of the old lifts of actors.

When all the theatres were filenced, Cox employed himfelf in compofing fmall interludes, called *drolls*, like fuch as were formerly acted at Bartholomew and Southwark fairs. The moft ferious of thefe pieces, fuch as Acteon and Diana, and Oenone, had a dafh of the comic in them, though, for the moft part, they were farces of one act, with finging and dancing; as *Hobbinol, Singing Simpfon,* and *Simpleton the Smith.** By the connivance of the ftate Cerberus's, to whom this adroit fellow flily gave an opiate or fop of *aurum palpabile,* he contrived to get his pieces acted to full houfes at the Red Bull Theatre, under the colour of rope-dancing. Cox acted the principal parts himfelf, and with fuch life, fpirit, and nature, that he
reftored

---

* Langbaine.

reſtored to the people the long-forgotten cuſtom of widening their jaws into riſibility;
for, to laugh, in thoſe days of hyprocriſy, was
a mortal ſin.   When he played young Simpleton the Smith at a country fair, he ſo delighted the noted maſter of a forge, in thoſe
parts, that he very gravely offered to take him
for his journeyman, and to allow him
twelvepence per week more than the reſt.
" I would accept your proffer with all my
heart, (ſaid Cox,) *but you I ſee have a good
ſhop of my own.*"

This comedian travelled all over the
kingdom with his company, which conſiſted, I think, of himſelf, a man, and a
boy.   The univerſities themſelves opened
their arms to entertain this maſter of merriment.   When he went to Stourbridge Fair,
Cox did not forget to renew his acquaintance with the heads of houſes.   At Oxford he ſo far got into the good graces of
a poetical butler, that he was pleaſed to
oblige him with a prologue, that he might
appear in form, as he had formerly ſeen

the

the members of a college, when they acted
a play at Chriftmas.*

By purfuing this method of itinerant exhibition, and by never ftaying long at a
place, this comedian acquired confiderable fums of money, and I have not the leaft
doubt that he fhared a good part of his
profits with his old fuperannuated friends
at Brentford. The players are, of all people, the moft alive to the feelings of humanity, and the readieft to relieve one a-
nothers wants. Let us confider Cox as
the good Samaritan, who poured balm into the wounds of poor Lowin and Taylor, and fometimes cheered their hearts in
the midft of their diftreffes. Thefe,
indeed, were greatly increafed after the beheading of the king and the extirpation of
monarchy. The players, however, tranf-
ferred their allegiance to the fon of their
unhappy fovereign, and, amongft their
friends and well-wifhers, drank a health,
we may reafonably believe, *to their king
over the water*. A toaft that might be
given

* Langbaine.

given *at that time* with propriety as well as loyalty.

In 1647, Shirley publifhed the plays of Beaumont and Fletcher, I believe, with a view chiefly to relieve the wants of the fur- viving actors, who had diftinguifhed them- felves in the principal characters of thefe writers. The names of Jofeph Taylor, John Lowin, Theophilus Bird, Robert Benfield, Stephen Hammerton,* Thomas Pollard,† and Richard Robinfon, are fub- fcribed to a dedication prefented to the Earl of Pembroke, the patron of drama- tic poetry.

In 1652, Taylor and Lowin, being arri- ved to a very great age, and in very indi- gent circumftances, publifhed Fletcher's comedy of the Wild-Goofe Chafe for their mutual advantage: it was ufhered into the

world

---

* This player was firft a famous reprefenter of wo- mens characters, and, afterwards, as much celebrated for a graceful actor of mens parts.

† Pollard was more fortunate than the reft of his af- fociates, having a fortune of his own, he retired into the country, and lived with his relations.

world with an advertifement, in which they modeftly intimated their wants, and called upon the benevolence of all who had a tafte for the drama.

I fhould not forget that Jofeph Taylor was the friend of Philip Maffinger; that he infcribed to him a copy of verfes on the fuccefs of his Roman Actor, in which tragedy Taylor performed the principal part.

My very learned and kind friend, the Reverend Mr. Bowle, of Idmifton, has informed me that he has read a copy of verfes of Shakerly Marmion, author of the Antiquary and feveral other dramatic pieces, to Jofeph Taylor, upon his prefentment of The Faithful Shepherdefs, in which he ftyles him his worthy friend.

The exact time, when Taylor and Lowin died, cannot be traced; but, it is certain, they paid the debt to nature fome few years before the Reftoration. Lowin died at Brentford, and Taylor at Richmond.

CHAP-

CHAPTER XVII.

King Henry VIII.

Reasons why this play was written in the reign of Queen Elizabeth.—King James's dislike to the family of Tudor accounted for.—His love of poetry and regard for Shakspeare. — The author's difficulty in drawing a portrait of Henry VIII. *— Merit of the play. — The prologue and its author. — Interview of two kings in the vale of Arde. — Buckingham and Wolsey.—Passages explained.—Generosity of the French king.— Somerset's contempt of the French. — Word* royal *explained.—And the word* fierce.*— Character of the Emperor Charles* V. *— Wolsey's immense revenues. — Cibber's Wolsey.—Mossop and Digges.—The author's admirable portraitures of English princes.— Betterton's excellent acting of Henry* VIII. *— The Wolsey of Harris. — His various merit in comedy and tragedy.—Booth's Harry* VIII.*—Quin, Harper, Price, and Nokes.*

MR.

MR. Malone has laboured ſtrenuouſly, and, I think, ſucceſsfully, to prove that the hiſtorical play of Henry VIII. muſt have been acted during the life-time of Queen Elizabeth. Several paſſages of the play may be produced, which, from their internal evidence, would farther convince us that the author could not have projected ſuch a piece in the reign of James I.

But there is yet a ſtronger reaſon for inſiſting upon this argument than what has been hitherto produced: our author could not be unacquainted with the extreme averſion which James had entertained, long before he mounted the throne of England, to his predeceſſor; an averſion that could not be extinguiſhed by her deceaſe.

Upon his acceſſion to the crown, nobody durſt appear before him in a mourning habit for that princeſs. Sully, the French ambaſſador, who had been particularly enjoined by his maſter Henry IV. to pay that decent reſpect which was due to the memory

memory of his friend and ally, was obliged to throw afide the mourning drefles
he had purchafed for himfelf and retinue,
upon being informed that, if he perfifted
in his defign, he would not eafily gain an
audience of the king. James's averfion to
the family of his predeceffor was univerfally
known; and, though he pretended to be
angry with Sir Walter Raleigh for the fevere character of Henry VIII. which he had
given in the preface to his Hiftory of the
World, yet it was well known that his
own opinion coincided with that of the
hiftorian.

The king's diflike to the Tudor family
was not founded on mere caprice. Henry
VIII. in his laft will, had, as far as was in
his power, by not mentioning them, ex-
cluded, from the throne of England, the
whole Scottifh race; for he preferred the
defcendants from his younger fifter, of the
houfe of Brandon, to the offspring of Mar-
garet, the elder fifter, who was married to
James IV. of Scotland. Queen Elizabeth,

befides the putting his mother, under the
form of law, to an ignominious death, had
treated James himfelf with infufferably affumed haughtinefs and fuperiority. She
deferred the nomination of his fucceffion
to the throne of England to the laft moments of her life.

The king, who was a lover of the mu-
fes, and had facrificed to them himfelf in
his early days, conferred marks of royal
favour upon Shakfpeare, almoft as foon as
he took poffeffion of his new dominions;
and the poet was too good a courtier to
write a play upon a fubject which was to
include a laboured panegyric on the king's
hated predeceffor and her family.

It was no eafy tafk for an author to com-
pofe a dramatic piece which fhould comprehend feveral tranfactions of a monarch
recently dead, who had rendered himfelf fo
odious to his fubjects. To bring upon the
ftage, before the reigning queen, his daughter, a character fo doubtful, at leaft, as
her royal father; to prefent a ftrong refemblance

blance of many of his moft ftriking features, without alarming his fovereign, or
difgufting the fpectators; was an undertaking worthy the genius of Shakfpeare; and
in which, notwithftanding the apparent
difficulty, he has admirably fucceeded.

Although this play, on a fuperficial
view, contains nothing but a tiffue of
pomp and ceremony, made out of mafques
and trials, a coronation and a chriftening,
it abounds in ftriking events, which embrace the fates of important characters,—
with paffions which excite our terror and
commiferation, and with profound mora-
lity, which tends to moderate, to humble,
and to rectify, the mind.

The prologue, like moft compofitions
of that fort in our author's days, is little
more than good fenfe put into meafured
profe. Our laft editors, and their affif-
tants, fufpect, with reafon, that it was not
entirely the work of Shakfpeare. Ben
Jonfon, it is fuppofed, wrote the greateft
part of it, if not the whole. Every body

will

will perceive that the beginning bears no resemblance to that reserve and modesty with which our poet ever addressed an audience.

> I come no more to make you laugh : things now,
> That bear a weighty and a serious brow,
> Sad, high, and working, full of state and show,
> Such *noble* scenes as draw the eye to flow,
> We now present.———

Great part of the prologue is composed of severe satire on plays which abound with the noise of targets, of drums and trumpets, and the exhibition of fools, whose coats are *guarded with yellow*; and, as our author comes properly within this censure, Jonson, in all probability, maliciously stole an opportunity to throw in his envious and spiteful invective before the representation of his rival's play.

In all probability Henry VIII. was revived soon after the coronation of James and his Queen, Anne of Denmark. Jonson, by his connection with the court, might occasionally be useful towards conducting the pageantry of the scenes. Whether Jonson's

Sejanus

Sejanus was acted before Henry VIII. was
revived, is not now to be known; but,
much about that time, a peace feems to
have been patched up between Jonfon and
the players, and, moft likely, by the me-
diation of our gentle bard; for Shakfpeare
not only acted a character in Sejanus, but
wrote part of the tragedy as it was originally
performed.

Act I.   Scene I.
Dukes of Norfolk and Buckingham.

BUCKINGHAM.

Thofe fons of glory, thofe two lights of men,
Met in the vale of Arde !

Since this interview of Henry of England and Francis king of France, in the
vale of Arde, nothing has taken place between any European monarchs that can be
compared to it in magnificent fhow and
performance of military exercife: the nobility of both countries were fo oftenta-
tioufly prodigal, and fo emulous in fplen-
dour and drefs, that the place where the
two kings met was called *the field of the cloth*

of

of gold. In confequence of this rivalfhip in grandeur, they involved themfelves in fuch expence, that the penury of their whole lives afterwards could not repair the profufion of a few days.

I D E M.

——All the time
I was in my chamber a prifoner.

The poet has not put in the mouth of Buckingham the true reafon of his abfence from this interview at Arde. ——— The duke was very rich and loved œconomy,—a quality by no means pleafing to an arbitrary court, by which independence is ever viewed with fufpicious eyes. He, finding the preparations for this folemnity amount to immenfe fums, threw out expreffions of difpleafure againft Cardinal Wolfey, whom he accufed as the contriver of the parade. Lord Herbert, Hollingfhead, and Polydore Virgil, agree in this circumftance, and thence we may date Wolfey's animofity to the duke.

N O R F O L K.

NORFOLK.

Pomp, till this time, was fingle, but now marry'd
To one above itfelf.

That is, pomp was now overmatch-
ed. The meeting of two fuch mighty
monarchs, and their queens, with a retinue of men and women, the moft illuftrious for birth, rank, courage, beauty,
and every accomplifhment, leffened and
difgraced all pomps and ceremonies preceding.

The poet, in the purfuit of a noble
thought, fometimes overftrains himfelf,
and miffes the mark he aims at. The
whole defcription of this celebrated meeting
is rich in matter, though harfh in expreffion. It is laboured with art, but often
rugged, and fometimes bordering on obfcurity.

IDEM.
————Their very labour
Was to them a painting.

That is, it brought colour into their
cheeks.

IDEM.
————Still him in eye,
Still him in praife.

Z 4 Henry

Henry and Francis were univerfally faid to be the handfomeft men of the age in which they lived, and moft expert in military exercifes. In the feveral engagements at tilts and tournaments, whether owing to their fuperior fkill and bravery, or the addrefs and politenefs of their rivals, they conftantly bore away the palm from all competitors. An inftance or two of Englifh courage and French generofity, which happened during this memorable tranfaction, and can only be known by recurring to Chronicles or larger hiftories, may not, perhaps, be unwelcome to the reader.

It muft be confeffed that the King of France, in the generofity and franknefs of his temper, greatly excelled his oftentatious rival. Francis felt himfelf hurt at the various and unneceffary precautions obferved when he vifited Henry; the number of the guards, on both fides, was carefully reckoned; every ftep was meafured with the utmoft fcrupulofity. Tired out with thefe difgufting forms and ceremonies,

ceremonies, Francis, one day, took with
him two gentlemen and a page, and rode
directly to Henry's quarter at Guifnes.
The guards manifefting furprife on feeing
the monarch approach them, he called a-
loud to them, " You are my prifoners!
Carry me to your mafter." Henry was
aftonifhed at the prefence of his brother-
king, and quite overcome with this unexpected example of generous confidence,
took him in his arms, and told him he had
played him a moft agreeable trick, and that
he now furrendered himfelf his prifoner
from that moment.

The Earl of Somerfet gave an inftance
of intrepidity and quicknefs of apprehenfion, which deferves to be remembered. It was one preliminary article
of the interview, That the French and
Englifh fhould not, in number, exceed each
other. It was found, on examination,
that the French greatly out-numbered the
Englifh. Somerfet, inftead of taking um-
brage at this apparent breach of articles,
cried

cried out aloud, " Let them pafs! it is plain they have not the fpirit to truft us, though we have the courage to truft ourfelves with them."

NORFOLK.

—— —— All was *royal*
To the difpofing of it.

By the word *royal*, in Shakfpeare, we are to underftand fomething fupremely excellent; as in Macbeth, Act II.

——Our fears, in Banquo,
Stick deep, and in his *royalty* of nature
Reigns that which would be fear'd.

The word Ϲασιλευ]ερον, in Homer, has the fame import; and is fo applied by Theoclemenes the fugitive, in his exclamation to Telemachus, on obferving an omen, which he interprets in his favour :

Ὑμε]ερϐ δ'ουκ εστι γενευς Ϲασιλευτερον αλλϐ
Εν δημω Ιϑακης. ODYSS. LIB. XVII.

In Wolfey's fpeech to Sir William Kingfton, juft before he expired, it is to be obferved that the word *royal* ftands for confirmed obftinacy of temper.

" He

" He was a prince, faid the dying cardinal, of a moft *royal* carriage, and hath a
princely heart; and, rather than he will
mifs for any part of his will, he will endan-
ger half his kingdom."

B U C K I N G H A M.

———— What had he to do
In thefe fierce vanities ?————

Mr. Steevens is of opinion that *fierce* is
ufed here as the French word *fier*. Dr.
Johnfon goes farther, and fuppofes it might
poffibly mean the mimical ferocity of the
combatants; and this is nearer the author's
intention, I believe : for thefe mock fights
often produced very terrible confequences ;
many combatants, in the vale of Arde,
were unhorfed; Henry II. fon of Francis,
was killed, by the fplinter of a fpear, in a
tournament. So many lives were occafionally loft at thefe trials of perfonal
prowefs, that, utterly to difcourage and
put an end to them, the popes iffued canons
and decrees againft them, as practices unlawful and unchriftian ; and, when nothing
elfe could prevail, finally to extirpate them,
they

they denied chriftian burial to thofe who died in fuch encounters.

In Timon of Athens, *fierce* means, I think, *exceſſive, extreme,* or *terrible.* The fteward, fpeaking of Timon's fall from the higheft profperity to the loweft ftate of poverty, fays,

O the *fierce* wretchednefs which glory brings !

BUCKINGHAM.

——Why the devil,

Upon the French going out——

That is, upon the French confenting to fettle the terms of accommodation, to meet the Englifh in the vale of Arde, by an interview with the two kings.

NORFOLK.

France hath flaw'd the league.

To have a juft knowledge of Henry's and his minifter's characters, it is neceffary to throw in fome light from hiftory :

Though the Duke of Norfolk charges the French with breaking the folemn compact entered into between the two kings, at their interview, from which they parted

with

with the moft folemn proteftations of
friendfhip, the diffolving of the treaty
cannot be afcribed to Francis. Charles V.
Emperor of Germany, the moft fubtle, in-
terefted, and difingenuous, prince of his
time, was alarmed at the late interview, and
confequent confederacy, of two fuch po-
tent monarchs. When Henry, before he
returned to his dominions, paid a vifit to
him at Gravelines, the politic Charles, who
faw through the capricious temper of his
vifitor, foon found means to efface that
friendfhip to which the fincere and noble
temper of the French king had given birth.
But, that which was more effential to his
intereft, he gained over Wolfey to his fide,
by promifing to affift him in acquiring the
papacy, and by putting him in poffeffion
of the revenues of two bifhoprics in Caf-
tile. The exorbitant incomes which the
cardinal enjoyed were not greatly inferior
to the revenues of the king himfelf. The
Duke of Buckingham hints at the cardinal's

nal's penfion from the emperor in a following part of the fcene:

> ————I'm fure the emperor
> Paid 'ere he promis'd.

Enter the cardinal with the purfe borne before him.

The cardinal, in his paffage, fixeth his eye on Buckingham, and Buckingham on him, both full of difdain.

The inftruction which Shakfpeare, in this quotation, has given the actors, is not fo generally obferved as it ought. The afpect of Wolfey, to Buckingham, fhould at once be fteady and deliberate, fcornful and reproaching. Buckingham's look, in return, fhould be fierce, indignant, and im-
patient. The cardinal, in paffing by the duke, fhould ftill keep his eye fixed upon him, as if demanding fome falutation or mark of refpect ; but, on the duke's per-
fifting filence, he turns to his fecretaries, and enquires of them concerning the exa-
mination of the duke's furveyor, in a tone not quite loud enough to be heard by the duke.

Colley

Colley Cibber has been much praifed for his affuming port, pride, and dignity, in Wolfey; but his manner was not correfpondent to the grandeur of the character. The man who was familiar in the greateft courts of Europe, and took the lead in the councils and defigns of mighty monarchs, muft have acquired an eafy dignity in action and deportment, and fuch as Colley Cibber never underftood or practifed. If fpeaking with feeling and energy were all the requifites in the cardinal, Moffop would have excelled greatly; but, in fpite of the robe, which was of fome advantage to him, his action, ftep, and whole conduct of his perfon, were extremely aukward, and unfuitable to the accomplifhed ftatefman, the companion of princes. Mr. Digges, if he had not fometimes been extravagant in gefture and quaint in elocution, would have been nearer the refemblance of the great minifter than any actor I have feen reprefent it.

Scene

Scene II. Council Chamber.

Enter King Henry leaning upon Wolfey.

Shakfpeare is eminent in the drawing of his moft diftinguifhed hiftorical charac- ters : here, more particularly, genius guides his pencil. If we compare his fe- veral portraits of our Englifh kings with their actions, as recorded in hiftory, we fhall perceive a ftriking and faithful re- femblance. They are as powerfully dif- criminated by their peculiar paffions, vir- tues, follies, and faculties, as the heroes of the greateft poet of the ancients. The gloomy turbulence of John ; the rafhnefs and effeminacy of Richard II. the jealous anxiety for the crown in Henry IV. the generous and warlike fpirit of Henry V. the piety and imbecillity of Henry VI. the fubtlety, perfidy, cruelty, and courage, of Richard III. and, laftly, the ftrutting gran- deur, imperious fpirit, and undifguifed, though boifterous, temper of Henry VIII. --thefe characters are fo juftly and fkilfully fe- parated from each other, by the author, that

no name is wanted to diftinguifh them from
each other.

Betterton, was taught the part of
Harry VIII. by Sir William Davenant,
from his remembrance of the performance
of the admired and accomplifhed Lowin.
Old Downs gives it as his opinion, that
nobody can ever approach to the great excellence which Betterton difplayed in acting the king. ' Wolfey (fays the fame ftage-
hiftorian) was fupported with great pride,
port, and mien, by *Harris,* an actor, of
whom we fcarce know any thing, except
that he played a variety of characters in tragedy and comedy, and fuppofe, from that circumftance, he muft have enjoyed very comprehenfive abilities for the ftage.' I find
his name, in Downs, to Romeo, and to Sir
Andrew Aguecheek in Twelfth Night,
which are parts as diftant, in dramatic features, as Hamlet and the Grave-digger.
Harris was the actor of thefe and many
other parts of equal diffimilarity. Cibber,
I fuppofe, had not feen him, for his name

is not in his apology. I imagine he left the
ſtage much about about the time the companies of Drury-lane and Dorſet-gardens were,
by the king's command, united. Harris's
name is not to be found in the dramatis
perſonæ of any play ſince that period.
He had formerly been joint-director of the
duke's company with Lady Davenant and
Betterton, and might poſſibly be offended
that, in the treaty between Betterton, in
conjunction with Davenant's ſucceſſors,
and Hart and Kynaſton, of the king's theatre, he was left out.*

His merit, in ſeveral characters beſides
Wolſey, is noticed by Downs; particularly in Sir Poſitive Atall in the Imperti-
nents of Shadwell, taken from Moliere's
Les Facheux, and the part of the maſter,
in The Man's the Maſter, by Davenant.
His talents were not confined to acting a-
lone; ſinging was another of his quali-
fications: he and Sandford ſang a humorous ballad-epilogue in the character of

two

---

* By looking carefully over the Roſcius Anglicanus, I
find that Harris was originally of the king's company,
but ſoon left it to join Betterton.

two ſtreet ballad-ſingers ; the ſame, I believe, which, many years afterwards, was
ſung by that droll, honeſt, agreeable, fellow, Jemmy Bencroft, and Nat Clarke.—
I call him Jemmy, becauſe it will better revive his memory, among his ſurviving
friends, than by the addition which he afterwards merited of James Bencroft, Eſq.
patentee of Covent-Garden theatre.

In the play of The Man's the Maſter,
Harris had the misfortune to wound Cademan in the eye, by uſing a ſharp inſtead of
a foil, which diſabled him from acting ever
after. Cademan received a penſion from
the players, on that account, we may rea-
ſonably ſuppoſe, as long as he lived, for
he enjoyed it in 1708, thirty-five years after the accident.

Booth ſucceeded Betterton in Henry VIII.
To ſupport the dignity of the prince, and yet
retain that vein of humour which pervades
this character, requires great caution in the
actor. Without particular attention, Harry
will be manufactured into a royal bully or

ridiculous

ridiculous buffoon. Booth was particularly happy in preferving the true fpirit of
the part through the whole play. Mr. Macklin, who had the good fortune to fee him feveral times in Harry, has declared that he
fhone in the character with particular luftre.
Quin, who had the good fenfe to admire
and imitate Booth, and the honefty to own
it, kept as near as poffible to his great ex-
amplar's portrait; but Quin was deficient
in flexibility as well as ftrength of voice;
he could not utter impetuous and vehement anger with vigour, nor dart tremendous looks; all which were fuited
to the happier organs and countenance of
Booth. He was, befides, a ftranger to
grace in action or deportment. — Booth
walked with the eafe of a gentleman and
the dignity of a monarch. The grandeur and magnificence of Henry were, in
Booth, fuftained to the height.

How the managers took it into their heads
to give this part to Harper, during Booth's
laft illnefs, I cannot conceive, unlefs his
being

being a fat man was the great recommendation. I could never feparate honeft Job-
fon, the cobler, from the prince: he put
me in mind of the old ballad of King
Harry and the cobler. I fhould not forget that, when Betterton and Harris
acted the king and the cardinal, the little
character of Lord Sands was played by
Price, frequently mentioned by Downs,
as a moft admirable low comedian.——
Why Nokes perfonated fo ferious a
part as the duke of Norfolk, I cannot
conceive: perhaps it was not the great comic actor, but that Nokes who was famous
for playing womens characters.

A a 3   CHAP-

CHAPTER XVIII.

Shakſpeare's hiſtorical plays. — Warnings to prince and people. — Court oppreſſion and miniſterial juggling. — Queen Katharine an advocate for the people. — A horrible tax. — Loans and benevolences. — Duke of Suffolk and Green. — Poverty and neceſſity. —The cunning of miniſters.—Tractable o-bedience explained. — Sick interpreters. — George I. and his courtiers. — The duke of Buckingham's eloquence. — His title to the crown. — Mrs. Porter. — Mrs. Pritchard. — French Faſhions adopted by the Engliſh. — Maſquerade; game of mum-chance.—Banquet with two hundred covers. — Buckingham's condemnation. — Duke of Norfolk's tears.—Earl of Kildare.—Wolſey's malice. — Buckingham deprived of his right. — Reaſon of the king's jealouſy and the people's love.—Wilks in Buckingham.—Archbiſhopric of Toledo. — Suffolk's character.

THE

THE plays of Shakfpeare, which are
founded on Englifh hiftory, are, in
my opinion, amongft our moft valuable
dramatic compofitions. They contain excellent advice and perpetual warnings to the
kings and people of this country. In thefe
ineftimable records they will find a reflecting
mirror of their anceftors, probably of themfelves.—Exact pictures of the prefent and
future times I cannot mean; but fuch general refemblances of character, in prince and
fubject, as muft neceffarily arife in a mixed
government, like ours; where incroachments, on one fide, muft perpetually meet
with refiftance on the other, and will infal-
libly produce events not very unlike thofe
which are defcribed fo affectingly by our
inimitable poet.

The fcene before us prefents a true picture of court oppreffion and minifterial
juggling. The author has related the matter in queftion with fome tendernefs to the
memory of Henry, and this affords ano-

ther

ther reaſon why we ſhould ſuppoſe the play
was written before the acceſſion of James
I. Queen Katharine is judicioufly choſen
to repreſent, to the throne, the grievances
of the people, who were burdened by a
moſt illegal and oppreſſive impoſt. Shakſpeare here aſſumes the part of the honeſt
politician and good citizen. In the conduct of the ſcene, he gives a caution to all
ſucceeding princes againſt the undue and
illegal exerciſe of their power.

Henry, by his mere arbitrary will, and
without aſſembling a parliament, had iſ-
ſued out commiſſions, by which he commanded to be levied four ſhillings in the
pound from the clergy, and three ſhillings
and four pence from the laity. But this
unprecedented and horrible taxation ſo diſ-
guſted the people, in all parts of the kingdom, that the king was obliged to revoke
the powers he had given, and had re-
courſe to another unjuſt practice of
raiſing money on loans or benevolence:
the name was ſofter, but the exaction e-
qually

qually oppreſſive and unlawful. When
the act which had paſſed in the reign of
Richard III. by which all ſuch methods of
raiſing money were aboliſhed, was oppoſed
to this mode of taxation, to the diſgrace
of the king and his miniſters, it was an-
ſwered, ' That Richard being an uſurper,
his parliament was an unlawful aſſembly,
and their acts of no validity,' which was
plainly to declare that an arbitrary tyrant
was more careful to diſtribute juſtice and
equity to his ſubjects than a lawful prince.

N O R F O L K.

The clothiers all, not able to maintain
The many to them 'longing, have put off
The ſpinſters, carders, fullers, weavers, who,
Unfit for other life, and compell'd by hunger,
And lack of other means, are all in uproar.

The duke of Suffolk, who was much beloved, prevailed on many of the wealthieſt
clothiers to ſubmit to the royal impoſi-
tion ; but, on this compliance, they diſ-
charged all their workmen and manufacturers under the pretence that they could
not now maintain them. This occaſioned

a

a great infurrection in the county of Suffolk. The duke ventured his perfon a-
mong them, and afked who was their lea-
der. One Green ftepped forward and anfwered, " They had two : *Poverty and Neceffity.*" The king, notwithftanding his
arbitrary and boifterous difpofition, was
obliged to pardon all who had oppofed his
illegal impofitions. This, I believe, was
the only inftance of Henry's retracting his
once-fettled purpofe.

WOLSEY.

———————— Pleafe you, Sir,
I know but of a fingle part in aught
Pertains to the ftate.

I am but one, of many counfellors, who,
of equal power with myfelf, advifed this
unhappy bufinefs. This is too often the
language of a minifter, who, though univerfally known to govern his mafter, and
take the lead in all tranfactions, yet, when
queftioned about any ftate matter, declares
he acts only in his proper department.

QUEEN.

———This makes bold mouths,
Tongues fpit their duties out, and cold hearts freeze
Allegiance;

Allegiance ; their curfes now
Live where their prayers did ; and it comes to pafs
That tractable obedience is a flave
To each incenfed will.———

The latter part of this fpeech is thus
ingenioufly explained by Mufgrave; " Thofe
who are tractable and obedient muft give
way to others who are angry."

But the queen has defcribed the confequences which oppreffion and injuftice
are apt to produce, and therefore intimates
that the very perfons, who, before this
impofition, were obedient and tractable
fubjects, are now changed into refolute op-
pofers of government, from motives of
juft refentment.

W O L S E Y.

I have no farther gone in this, than by
A fingle voice, and that not paft me, but
By learned approbation of the judges.

Shakfpeare has, in this, followed exactly the thread of hiftory. The judges,
fays Hume, went fo far as pofitively to af-
firm, " The king might exact any fum of
money he pleafed." We need not be furprifed

prifed that his majefty's privy council gave
an affent to this decree, which annihilated,
at once, all the privileges of the fubject.
It fortunately happened, in this inftance,
though the parliament in general confpired
with the king, through his whole reign,
to fix fhackles on the people, tyranny was
obliged to forego its hold.

W O L S E Y.

——What we oft do beft
By fick interpreters, once weak ones,
Is not ours, or not allow'd.

By fick interpreters, we are to underftand
peevifh or ill-natured expofitors, men, who,
from an overheated temper, or melancholy difpofition, put a wrong conftruction
upon public meafures.

I D E M.

A word with you. [*Speaking to the fecretary*]
Let there be letters writ, to every fhire,
Of the king's grace and pardon.
——————— Let it be nois'd
That, through our interceffion, this revokement
And pardon comes.

The minifter's filching from his royal
mafter the honour of beftowing grace
and

and pardon on the fubject, appeared fo grofs
and impudent a prevarication, that, when
this play was acted before George I. at
Hampton-Court, about the year 1717, the
courtiers laughed fo loudly at this minifterial craft, that his majefty, who was unacquainted with the Englifh language,
afked the lord-chamberlain the meaning of
their mirth ; upon being informed of it,
the king joined in a laugh of approbation.

> K I N G.
> ——————— And when we,
> Almoft with liftening ravifh'd———

The duke of Buckingham's eloquence
has been recorded by the old hiftorians,
who pretend to fay he inherited the gift
from his father, once the bofom counfellor
of Richard III. who made ufe of his art in
fpeaking to cajole the citizens of London,
and to perfuade them that his title to the
crown was better founded than that of his
nephew.

> S U R V E Y O R.
> ——— ——— If the king
> Should die without iffue, he'd carry it fo
> To make the fceptre his.

It

It was this nobleman's misfortune to have a remote title to the fucceffion of the crown. He was defcended, by a female, from the duke of Glofter, youngeft fon of Edward III.

In the fcene before us, the deportment of the actors, when the play was revived in 1727, was much approved. Booth did not command attention more by attraction of figure and juft elocution, than by the propriety of his action and the ftatelinefs of his ftep. The bufinefs of Wolfey, in this fcene, being confined to addrefs, caution, and management, was not unfuitably reprefented by Colley Cibber. But the dignity and grace of a queen were never, perhaps, more happily fet off than by Mrs. Porter. There was an elevated confequence in the manner of that actrefs, which, fince her time, I have in vain fought for in her fucceffors.

Her firft fpeech to the king, after kneeling to him, was uttered with fuch intelligence and fenfibility, that fhe commanded the applaufe as well as attention, of the audience,

dience. The words are fimple, and, feem-
ingly, unimportant; but fhe underftood
her author well, and, in delivering them,
conveyed the prime duties of the kingly
office with energy.

> *That you would love yourfelf, and, in that love,*
> *Not unconfidered leave your honour, nor*
> *The dignity* of your office, is the point
> Of my petition.

Her conduct, in the whole fcene, was a
mixture of graceful elocution and dignified
behaviour.

Mrs. Pritchard, in Queen Katharine,
was eafy in her addrefs and natural in her
expreffion, but unaccompanied by that
grace and dignity which her predeceffor,
Mrs. Porter, knew fo well to affume.

Scene III.

LORD   CHAMBERLAIN.

> ————All the good our Englifh
> Have got by our laft voyage is but merely
> A fit or two o'th' face.

Our neighbours of France have, time
out of mind, conftantly led the way in new
fafhions

fafhions and fopperies; and we have as
conftantly imitated and reproached them
for it. Grimace of countenance is here fa-
tirized. Dryden, in the epilogue to his
Aftrologer, charges a mimic of French ab-
furdities with a different kind of affecta-
tion :

Up ftarts a monfieur, new come o'er, and warm
In the French ftoop and pull-back of the arm.

Scene IV.

SERVANT.

————————A noble troop of ftrangers,
For fo they feem; they've left their barge and landed,
And hitherto make as great ambaffadors
From foreign princes.

This vifit of the King and Courtiers,
mafqued, to the Cardinal, is taken from
Hollingfhead ; our poet has artfully introduced Anne Bullen to attract the notice of the King for the firft time, an incident, which is not in the original. The
mafkers, fays the Chronicle, were dreffed
moft gorgeoufly, and brought with them a
large

large gold cup filled with crowns and other
pieces of gold, which were to be played
for at a game called *mum-chance*, I suppose
from the silence observed during play, and
the chance of the die. The maskers poured out of the cup, before the Cardinal,
their winnings and losings, which a-
mounted to about two hundred crowns. —
' At all,' said the Cardinal; and, throwing the die, he won the whole. *

C A R D I N A L.

There should be one amongst them, by his person,
More worthy this place than myself.

This incident is likewise taken from
Hollingshead, though Shakspeare has properly enough graced Wolsey with the good
fortune to select his royal master from the
rest.   He really mistook Sir Edward Nevil,
who was disguised with a black beard, for
the king, who laughed at the blunder,
and immediately pulled off his mask.

---

* Hollingshead, Vol. II.

WOLSEY.

Sir Thomas Lovel, is the banquet ready
In the privy-chamber?

At this after-banquet, where the king
himfelf prefided, no lefs than two hundred
covered difhes were placed on the table.

Act. II.   Scene the firft.

The account of the D. of Buckingham's
trial is faithfully and pathetically defcribed
from our old Chronicles. The Duke of
Norfolk, who was lord-high-fteward at
this memorable trial, on pafling fentence
upon the noble prifoner, could not refrain
from fhedding tears; perhaps reflecting
that Buckingham's misfortune might one
day be his own.

GENTLEMAN.

———— ———— Certainly,
The Cardinal is the end of this.

That is, Wolfey was the chief promoter of Buckingham's fall.

SECOND GENTLEMAN.
'Tis likely,
By all conjectures: first Kildare's attainder——

The case of Lord Kildare will, perhaps, more than any other circumstance, throw a light upon the real character of the cardinal.

The Earl of Kildare, was accused, before the king and council, of divers high crimes, by Wolfey. He answered the cardinal's accusation with such force, that he cleared himself to the king's satisfaction. — He was afterwards tried and condemned, and imprisoned in the Tower; but the king was prevailed upon to grant 'him a pardon. Wolfey, notwithstanding, had the insolence and cruelty to send orders to the lieutenant of the Tower to see him executed privately there: he, being the earl's friend, informed the king of the cardinal's orders; who in great wrath reproved Wolfey, and discharged the earl from his imprisonment.*

BUCK-

* Lord Herbert.

BUCKINGHAM.

There cannot be thofe numberlefs offences
'Gainft me I can't take peace with : no black *envy*
Shall make my grave.

Mr. Steevens has rightly obferved, though
he adduced no inftance of it, that Shakfpeare fometimes ufes the word *envy* inftead
of *malice* or *hatred.* Wolfey, in a fubfe-
quent fcene with the King and Campeius,
applies the word in the fame fenfe as here :
fpeaking of the intended trial for the divorce, he fays,

Who can be angry now ? what *envy* reach you ?

' What malicious tongues will now dare
to reproach your conduct, fince you have
fubmitted to a fair and impartial trial ? ' —
The Duke, moft feelingly and like a Chriftian, declares, that malice fhall have no
fhare in his latter end : ' I fhall deprive
bad minds of the power to flander my laft
moments with a report of my dying with a
rancorous or unforgiving temper.'

BUCKINGHAM.

———————— I was lord-high-conſtable
And Duke of Buckingham.

The office of high-conſtable of England
expired with this nobleman.

IDEM.

———————— I had my trial,
And muſt needs ſay a noble one.

The king, knowing that the evidence a
gainſt the unfortunate duke was ſo full and
complete that he could not poſſibly be ac-
quitted, ſent him word that he ſhould enjoy all the advantages which the law would
allow him. However, the king robbed
him, in one material inſtance, of his
right; as a peer of the realm he had a juſt
claim to be tried by all the peers. The
Duke of Buckingham's jury conſiſted only
of a duke, a marquis, ſeven earls, and
twelve barons.

Although there is no reaſon to doubt the
juſtneſs of the ſentence paſſed upon Buck-

B b 3   ingham,

ingham, his crimes proceeded rather from levity and folly than deliberate malice. The people loved him, and were in hopes the king would have extended mercy to him. But his alliance to the crown prevented all hopes of pardon. Henry's jealoufy of all claims of that kind rendered him implacable. His father, Henry VII. murdered the Earl of Warwick for no other reafon but his having a better title to the crown than himfelf. The greateft crime, too, of Mary Queen of Scotland, in the eyes of Elizabeth, was the goodnefs of her title; and James, her fon, fhamefully perfecuted Lady Arabella Stewart, becaufe fhe was a-kin to the royal family.

To the reader of this play the part of Buckingham may feem to be of little or no confequence; but there is an affecting pathos in it which the actor of merit will difcover and exemplify in action and elocution. When the play was revived, as above related, the incomparable Wilks thought Buckingham worthy his attention.

In

In the firſt ſcene, at the opening of the
play, the reſentment and indignation of the
character to Wolſey broke out, in Wilks,
with an impetuoſity reſembling haſty ſparks
of fire; his action was vehement, and his
motion quick and diſturbed. His demeanour, when condemned, was gentle,
graceful, and pathetic; his grief was
manly, reſigned, and temperate: ſuch as
became the nobleman and the Chriſtian.

FIRST GENTLEMAN.

—Merely to revenge him on the emperor,
For not beſtowing on him, at his aſking,
The archbiſhopric of Toledo.

Nothing could ſatisfy the unbounded
ambition and avarice of Wolſey. — Shakſpeare is juſtified in alledging this fact. The
Archbiſhop of Toledo is primate of Spain,
great chancellor of Caſtile, and proprietor
of ſeventeen towns and a great number of
villages ; his yearly revenue is computed at
75000l. The King of Spain generally re-
B b 4   ſerves

ferves it for the youngeft branch of his family.

Scene II,

NORFOLK.

—— This imperious man will work us
From princes into pages.

Wolfey had no lefs than nine noblemen
in his retinue.

SUFFOLK.

As I am made without him, fo I'll ftand.

Charles Brandon, Duke of Suffolk,
who married the Queen - dowager of
France, fifter to Henry VIII. was one of
the moft amiable noblemen of the age he
lived in : brave, generous, condefcending,
and humane, his popularity was the well-
earned tribute of his virtues. That Henry,
though precipitate, tyrannical, and cruel,
was capable of fincere and cordial friendfhip,
is apparent from his inviolable attachment
to Suffolk and Cranmer : the latter he pro-
tected from all his powerful enemies, and
the

the former he loved with a friendſhip that was inviolable.   When news was brought of Suffolk's death, he was ſitting in coun-cil.—He embraced the occaſion to expreſs his deep regret for the loſs of his brother, and to bear teſtimony to his virtues : he averred that, during the whole period of their friendſhip, which grew up from in-fancy, he had never attempted to injure an adverſary, nor had ever, in his hearing, dropped a word to the diſadvantage of any man.   Then, looking round him, he ſaid, with ſome emotion, ' Is there any of you, my lords, can ſay ſo much ?'   When Hen-ry ſpoke theſe words, he diſcovered in their faces that confuſion which is the compa-nion of conſcious guilt.

CHAPTER

CHAPTER XIX.

Word goodnefs *explained. — Pace, why called a fool. — Validity of the King's marriage tried.—Clement* VII.—*The Queen not placed properly at the trial.— Character of Ferdinand King of Spain.— Mrs. Porter's elevated manner.—Booth's ʽ Go thy ways, Kate.' —Quin. — The King's fcruples.— Mrs. Pritchard. — Mrs. Porter. — Booth and Macklin. — Henry's confeffor. — The King's true reafons for a divorce.—ʽ Weigh out afflictions' explained.—Fuller's character of Henry.— Reafons for Wolfey's behaviour in the bufinefs of the divorce.—Henry's fymbol of difpleafure.*

WOLSEY.

W O L S E Y.

Muſt now confeſs, if he have any *goodneſs*,
The trial juſt and noble.

THE word *goodneſs* ſtands here for *im-partiality, juſtice,* or *equity.*

C A M P E I U S.

Kept Pace a foreign man.

It is no uncommon practice of miniſters, when they cannot mould an officer of ſtate to their own faſhion, to keep him at diſtance from the court, under ſome honourable title abroad.

W O L S E Y.

——————— He was a fool,
For he would needs be virtuous.

The Cardinal means, that Pace would have the aſſurance to think for himſelf. — And, for this perverſeneſs, Wolſey ruined him.

HENRY.

——————— O my lord,
Would it not grieve an able man to leave
So fweet a bedfellow ?

It is remarkable that Henry and Queen
Katharine lay in the fame bed till the trial
for the validity of the marriage was o-
pened.

Scene between Anne Bullen and the Old
Lady.

OLD LADY.

Pluck off a little.

The Lady, in my opinion, means, ——
' Draw afide that affected veil of modefty
you have put on. Do not difguife your
fentiments with artificial coverings.'

CHAMBERLAIN.

——————— And who knows yet,
But from this lady may proceed a gem
To lighten all this ifle ?

This gem was Queen Elizabeth ; and
this may ferve amongft other proofs that
the

the author wrote this play during the life
of that princefs.

OLD LADY.

How taftes it ? Is it bitter ? Forty-pence—no.

The fee of an attorney for advice, as
well as term-fee, was then, as now, 3 s.
4 d.

Act. II.   Scene IV.
The Trial.

The trial of the validity of a king's marriage, before perfons delegated for that
purpofe, in a court where the royal perfons were fummoned, and did actually appear, was an occurrence new and extraordinary, which drew the attention of all
Europe. The legality or illegality of mar-
riages amongft the great, before that period, had been determined at the court of
Rome by the fole power of the pontiff. —
Nor would Clement VII. the then reigning pope, have parted with fuch a privilege, had not the reformation, which be-

gan

gan about twelve years before the trial by
Luther, made fuch an alarming progrefs as
induced him to act cautioufly with a prince of
Henry's refolute and undaunted temper. —
However, the pope ftill kept in his hands
the power of fhortening or lengthening the
procefs, and of eftablifhing or diffolving
the court, which was opened, at Black-
Friers, May 31, 1529.

In the diftribution of the feveral perfons
who compofed this learned and illuftrious
affembly, Shakfpeare had, I think, with
great propriety, feated the Queen at fome
diftance from the King. Why modern
managers fhould all concur to make an alteration in his ftage-œconomy I can difcover no good reafon : for if, in the infancy
of the ftage, when they had fcarcely room
to difplay their figures to advantage, they
could place a throne or feat for fuch a per-
fonage as a Queen, furely, with a much
larger area, every embellifhment and neceffary decoration need not be omitted. —
Befides, as it is now managed, the Queen

is fuppofed to wait like a common fuitor
or culprit till fhe is fummoned into the
court: whereas the rifing from her feat,
when called by the Crier, would be attended with more confequence, and give an
opportunity to the actrefs by her deportment to gain the attention of the fpectators.

Q U E E N.

Sir, I defire you do me right and juftice,
And to beftow your pity, &c.

The greateft part of Katharine's fpeech
is indeed faithfully tranfcribed from our
Chronicles, but much heightened by pathetic expoftulation, warmth of paffion,
and dignity of refentment.

Q U E E N.

——————— Ferdinand,
My father, King of Spain, was reckon'd one
The wifeft prince that there had reign'd by many
A year before.

If poffeffing the art of acquiring territories by fraud, perfidy, cruelty, and injuftice ;

tice; if the putting in practice every machination to circumvent and betray; can be termed the arts of wisdom, Ferdinand, called the Catholic, King of Spain, was of all kings the wifeft. Strange, that the commiffion of enormities, which would fubject a private man to an ignominious punifhment, fhould be efteemed meritorious in a crowned head!

WOLSEY.

——————— I do profefs,
You fpeak not like yourfelf.

The Cardinal's defence of his conduct is temperate and artful. Shakfpeare, who in this play treads no ground without warrant, has in this fcene alfo traced our beft Chronicles.

QUEEN.

——————— I muft tell you,
That you tender more your perfon's honour
Than your high profeffion fpiritual.

Wolfey was fuppofed not to have favoured the caufe of the queen, from private animofity :

animosity: she had publicly reproached him with his licentious manner of living.

Mrs. Pritchard's Queen Katharine has been much approved, and especially in this scene of the trial. She certainly was in behaviour easy, and in speaking natural and familiar; but the situation of the character required more force in utterance and more dignity in action. Mrs. Porter's manner was elevated to the rank of the great person she represented. Her kneeling to the King was the effect of majesty in distress and humbled royalty; it was indeed highly affecting; the suppression of her tears when she reproached the Cardinal, bespoke the tumultuous conflict in her mind, before she burst into that manifestation of indignity, she felt in being obliged to answer so unworthy an interrogator.

KING.

Go thy ways, Kate!

Mr. Macklin, our theatrical Nestor, will tell us, that Booth pronounced these

four fhort words with fuch happy em-
phafis, conveying at once characteriftical
humour and liberal acknowledgement of
Katharine's virtuous excellence, that the
audience not only applauded, but admired, the fpeaker.

Quin borrowed fomething of Booth's
manner in uttering this valediction; but I
am afraid he mixed in it a little of Falftaff's ftyle.

K I N G.

——————— Oft have hinder'd
The paffages made towards it.

That is, ' You have rather thrown ob-
ftacles in the way of this bufinefs than
promoted it.'

I D E M.

My confcience firft receiv'd a tendernefs
And *prick*.

Prick of confcience, fays Dr. Johnfon,
was the term in confeffion; and the fweet
prick of confcience was transferred from
the popifh priefts to the Calvinift paftors,
efpecially thofe of Scotland.

I D E M.

I D E M.

—————— For her male iſſue,
Or died when they were made, or ſhortly after
This world had air'd them.

The King, it is ſaid, was ſtruck with
this misfortune, becauſe the curſe of being
childleſs is the very threatening of the Mo-
ſaical law againſt thoſe who eſpouſe the
brother's widow.

I D E M.

————— I began, in private,
With you, my lord of Lincoln.

The Biſhop of Lincoln was Henry's
confeſſor.

I D E M.

How under my oppreſſion I did *reek*.

Reek is a coarſe, though ſignificant,
metaphor, taken from a man's ſweating
under a heavy burden.

I D E M.

To you, my lord of Canterbury.

Warham was then Archbiſhop of Canterbury, and not Cranmer, as hinted in
ſome editions of this play.

I D E M.

Prove but our marriage lawful, ————
———————— we are contented
To wear our mortal ſtate to come with her,
Kath'rine, our queen, before the primeſt creature
That's paragon'd in the world.

Notwithſtanding this very public and
ſolemn proteſtation, which I think Shakſpeare has faithfully tranſcribed from the
Chronicle, Henry's private reaſons, which
he ſent to the pope, contain very different motives. The following is a tranſlation from a curious Latin record :

" There are, beſides, ſome particular
reaſons to be laid before his holineſs in
private, though not proper to be committed to writing ; upon which account,
as well as by reaſon of ſome diſtempers
which

which the queen labours under, without hopes of remedy, as, likewife, through fome certain fcruples which difturb the king's confcience, *his majefty neither can nor will, for the future, look upon her, or live with her, for his lawful wife, let the confequence be what it will.*"

The king's ardent paffion to have male iffue feems to have been the great motive for his divorce from Katharine. He had a fon, by her, chriftened Henry, who died two months after his birth: and this, he ufed to fay, was a judgement upon him for marrying his brother's wife. The fame eager defire to have a male child, and his difappointment, occafioned his unconquerable averfion to Anne Bullen. This unhappy lady was delivered of a dead male; thence, it is fuppofed, he fought all methods to ruin her.

I D E M.

My learned and well-beloved fervant, Cranmer, Pr'ythee return————

Quin

Quin fpoke this apoftrophe to Cranmer in a low voice, but fo melodioufly and well-tuned, as to be heard diftinctly in every part of the theatre.

I D E M.

——Break up the court.

Notwithftanding Shakfpeare has, in this paffage, feemed to have diffolved this famous affembly, it actually continued to fit and do bufinefs for fome time. The king was fo angry at their dilatory proceedings, that he employed the duke of Suffolk as a meffenger to them, who fharply reproved their ftudied procraftination ; and, vehemently ftriking the table with his hand, he told Wolfey, " That it never was well with England when cardinals had the management of affairs." — Wolfey replied fhortly, " That, if it had not been for one cardinal, the duke of Suffolk would not have kept his head on his fhoulders."*

Act

* Fuller.

Aɛt III.   Scene I.

Queen Katharine, Wolfey, and Campeius.

This fcene is omitted, in the reprefentation, as tedious and unneceffary.   However, as it farther difplays Queen Katharine's temper and difpofition, and contains
many characteriftical features of that unhappy lady, it well deferves our attention.   It is, in general, a tranfcript from
Hollingfhead, paraphrafed and enlarged
with correfpondent matter.

QUEEN.
————I was fet at work
Amongft my maids——

When Queen Katharine was informed that
the cardinals Wolfey and Campeius defired
audience, fhe came to them with a fkein
of thread about her neck ; nor would fhe
retire with them into her private chamber,
as they requefted, till after a conference
fuch as the poet has given us.

IDEM.
————Nay, forfooth my friends,
They that muft weigh out my affliɛtions.

This *weighing out of afflictions* is, I think,
a metaphor taken from the unloading of a

fhip.

ſhip. Thoſe friends, who are moſt capable of eaſing me of afflictions, are at a great diſtance from me.

QUEEN.

Almoſt forgot my prayers to content him !
And am I thus rewarded ?

Fuller's ſhort character of Katharine is no ill anſwer to the lady's complaint :

" *Queen Katharine's age was above her huſ-band's, her gravity above her age, more pious at her beads than pleaſant in her bed, a better woman than a wife, and a fitter wife for any prince than Henry.*"

Scene II.

Lord-Chamberlain, Norfolk, Suffolk, and Surry.

CHAMBERLAIN.

The cardinal's letter, to the pope, miſcarried,
And came to the eye of the king, wherein was read
How that the cardinal did intreat his holineſs
To ſtay the judgement of the divorce.

This is conformable to Hollingſhead's relation.

Hiſtorians

Hiftorians are at a lofs to account for
Wolfey's behaviour in the trial for the divorce.   He certainly had the whole management of the bufinefs in his own power; for Campeius was but fecond in the
commiffion, and, confequently, he might
have terminated the matter to his mafter's
wifh.   At this diftance of time it is difficult to afcertain the real motive by which
Wolfey was influenced.   The king's paffions, he knew, would brook no controul:
it was dangerous to oppofe them.   But, it
fhould be remembered, that the cardinal's
ambition aimed at the triple crown, and that,
during the trial, Pope Clement was feized
with fo dangerous an illnefs that it was feared it would terminate only with his life.
Wolfey, who had before been twice a can-
didate for the papacy, again had his hopes
renewed.   Had he decided the bufinefs of
the divorce in favour of the king, he would
have loft the interpofition of the emperor,
Queen Katharine's nephew, without whofe
intereft he could not poffibly fucceed.   Clement's

ment's recovery put an end to Wolfey's dream of the papacy, and expofed him to the refentment of Anne Bullen and her party, who took indefatigable pains to incenfe the king againft him. This part of Wolfey's hiftory, refpecting the papacy, has not, except in one place, been touched upon by Shakfpeare.

SUFFOLK.

——I do affure you
The king cry'd Ha! at this.

CHAMBRLAIN.

——Now God incenfe him,
And let him cry Ha! louder.

Henry's fign of difpleafure was ufually marked by a loud explofion of the interjection Ha! or Ho! and this behaviour, more fuitable to the hog-driver than the prince, ferved to terrify and keep in awe his flavifh and timorous courtiers. For this prognoftic was matter of the utmoft difmay to them.

There is a ftory, in Fuller's Worthies, of a weak effeminate boy, who perfonated Henry VIII. in a certain play written on

that

that ſtory, who cried ho! in ſo feeble a
tone, that one of his brother-performers
told him, ' that he acted more like a
mouſe than a man; and that, if he ſpoke
ho! with no better ſpirit, his parliament
would not grant him a penny of money.'

CHAP-

CHAPTER XX.

Cibber snuffing a candle. — Nobles betting for and against Wolsey's favour with the King. — Wolsey's immense riches. — Henry's anger, as expressed by Booth. — Surry's impetuosity. — His character. — Curious article against Wolsey. — Cranmer, Archbishop of Canterbury. — Explanation of ' cherish those that hate you.' — The great art of Shakspeare in a scene of the 3d act. — Cibber and Mossop criticised. — Digges commended. — Wolsey's present of a fool to the King. — Banished to his diocese by Norfolk. — Arrested for high treason. — His death. — Wolsey's ambition to be pope. — Hume refuted. — Wolsey's love of learning and encouragement of learned men. — Erasmus and Wolsey. — The latter's selfishness, pride, and cruelty. — His superstitious and vindictive temper. — Soft music. — Vision of angels. — Bayes's grand dance. — Queen Katharine's character. — Mrs. Pritchard

*Pritchard and Mrs. Porter.— Mrs. Willis
and Theophilus Cibber.—Gardiner's character.— Jonson's, Hippisley's, and Taswell's,
representation of him. — The King, Surry,
and Norfolk. — Power of brass to invigorate
the eye-sight. — Plutarch and Macrobius.—
Character of Queen Elizabeth, as drawn by
Shakspeare.— Dr. Hurd and Mr. Hume.—
England most indebted to her worst princes.--
Calderone's Spanish play on the subject of
Henry VIII.*

W O L S E Y.

This candle burns not clear; 'tis I must snuff it,
And out it goes.

THE action of Colley Cibber, in speaking this, I have heard much commended : he imitated, with his fore-finger
and thumb, the extinguishing of a candle
with a pair of snuffers. But surely the
reader will laugh at such mimicry, which,
if practised, would make a player's action
as ridiculous as a monkey's.

Enter

Enter the King, reading a fchedule.

The whole fcene, to the end of the third
act, is the genuine contrivance of the poet. — Though the King had given Wolfey
evident marks of his difpleafure, and often
rated him in his boifterous manner,—and
particularly once, at Grafton, in North-
amptonfhire, when the nobility, who hated him, laid bets for and againft his re-
taining the King's affection, — yet, at that
time, we have authority to fay, Wolfey
ftood his ground fo well, that he departed
from the King's prefence with marks of
favour rather than difpleafure. — This was
the laft time of Henry and Wolfey's meeting.

KING.

What piles of wealth hath he accumulated !

It is impoffible to read the inventory of
Wolfey's riches, as it ftands in our Chronicles, without aftonifhment and indignation.—The walls of his palace were covered
with

with cloth of gold or cloth of filver; his
cupboard contained maffy plate of gold.—
A thoufand pieces of fine Holland, and
the reft of the furniture in proportion. —
To eftimate his riches at half a million
will not, by thofe who carefully attend to
authentic hiftorians, be fuppofed to over-
rate them. How impoverifhed and wretched muft the people be, when a prodigal
king, a grafping minifter, and a flavifh
parliament, all combined to drain them of
their money!

N O R F O L K.

——————— My lord, we have
Stood here obferving him. Some ftrange commotion
Is in his mind.

The defcription of Wolfey's deportment
during the perturbation of his mind, fo
ftrongly depicted in his foliloquy, is an e-
vident proof, that, although Shakfpeare
was not a fkilful actor himfelf, he knew
perfectly what was due to character. He
has here given a leffon to the reprefenter of
Wolfey

Wolfey which the moft confummate player may be proud to learn.

KING.

———— And then to breakfaft— *with What appetite you may.*

Henry's anger fhould be referved by the actor till he pronounces, ' With what appetite you may.' This is confirmed by what the Cardinal fays immediately after the King's departure :

What *fudden* anger's this ?

The tremendous look which Booth put on, with his rapid and vehement expreffion, fully correfponded with the defign of the author.

NORFOLK.

Deliver up the great feal.

The King fent for the great feal, but Wolfey refufed it, as Shakfpeare has recorded it ; nor did he return it till the King wrote to him, and commanded him to deliver it.

SURRY.

S U R R Y.

———————— By my foul,
Your long coat, prieft, protects you ; thou fhould'ft
elfe
Feel my fword in the life-blood of thee.

In this vehement burft of paffion, the
writer has drawn the characteriftical blemifh
of Surry : brave, learned, generous, and accomplifhed, with many fplendid qualities,
which equally gained him the love and admiration of his own countrymen and foreigners, he was fometimes betrayed into
that warmth of temper which juftly expofed him to reprehenfion. In a difpute once
with Wolfey, he was fo far tranfported beyond himfelf as to draw his dagger.*

The refentment which the earl felt to the
minifter, on account of the part he bore in
the trial of his father-in-law, the Duke of
Buckingham, induced our poet to make
ufe of his agency to reproach the Cardinal,

Vol. I.   D d   with

————————————————————

* The people of England can, at this time, boaft of
an Earl of Surry, who is a true friend of liberty, and
an undaunted fupporter of the conftitution of his country, who enjoys all the virtues of his great anceftor unmixed with his exceffes.

with more impetuofity and bitternefs than
he allotted to any of the other peers.

S U R R Y.

Firft, that, without the King's confent,——
You wrought to be a legate.

The affuming the power of a legate was
expreflly contrary to an act paffed in the
reign of Richard II. and left the offender
out of the king's protection. It was,
however, difingenuous and cruel to try
the Cardinal, upon an obfolete act, and for
exercifing that power, in the face of the
world, with the King's confent and approbation.

Amongft above forty articles, which
were laid to his charge, there was a very
fingular one: ' That, knowing himfelf
contaminated with the great pox, he had
the impudence to breathe in the King's
prefence.'

W O L S E Y.

———— My high-blown pride
At length broke under me.

The

The props, by which Wolfey's mind was fupported, were pomp, pride, grandeur, ftate, and magnificence : thefe once failing, the man had nothing from within to fupport his fpirit, he had no whifpering comforts from an unfullied confcience to bear him up againft the tide of adverfity which was ready to overwhelm him.

W O L S E Y.

Vain pomp and glory of the world, I hate you !

With what facility do we renounce what we can no longer keep ! And how like children do men behave, when they give up thofe playthings from which they are debarred !

I D E M.

May have a tomb of orphans tears wept on him.

' May his tomb be wafhed with orphans tears, in gratitude for his acts of juftice to them.'

Wolfey himfelf exercifed the office of chancellor without reproach.

D d 2

CROMWELL.

—— That Cranmer is return'd with welcome,
Inftall'd Lord Archbifhop of Canterbury.

This is a fufficient proof, that Suffolk,
in a former part of the fcene, meant that
Cranmer was really returned with a full
approbation of his opinions; and not, as
Mr. Tyrwhit fuggefted, that he was come
back only by his fchedules, or tranfcripts,
confirming the validity of a divorce, from
foreign univerfities; neither is it likely
that Cranmer would fend that by another
which he could bring himfelf.

WOLSEY.

Cherifh thofe hearts that *hate* you.

Dr. Warburton alters *hate* to *wait*; but
this editor is known to be an arbitrary
foifter of his own fancies into the text. ——
He fays Wolfey neglected his dependents;
the contrary, in general, is true; when
he and his retinue parted, mutual mani-
feftations of grief and tendernefs were feen

on

on both fides. ' Cherifh thofe hearts that
hate you' was fpoken in condemnation of
his own conduct, who had provoked the
nobility by his pride and infolence, rather
than he would foothe them by gentlenefs.
His profecution of Buckingham brought
againſt him the family of Norfolk and all
their friends. But, again, ' Cherifh thofe
hearts that hate you' is, according to the
precept in the Gofpel, ' Blefs them that
curfe you.' This is a leſſon which Shakfpeare puts into the mouth of a heathen :
Flavius, the fteward, on the fight of Ti-
mon, his mafter, in mifery, amongſt o-
ther reflections, breaks out into this :

How rarely does it meet with this time's guife,
When man was wifh'd to love his enemies !

I D E M.

Had I but ferv'd my God with half the zeal
I ferv'd my king, he would not in mine age
Have left me naked to mine enemies.

This fentence, fays Dr. Johnfon, was
really uttered by Wolfey; but the words
D d 3   which

which he fpoke after this fentence, as related by Hollingfhead, are equally pathetic, and are well worth preferving : " But
it is the juft reward that I muft receive for
the diligent pains and ftudy that I have
had to do him fervice, not regarding my
fervice to God, but only to fatisfy his
pleafure."

When we look back, and confider the
foregoing fcene, from the entrance of the
Cardinal to his concluding fpeech at the
end of the third act, we muft confefs that
the poet has wrought up the whole with
great dramatic fkill. The hiftorical incidents, or events, are rendered extremely
interefting, while the characters and paffions of the great perfonages introduced
fupport the dialogue with uncommon vigour. The art of Shakfpeare has, in the
conclufion, rendered the man, who had
been the object of our difguft and hatred, the
fource of tendernefs and commiferation. —
If the rough and bitter terms of reproach,
in the mouths of princes and nobles,
fhould

fhould difpleafe a modern tafte, it fhould be confidered, that the author draws a faithful picture of manners fuch as he found authenticated in hiftory, and fuch as, with very little variation, would in a fimilar fituation take place in all times; for paffions will eternally be the fame, and fpeak nearly the fame language.

If the reprefentation of this fcene has, in general, fallen fhort of the writer's intention and the fpectators expectation, we muft, in a great meafure, attribute that to the difficulty of performing it with excellence. Colley Cibber's pride and paffion, in Wolfey, were impotent and almoft farcical. His grief, refignation, and tendernefs, were inadequate, from a deficiency of thofe powers of expreffion which the melting tones of voice, and a correfponding propriety of gefture, can alone beftow.— Moffop was a powerful and energetic fpeaker of fentiment, and, fometimes, happy in the utterance of paffion. But his ftatelinefs, in a part of this fcene, was without dig-

D d 4   nity,

nity, and his tendernefs without pathos. Digges affumed uncommon grandeur of deportment, which fometimes degenerated into bombaftical ftrutting. To the refigned portion of the character, the grave tones of his voice were not ill-fuited. Had he kept within thofe modeft bounds prefcribed by Shakfpeare, he would have drawn an excellent outline of the imperious Wolfey.

Act IV.

Scene II.　Queen, Griffith, &c.

Notwithftanding his favage difpofition, the king could not at once abandon his favourite minifter. At different times he condefcended to fhew him tokens of his favour and returning friendfhip. The cardinal was fo tranfported with joy on his royal mafter's fending him a ring, which he conceived to be a certain evidence of his protection, — that he difmounted from his horfe and would receive it on his knees. To manifeft his gratitude, he fent to the king, as the moft valuable of all gifts, his *fool, Patch*, whom he had cherifhed as one

referve

referve of happinefs, or, at leaft, amufe-
ment, in his misfortunes; but the poor
cardinal was ftill wedded to vanity and oftentation: he travelled to York, whither
he was obliged to go by order of the duke
of Norfolk, who threatened, " If he refufed, to tear him in pieces with his
teeth.*" He travelled, I fay, with a retinue of one hundred and fixty perfons in
order to be inftalled. The preparations,
for this inftalment, were exceedingly magnificent, and beyond all reafonable limits.
This unhappy relifh for human grandeur
was, in all probability, the immediate caufe
of his ruin. Had he remained quiet in
his diocefs, his enemies would, perhaps,
have been at a lofs for matter to excite the
king's anger againft him; but, on the report of his oftentatious manner of living,
Anne Bullen, inftigated by the duke of
Norfolk, her uncle, never ceafed to ply the
king with accufations againft him, till, at
laft,

---

* Vide Cavendifh.

laft, Henry, notwithftanding he had granted him a pardon drawn up in the moft ample terms, commanded the earl of Northumberland to arreft him for high treafon,
and bring him to his trial. Wolfey, who
knew that his mafter never ruined any man
by halves, dreaded the confequence fo
much, that, Cavendifh fays, he difpatched
himfelf by a powerful dofe. — He had no
lefs, fays Hollingfhead, than fifty ftools in
one day.

QUEEN.

————Ever ranking himfelf
With princes.

The man whofe ambition aimed to be
fuperior to all crowned heads, by getting
poffeffion of the papal tiara, could never
confider himfelf as a fubject; efpecially
when he was accofted and faluted by the
flattering titles of friend, father, and coun-
feller, by emperors and kings. Hume is
of opinion that, if Wolfey had once gained
the papacy, he would have had it in his
power to have amply repaid his mafter for

all

all marks of favour he had beftowed on him.
From the arrogance of the man I fhould
rather fufpect he would have acted the part
of Thomas-a-Becket, who, from a faithful fervant to his prince, while a layman,
proved, when raifed to the fee of Canterbury, the greateft oppofer of his royal
mafter's will.   But, not to dwell upon conjecture, let me afk if Wolfey's promotion
would have altered the ftate of Italy?
Would not the emperor be ftill as powerful there as he was before the cardinal's
exaltation? Would he not have found it
as eafy to humble him as the preceding
pope, whom he had befieged in his capital
and reduced to the laft extremity? Wolfey
muft, of neceffity, have adapted his poli-
tics to his fituation.

QUEEN KATHARINE.

———————— One that by fuggeftion
Ty'd all the kingdom.

I know no word more forcible, to
exprefs what feems to be the author's
meaning, than *ty'd*.   The infinuations
of

of an unfeeling minifter, to perfuade his royal mafter to chain down the minds of his fubjects, cannot be put into ftronger language. Dr. Farmer's propofed alteration of *tith'd* is inferior in its original meaning, and deficient in its general application. Dr. Farmer is a moft refpectable name on every account; but Mr. Tollet has very juftly defended a reading which is fupported by all the editions.

GRIFFITH.

———— From his cradle,
He was a fcholar, and a ripe and good one.

Wolfey's love of learning, and his conftant encouragement of it, was the moft amiable part of his character.

To the revival of learning in this nation he contributed more than all our clergy and nobility. His mind was fufceptible of that reputation and glory which the encouragement of the fine arts and the belles-lettres can only beftow, an honour fuperior to the noify fame of military atchievements. Wolfey

fey was one of the felect few of his age who
enjoyed a juft and elegant tafte for literature. An hiftorian* has preferved fome ex-
tracts from a method of teaching and edu-
cating youth, addreffed by him to the mafters of a fchool which he founded at Ipfwich, in which he has difplayed fo good a
ftyle, fuch folid judgement, and a tafte fo
refined, that it reflects the higheft honour
upon the writer. When Wolfey fpeaks
of the fifth clafs, there is, in his inftruc-
tions, fomething fo truly liberal, that I
cannot forbear tranfcribing the paffage : —
' *Imprimis, hoc unum admonendum cenfueri-*
mus, ut neque plagis feverioribus, neque vul-
tuofis minis, aut ulla tyrannidis fpecie, tenera
pubes afficiatur : hac enim injuria, ingenii
alacritas aut extingui, aut magna ex parte
obtundi folet.' ' Above all things, I think
it proper to admonifh you, that tender
youth fhould not be afflicted with fevere
fcourgings, with boifterous threatenings,
nor

---

* Guthrie.

nor with any fpecies of tyranny. For, by
fuch treatment, a lively genius is either
quite overwhelmed, or in a great meafure
blunted.'

In the conclufion of advice to the fe-
venth clafs, wherein he recommends the
indulging them with fuitable amufements,
he difcovers a moft amiable and benevolent
fpirit. Milton, in his letter to Mr. Hart-
lib on education, has happily extended
and improved this part of the Cardinal's
plan.

I D E M.

Exceeding wife, fair-fpoken, and perfuading.

In confirmation of this part of Wolfey's
charaƈter, we have the authority of Eraf-
mus. " His manners (fays this writer in
his Epiftles) betray nothing of his birth;
he diligently employs himfelf in reviving
the liberal arts." In fine, York-place,
like the houfes of Lucullus, Cicero, Atti-
cus, and other great men of Rome, was an
agreeable retreat for all men of letters,
without

without diftinction. For the compiling a
collection of books and MSS. that might
vie with the Alexandrian library, he employed learned men, all over Europe, or
wherever he could find them. No mechanic
ever toiled more affiduoufly, in his profeffion, than Wolfey did to adorn England
with luminaries of learning. This anxiety of the Cardinal, to encourage literature,
and to introduce the beft fcholars in Europe
amongft his countrymen, feems utterly in-
compatible with Dr. Middleton's account
of Wolfey's fpeech to the clergy, in which
he publicly forewarned them, that, if they
did not deftroy the prefs, the prefs would
deftroy them.*

I D E M.

—— Ever witnefs for him,
Ipfwich and Oxford ! one of which fell with him ;
The other, though unfinifh'd, yet fo famous,
So excellent in art, and ftill fo rifing,
That Chriftendom fhall ever fpeak his virtue.

There

---

* Dedication to Middleton's Letter from Rome.

There is, in this eulogium of Chrift-church college, at Oxford, fomething, furely, that looks prophetical. No other feminary in Europe has perhaps been fo fertile in perfons famous for ufeful learn-ing, extent of genius, and elegance of tafte in the belles lettres.

It is with a degree of pleafure I have fe-lected, from the beft hiftorians, paffages to confirm that draught of the fhining part of Wolfey's portrait given by Shakfpeare. But it cannot be controverted that the dark fhades of it wanted the brighteft tints to fet them off. The eminent fuperiority of his genius he principally employed to the advancement of his own power, inte-reft, and grandeur; his ambition was as infatiable as his avarice, and with them his pride and cruelty went an equal pace. He gave certain indications of a little mind, for he was fuperftitious and vindictive.

One of thofe enormous croffes, which always accompanied him wherever he went, happening, at an entertainment, to
fall,

fall, and hurt one of his retinue, he afked whether the blow had fetched blood ? and, being anfwered in the affirmative, he cried out *Malum omen !* and retired to his chamber.

During the time that he was a fchoolmafter, a quarrel happened between him and Sir James Paulet, who, to giatify his anger, had Wolfey put into the ftocks. — Many years after this fray, when the Cardinal was advanced to the poft of lord-high-chancellor of England, he fent for Paulet; and, after reproaching him fternly for his former behaviour to him, he, by his own authority, obliged him to remain in London five or fix years. *

QUEEN KATHARINE.

Caufe the muficians play me that *fad note*
I nam'd my knell.

Sad note is, ' that foft and melancholy air which pleafes me.'

VOL. I.   E e   The

—————————————

* Hollingfhead.

The Emperor Charles V. Katharine's nephew, when retired to the monaftery of Juft, in Eftremadura, caufed the folemn dirge to be played before him which was to be performed at his funeral obfequies.

The Vifion of Angels.

No dramatic author ever took fuch in-defatigable pains to feed the eye and the ear, as well as the underftanding, as Shak-fpeare. What effect this vifion might pro-duce on the audience originally is not now to be learned. That it was reprefented be-fore Mrs. Betterton, when fhe acted Qu. Ka-tharine, foon after the Reftoration, is certain. Though the author fhews fancy in this lit-tle pantomime, yet it feems fitter, at prefent, to tempt an audience to mirth and ridicule than to ferious attention. The grave congées, folemn dancings, and ftately courtefies, of thefe aërial beings, put us in mind of Bayes's grand dance; and per-haps the Duke of Buckingham borrowed a hint of it from this vifion. In the third

act

act of the Rehearfal, Bayes, chiding
the players for their aukwardnefs, tells
them they ' dance worfe than the fat fpirits
in the Tempeft or the angels in Henry
VIII.'

MESSENGER.

An't like your grace ————

KATHARINE.

———— You are a faucy fellow.

The Meffenger, forgetting to pay Katharine the refpect due to majefty, raifes her
indignation even in her laft agony; and
this is truly a part of that lady's character. All the homage, which was paid
to her before the divorce, fhe determined to preferve to the laft. The king
employed commiffioners to fettle her houfe
as Princefs-dowager of Wales, who would
have placed fervants about her, to treat her
as fuch; but this impofition fhe rejected
with difdain.

The virtues of Queen Katharine are celebrated by all hiftorians. Her form was
little

little calculated to retain the affections of such a man as Henry; but, though he could not love her, such was her conformity to his will, and such the innocence of her life, he ever spoke of her with great respect, and professed the highest reverence of her virtues.

That Katharine should persist in denying, with an oath, the consummation of her marriage with Prince Arthur, considering the evidence which was produced of it, historians in general seem to wonder: but, when we reflect what herself and her daughter, the Princess Mary, might lose by owning the completion of the marriage, we shall rather, I believe, pity her situation, which reduced her to so unhappy a dilemma, than condemn her perseverance. The absolution of a confessor might operate like a charm upon her mind; nor is it, I hope, uncharitable to suppose, that such a cordial would not be refused.

During this truly-pathetic scene, the behaviour of Mrs. Pritchard, the representer

fenter of Katharine, was refpectable ; but
her beft efforts could not reach the grace and
dignity of gefture, much lefs the heart-
touching tendernefs, of Mrs. Porter. In
this actrefs it was obferved, that a very
bad voice did not obftruct the forcible
expreffion of exceffive grief.

Act. V.   Scene the firft.

Shakfpeare has felected fuch parts of
Henry's life as would rather reflect honour
than difgrace on his memory. Though,
in general, he had confined himfelf to that
period of his hiftory which is compre-
hended in about twelve or thirteen years,
from the attainder of Buckingham to the
chriftening of Queen Elizabeth, — he has,
notwithftanding, by the help of an ana-
chronifm, contrived to infert the infidious
plot of Cranmer's enemies to ruin him
in the king's favour, and Henry's generous refentment of their treachery.

CRANMER.

The *good* I ſtand on.

The *good* means ' the foundation of truth I rely on.'

KING.

————— Is the queen deliver'd ?
Say ay, and of a boy !

By what has been already ſaid, it appears the king moſt ardently wiſhed for male iſ-ſue.—This ſhort and quick interrogation ſtrongly marks it. Anne Bullen was, a-bout two years afterwards, delivered of a dead male child : and this circumſtance, above all others, alienated the king's affec-tion from her.

OLD LADY.

An hundred marks ! By this light I'll have more !

Mrs. Willis, a moſt excellent actreſs in low humour, played this ſmall, and, I be-lieve, generally thought, inſignificant part, many years. She threw into this old lady,

as

as well as into every thing fhe acted, fo
much truth and nature, that the audience
never difmiffed her without marks of approbation.

Let me here give an anecdote of her and
Theophilus Cibber.—I may not, perhaps,
find a place for it elfewhere. She lived to
a great age with its worft companion, poverty. A charitable collection was fet on
foot for her relief amongft the players, who
never turn their backs upon want and affliction. The. Cibber was then very young and
wild. When fhe applied to him his finan-
ces were fo low, that he denied her with the
excufe that he had a large family.   "O
dear, Sir, (faid Mrs. Willis,) how can that
be ? you have neither wife nor child." " It
may be fo,—but I have a large family of
vices, madam !"

C H A N C E L L O R.
Speak to the bufinefs, Mr. Secretary.

Mr. Theobald, forgetting that Shakfpeare had, in this inftance, broke through
his original defign, by introducing the con-

E e 4   fpiracy

fpiracy againft Cranmer, will have it that the chancellor of the fcene was Sir Thomas Audley, fucceffor of Sir Thomas More; but he died in 1544, two years before the plan was concerted to ruin the archbifhop, Wriothefly was Audley's fucceffor, and, confequently, the chancellor whom Shakfpeare meant.

G A R D I N E R.

Which reformation muft be fudden too!

So averfe was Gardiner to all innovation whatfoever, and fo firm a friend to eftablifhed error, in matters of mere indifference, that he oppofed, with all his might, the more accurate pronunciation of the Greek tongue, introduced by fome learned men into our univerfities. The Papifts adhered to the old method, and the Proteftants favoured the new. This was a reafon fufficiently powerful, with this hot zealot, to employ the authority of the king and council to fupprefs any propofed reformation in this particular, by perpetuating the corrupt found of the Greek alphabet.

phabet. The penalties of difobedience, inflicted by Gardiner, were whipping, degradation, and expulfion.

CROMWELL.

———Would you were half fo honeft!

Shakfpeare throws out no idle or ill-founded charges. When Gardiner was ambaffador at the court of France, being extremely averfe to the progrefs of any ecclefiaftical reformation, on which he found his mafter very intent, it was fufpected that he betrayed the intereft of Henry to the French king.

SURREY.

May it pleafe your majefty———

KING.

No, Sir, it does not pleafe me.

This angry interruption of the king is always uttered with vehemence. And this event falling out a year before the king's death, the author feems to point out Henry's fixed averfion to the earl, whom with his father, the duke of Norfolk, he profecu-

ted

ted with inexpiable rage. The pretended
crime of both was quartering the king's
arms with their own; a practice juftified
by the heralds. For this, and other fri-
volous pretences, the earl was tried by a
jury of commoners and condemned to die.
His defence was noble, becoming his birth
and his undaunted fpirit. He was executed about ten days before Henry died,
The humble fubmiffion of the duke avail-
ed him nothing : all his fervices, in defeat-
ing the Scots and fubduing feveral rebel-
lions within the kingdom, were forgotten.
The king apprehended that the duke and
his fon would difturb the fettlement of government which he had planned for Edward, his fucceffor ; he therefore determined to get rid of them both.—Nor could
his own approaching death, nor the fenfe of
the enormous cruelties he had committed,
foften his favage and obdurate mind. Being
unable to fign his name to the warrant for
the duke's execution, he made ufe of a
feal contrived for that purpofe : happily
the

the king died before the day appointed for
Norfolk's execution. The council thought
it would be unpopular to begin the new
reign with the death of fo great and popular a man as the duke of Norfolk.

GARDINER.

With a true heart and brother's love.

The king obliges Gardiner to embrace
Cranmer twice. The coldnefs of the latter, who could not conceal his hatred at
the firft embrace, caufes a fmothered
laugh in the fpectators : but when, at the
king's command, he is obliged to be more
in earneft, his apparently affumed alacrity
raifes a general burft of laughter and much
loud clapping.

The chafte manner of Ben Jonfon, the
actor, would admit of no farce or buffoonery, in perfonating the fplenetic Gardiner. He preferved all the decorum proper
to the character of a bifhop and privy-
counfellor. Hippifley went a ftep farther,
and added fome ftrokes of humour, which
approached to grimace ; and this caufed a

mirth

mirth unfuitable to the character of the perfons. But Tafwell's Gardiner degenerated
into abfolute trick and buffoonery, and,
when he followed Cranmer, at the clofe of
the fcene, to make the upper gallery fport,
he held his crutch over his head. This
was the more inexcufable in him, as he
wanted not judgement to inform him better, but he pitifully facrificed his knowledge of propriety to the pleafure of diverting the moft ignorant part of the audience, for which he fometimes paid very
dear ; for the judicious part of the fpectators exploded, by a hifs, fuch violent mifreprefentation.

Scene III.

PORTER.

He fhould be a brafier by his face, for, on my confcience, twenty of the dog-days reign in his nofe.

Our author feems fond of exercifing his
wit on pimpled faces and carbuncled nofes,
and Bardolph is introduced into the play
of Harry IV. for no other reafon.

' A brafier, fays Dr. Johnfon, fignifies a
a man that manufactures brafs, and a mafs
of

of metal occafionally heated to convey warmth; both are here underftood." I fhould think that here the latter only was meant. Of this, we are certain, that the ancients were of opinion that all manufacturers of brafs were remarkable for vigour in the eyes and happinefs of fight.

In the Odyffey, book the 13th, Homer calls brafs ευηνορα χαλκον, which is tranfla-ted *Vires honeftans æs.* In the Sympofiacs of Plutarch, book the 3d, there is a very curious obfervation upon the power of brafs to invigorate the eye-fight, and even to reftore loft eye-lafhes. I will give the paffage as I find it almoft verbally tranfla-ted by Macrobius, in the 7th book of his Saturnalia : " Qui in metallo æris moran-tur femper oculorum fanitate pollent, et quibus ante palpebræ nudatæ fuerant illinc conveftiuntur. Aura enim quæ ex ære procedit, in oculos incidens, haurit et ex-ficcat quod male influit, unde et Homerus modo ευηνορα χαλκον, modo νωροπα χαλκον, has caufas fecutus, appellat." Brafs feems

to

to have the fame power to exhilarate the fight that Venus had to give brilliance to the eyes of her fon :

Et lætos oculis afflarat honores.

VIRGIL.

CRANMER.

———— She fhall be
A pattern to all princes living with her,
And all that fhall fucceed.

This character of Elizabeth, drawn by Shakfpeare, is not unlike to that entertained by moft Englifhmen and *all* foreigners till very lately. It is now become almoft a fafhion to declaim violently againft her, and reprefent her as a moft difagreeable woman and a tyrannical princefs.

A very elegant writer has, in a dialogue between three eminent perfons, compofed a moft fevere inquifition into her private and public conduct. A detection of deformities faved from oblivion, the publication of which can anfwer no rational purpofe, might, I think, with fubmiffion, have been fpared. Erafe the name

name of Elizabeth from the catalogue of good Englifh monarchs, and I believe the acuteft fight will fcarcely be able to point out one from the Conqueft to the Revolution: I mean, by a good prince, one that confults, in the general tenor of his conduct, the real intereft of the people. It is pleafant enough to find, that Mr. Addifon, who, in all the writings in which he had occafion to mention this lady, fpoke of her with the higheft eulogium, is, in this dialogue, made to hold the fcalping-knife, and diffect her with a feverity and keennefs very different from his ufual ftyle of writing. This is very ftrangely accounted for by the reverend and learned writer, who tells us, that Addifon's public and private opinion of this great princefs were very difcordant. This exoteric and efoteric doctrine is extremely fanciful and dangerous; for, according to this principle, Dr. Hurd's name may, by fome future writer, be made ufe of as a panegyrift of Elizabeth; and Lord Bolingbroke, who

in

in his writings extols the character and political conduct of this queen beyond meafure, may be introduced as a moft bitter
fatirift againft her.

After all, if we examine her merit fairly,
it muft be from a different principle than
that which feems to have guided the pen
of this eminent writer. We fhould confider her as living at a time when the prerogative was fuperior to law, and not as if
fhe had reigned when the boundaries between the prince and people were fixed at
the Revolution. To bring her conduct to
a teft, on doctrines and cuftoms eftablifhed
at this late period, would be to try her on
an ex poft facto law.

Mr. Hume, in a comprehenfive and
mafterly manner, has fairly and accurately
drawn the portrait of Elizabeth. He has
candidly feparated the public from the private character; he has confidered her as a
rational being, placed in authority and entrufted with the government of mankind.
We may, fays this fagacious writer, find
it

it difficult to reconcile our fancy to her as a wife or a miſtreſs; but her qualities as a ſovereign, though with ſome conſiderable exceptions, are the objeƈt of undiſputed applauſe and approbation.

To enter into a full diſcuſſion of Henry's charaƈter is not the buſineſs of him who is not called upon to go farther than his original author. Shakſpeare has given the fair ſide of this prince, and ſuch as a daughter might behold without bluſhing. Had he given a ſecond part of Henry VIII. without great ſoftening, he muſt have preſented ſuch a piƈture, perhaps, as no audience could bear; and yet we muſt not preſume to doubt our author's ſkill in the art of colouring, or making that portrait not only bearable, but ſought after, which, in the hands of another, would perhaps be utterly diſguſting; witneſs the Life and Death of King John, and his Richard III. princes more offenſive to humanity than even Henry VIII.

To the worſt and moſt arbitrary kings
this nation has eventually been indebted for
its greateſt happineſs. John's exceſſive cruelty and oppreſſion produced Magna Charta.
The violence of Hen. VIII. freed England
from papal power and the popiſh religion.
To the weak and obſtinate efforts of Ja. II.
to extend the prerogative beyond law, we
owe the ſettlement at the Revolution and
the ſucceſſion of the Hanover line.

In a play, called La Ciſma de Inglaterra,
Calderone, the celebrated Spaniſh poet,
has treated of the ſubject of Henry's divorce. The characters of Henry, Wolſey,
and Queen Katharine, are not ill ſuſtained.
The King, indeed, he makes conſcious of
acting ill all through the play ; his violent
love for Anna Bullen is the only cauſe of
his divorcing Katharine, in which he is
ſupported and prompted by Wolſey. The
unhappy Bullen is proud, inſolent, un-
grateful, and laſcivious, as moſt Roman
Catholic authors repreſent her. Her in-
trigue with Carlos, the French ambaſſador,

dor, is difcovered by the King, who in his clofet overhears their difcourfe. In a rage, he orders her to be fent to the Tower; fhe is beheaded, and her dead trunk is foon after brought upon the ftage. In the parliament-fcene, which is by far the beft, the King gives his reafons for the divorce with a mixture of feigned regret and fome cold compliments to Katharine; he fwears to fupport the fucceffion of his daughter Mary, and, without any farther ceremony, bids the Queen fubmit to her fate and retire to a convent; then, turning to the parliament, he declares he will make that man fhorter by the head who fhall prefume to think that he is in the wrong:

> Y el vafallo que fintiere
> Mal, advierta temerofo,
> Que le quitare al inftante
> La cabeza de los ombros.

The Queen's anfwer is extremely affecting, and worthy the name of Calderone. — Her love to the King is not to be fhaken, notwithftanding

notwithſtanding the cruel ſentence he has
pronounced againſt her. With a proteſtation the moſt paſſionate, ſhe declares nothing can be terrible to her except his hatred. She diſclaims any appeal to the emperor, her victorious nephew ; nor can ſhe
think of entering a convent, for ſhe is his
married wife ; and concludes with calling
him her lord, her happineſs, her king,
and dear huſband.

Upon the whole, though we ſhould allow that the play has in it many poetical
beauties, yet it is, in *dramatic ſtamina,*
greatly inferior to the Engliſh play. Calderone breaks through the unities of time
and place as freely as our author.

END OF VOL. I.

INDEX to VOL. I.

Cibber,

Hale,

H.

Henry

John

Walker,

W.

ERRATA

ERRATA to VOL. I.

Page 1. l. 5. } for Fatal Tyranny, *read* Papal Tyranny.
   4. }

 46. The contents of Chap. IV. from *Rumney's opinion of Æschylus*, to the end, were inferted by miftake.

 106. for Maid for a Month, *read,* Wife for a Month.

 115. The contents of Chap. VII. are complete no farther than to the bottom of p. 133. they are wanting to p. 149.

 249. For fupercilious brow, *read,* fupercilious look.

 276. *At the end of the Contents of Chap.* XIV. dele "Overfight of the Author—Death of Glendower;" *thofe two articles being contained in the next chapter.*

 307. Inftead of balance of a watch's pendulum, *read* balance of a watch.